SUPPORT SERVICES
RENEWAL IN EDUCATION

HOW TO ORDER THIS BOOK

BY PHONE: 800-233-9936 or 717-291-5609, 8AM–5PM Eastern Time

BY FAX: 717-295-4538

BY MAIL: Order Department
Technomic Publishing Company, Inc.
851 New Holland Avenue, Box 3535
Lancaster, PA 17604, U.S.A.

BY CREDIT CARD: American Express, VISA, MasterCard

PERMISSION TO PHOTOCOPY–POLICY STATEMENT

Authorization to photocopy items for internal or personal use, or the internal or personal use of specific clients, is granted by Technomic Publishing Co., Inc. provided that the base fee of US $3.00 per copy, plus US $ .25 per page is paid directly to Copyright Clearance Center, 222 Rosewood Drive, Danvers, MA 01923, USA. For those organizations that have been granted a photocopy license by CCC, a separate system of payment has been arranged. The fee code for users of the Transactional Reporting Service is 1-56676/95 $5.00 + $ .25.

EDUCATIONAL LEADERSHIP FOR THE 21ST CENTURY

SUPPORT SERVICES RENEWAL IN EDUCATION

Leroy G. Baruth, Ed.D.
Reich College of Education
Appalachian State University

M. Lee Manning, Ph.D.
Darden College of Education
Old Dominion University

SERIES EDITOR: WILLIAM J. BAILEY

LANCASTER · BASEL

Support Services Renewal in Education
a **TECHNOMIC**® publication

Published in the Western Hemisphere by
Technomic Publishing Company, Inc.
851 New Holland Avenue, Box 3535
Lancaster, Pennsylvania 17604 U.S.A.

Distributed in the Rest of the World by
Technomic Publishing AG
Missionsstrasse 44
CH-4055 Basel, Switzerland

Copyright © 1995 by Technomic Publishing Company, Inc.
All rights reserved

No part of this publication may be reproduced, stored in a
retrieval system, or transmitted, in any form or by any means,
electronic, mechanical, photocopying, recording, or otherwise,
without the prior written permission of the publisher.

Printed in the United States of America
10 9 8 7 6 5 4 3 2 1

Main entry under title:
    Educational Leadership for the 21st Century – Support Services Renewal in Education

A Technomic Publishing Company book
Bibliography: p.
Includes index p. 255

Library of Congress Catalog Card No. 98-61633
ISBN No. 1-56676-203-0

CONTENTS

Preface to the Series ix

Preface xi

Acknowledgements xv

PART I: RESTRUCTURING AND RENEWING SUPPORT SERVICES PERSONNEL

Chapter 1: Support Services Personnel — 3
Overview 3
Support Services Personnel 4
Support Services in the 21st Century: Challenges and Changing Roles 22
Summary 32
References 32

Chapter 2: Renewing Support Services — 35
Overview 35
The Need for Renewal 35
The Possibilities for the 21st Century 44
Summary 61
References 62

PART II: FORMING PROFESSIONAL TEAMS AND EMPOWERING INDIVIDUALS

Chapter 3: Empowering Teams and the Teaming Process — 65
Overview 65
Empowerment and Beyond: Support Services Initiatives 65
Teams, Teamwork, the Team Process, and Support Services Personnel 69

Support Services Professionals as Team Agents 86
Summary 90
References 90

Chapter 4: Advocacy Agents   93

Overview 93
Advocacy Roles: Past and Present 93
Advocacy Roles: Beyond the Status Quo 94
Advocacy Roles the Future Might Bring 108
Summary 114
References 114

Chapter 5: Training and Educating Support Services Personnel   117

Overview 117
Professional Preparation 117
Increased Professionalism 130
Accountability Demands 131
Other Efforts to Educate Support Services Professionals 142
Summary 148
References 148

Chapter 6: Consultant and Leadership Roles   151

Overview 151
The 21st Century: Contemporary Roles 151
Consultants and Leaders: Prerequisites to Success 172
Summary 179
References 179

PART III: CHALLENGES AND PROSPECTS FOR THE 21ST CENTURY

Chapter 7: Support Services in a Culturally Diverse Society   183

Overview 183
The Melting Pot Ideology—Perspectives from the Past 183
The Salad Bowl Ideology—A More Enlightened and
   Contemporary Perspective 184
The Culturally Different 185
Lingering Problems Challenging the United
   States Society 188

*Roles of Support Services Personnel in Our Culturally
    Diverse Society* 191
*Traditional Personnel: Roles in an Increasingly
    Multicultural Society* 195
*Future Support Personnel and Their Roles in a
    Multicultural Society* 202
*The Need for Culturally Diverse Support
    Services Personnel* 208
Accountability and Professionalism 210
Summary 211
References 211

Chapter 8: Issues and Challenges — 215

Overview 215
Issues and Challenges 215
Issues 218
Challenges 227
Summary 237
References 238

Chapter 9: The Future of Support Services Personnel — 239

Overview 239
*The Reform/Restructuring Movement – Impetus and
    Opportunities for Support Services Professionals* .. 239
Indicators of a Bright Future 242
Summary 252
References 252

Index — 255

PREFACE TO THE SERIES

ANY ADULT, WITH even a small awareness of public affairs, living in the last decade of the 20th century knows two things about public education. First, a quality education is absolutely essential to individuals in a democracy facing the rapid changes of the future. Second, the present public education system has lost credibility with the majority of taxpayers. Interestingly enough, a recent survey shows that most parents think public schools are not doing their job, but that "their school" is satisfactory. Clearly, the advent of educational reform literature in the 1980s and 1990s offers many solutions; however, even more clearly, the public schools are very slow and reluctant to change. The theories offered on educational reform illustrate the problem—a large discrepancy between what is possible and what is common practice.

Short of rewriting the federal Constitution regarding the responsibilities of the states to provide for a free and public educational system, the American public schools need a total revamping of structure, philosophy, pedagogy, and professionalism. This professional educator's library is designed to explain why significant changes are needed and how changes can be made given the present constitutional authority.

How is this library different than the other polemics of reform? The literature is replete with articles, books, technical reports, national studies, state reviews, and speeches—not the least of which comes from politicians. The literature covers structure, instruction, curriculum, support services, and educational leadership; however, most of the topics in these documents are unrelated. Busy administrators and harassed teachers cannot pull all of this disparate advice together for total, quality, and comprehensive change. This book series library takes the basic components of an educational system and, in a coordinated manner, delineates how system reform can work.

Each author, an expert in his/her respective field, addresses three pertinent themes wrought from many hours of research and discussion: increased professionalism, accountability, and technology. Additionally, each author presents future oriented practices germane to their field. Our overriding vision is to develop scholarly practitioners for the 21st century, who demonstrate deliberative responses to the cultural demands placed on education.

WILLIAM J. BAILEY
Series Editor

PREFACE

THIS BOOK, ENTITLED *Support Services Renewal in Education*, focuses on the role of support services personnel during the 21st century. Traditionally, support services personnel included school psychologists, library/media specialists, counselors, and communication disorders specialists. However, the 21st century might bring other support personnel such as learning diagnosticians, accountability specialists, adult education specialists, home-schooling designers and coordinators, and perhaps even personnel working to coordinate school restructuring efforts. The increasingly complex and technological society, as well as the increased demands placed upon schools, calls for a reexamination of support services professionals' roles. For too long, classroom teachers and support services personnel have worked in isolation and have not benefitted from collaborative efforts. One aspect of this restructuring process includes changing support services personnel roles from being a resource person to being a professional empowered to work collaboratively and collegially in decision-making processes. A pervasive goal of this volume is to help support services personnel as they reconsider, restructure, and renew their roles to meet the demands of the 21st century.

Essential aspects of this volume include 1) explaining the rationale for restructuring roles and responsibilities needed to meet societal and educational challenges of a new century; 2) empowering support services personnel with the knowledge and skills to engage in participatory decision making; 3) developing the leadership skills necessary to initiate change and to lead others in the change process; 4) empowering support services personnel to work as significant members of a "community of scholars, learners, and researchers" in an attempt to restructure educational institutions and specifically restructure the roles of support services personnel; and 5) providing support services personnel with adequate professional training and preparation to function collaboratively and collegially in a rapidly changing society.

Support Services Renewal in Education suggests that professional educators are rapidly recognizing support services professionals' specialized knowledge, abilities, consultant abilities, and leadership skills. Likewise, their opinions are also changing toward roles and responsibilities that support services personnel can play and adopt in schools. For many years, educators called upon support services professionals only when specialized services were needed; however, this book suggests support services professionals should take more proactive stances and assume new roles: leaders, advocates, collaborators, consultants, and team members, to name a few.

OBJECTIVES

The authors' specific objectives for this book include the following:

(*1*) Readers will examine the roles and professional responsibilities of traditional and future support services personnel.
(*2*) Readers will understand the effects that increased professionalism, increased accountability, and rapid technological innovations will have on support services personnel.
(*3*) Readers will develop knowledge and the abilities necessary to work collaboratively and collegially as team members and leaders during teaming efforts.
(*4*) Readers will develop the knowledge and abilities to be effective change agents, advocates, consultants, and leaders necessary to assist administrators, classroom educators, other support services personnel, and learners to work toward agreed-upon specified goals.
(*5*) Readers will examine the challenges and prospects facing support services personnel and offer suggestions for preparing to meet rapidly changing demands.

ORGANIZATION OF THE BOOK

Restructuring and renewal will allow support services personnel to examine their professional roles and to develop a self-perception of being a fully participating member of the total educational effort. To provide these professionals with the ability and confidence to meet the challenges of restructuring and renewal, the book includes three parts divided into nine chapters, each part designed to address a particular facet of the professional life of the support services personnel.

Part I, "Restructuring and Renewing Support Services Personnel," has two chapters that take a broad look at support services personnel and their renewal. Chapter 1, "Support Services Personnel," introduces the book by looking at who support services personnel are and who they might be in the 21st century. Also, the chapter examines how challenges and changing roles will affect their professional lives. Chapter 2, "Renewing Support Services," looks at the concept of professional renewal and how possibilities for the next century might provide support services specialists with a sense of professional renewal.

Part II, "Forming Professional Teams and Empowering Individuals," has four chapters that examine empowering teams and individual professionals to meet changing expectations. Chapter 3, "Empowering Teams and the Teaming Process," proposes empowerment and beyond by examining effective team processes and also several dimensions contributing to support services professionals' effectiveness in team situations. Chapter 4, "Advocacy Agents," suggests support services personnel should assume advocacy roles such as outreach coordinators, technology advocates, and specialists addressing learning styles and cultural and gender differences. Chapter 5, "Training and Educating Support Services Personnel," examines the professional preparation of support services personnel in light of increased professionalism, new accountability demands, and possible competencies needed for the 21st century. Chapter 6, "Consultant and Leadership Roles," advocates that support services professionals should include consultants and leadership roles and also examines prerequisites to their professional success.

Part III, "Challenges and Prospects for the 21st Century," takes a look at issues, challenges, and prospects that support services professionals might face during the 21st century, especially in an increasingly culturally diverse nation. Chapter 7, "Support Services in a Culturally Diverse Society," examines a topic growing in significance, our nation's increasing cultural diversity, which will challenge support services personnel and other educators to address cultural differences and to take a stand against problems facing our nation such as racism, stereotyping, and discrimination. Chapter 8, "Issues and Challenges," looks at concerns facing support services personnel and offers possible solutions and answers. Chapter 9, "The Future of Support Services Personnel," takes a futuristic perspective and suggests opportunities for support services personnel and also offers several indicators suggesting a bright future.

ACKNOWLEDGEMENTS

AS WITH ANY writing project of this magnitude, a number of people deserve special thanks for their work and patience. The authors wish to thank Betty Levin of Old Dominion University for her computer skills and her actual work on the book, Debbi Tibbette and Regina Presnell of Appalachian State University for much of the word processing, Bill Bailey for serving as series editor and for developing the concept of a series of books focusing on education in the 21st century, and the many professionals at Technomic Publishing Company for their assistance with all phases of the publication process.

PART I

Restructuring and Renewing Support Services Personnel

CHAPTER 1

Support Services Personnel

OVERVIEW

SUPPORT SERVICES PERSONNEL, for many decades, played helping or "supportive" roles when classroom educators had learners with disabilities or particular learning needs. Most people can remember a counselor intervening for a problem or discussing career choices, a school psychologist who tested or diagnosed learning problems, or a speech correctionist who worked to correct an articulation problem. These professionals played valuable roles in schools and helped learners with specific problems, which the classroom teacher did not have the time or skill to address.

While these traditional support professionals will likely continue to provide valuable services in the 21st century, other support roles will likely develop, roles that address more acute learning problems or perhaps contribute to school effectiveness in other ways. Several indicators suggest support services professionals will experience significant changes—changing mind-sets toward support services professional roles; the reform and restructuring movement; educators being empowered to make professional decisions; support services professionals assuming roles as change agents; and the many social, economic, and political changes affecting our nation and its schools. Still other impetuses—major themes of this book such as increased accountability, enhanced professionalism, and technological innovations—will change support services professionals' roles.

The late 1990s and early 21st century undoubtedly will be a time of change, both within the profession and in the way the nation views education. Both learners and the profession will be the beneficiaries when support services professionals begin to assume more proactive roles—taking initiatives before being called upon, assuming consultant roles in specialty areas, and taking leadership efforts and other roles that traditionally have not been assumed. These are challenging times where support services professionals have numerous opportunities to respond to calls for change, especially at a time when a movement is under way to restructure and reform educational practices. This chapter examines traditional support services professional roles, predicts new roles for the coming century, and looks at contemporary challenges and changes.

SUPPORT SERVICES PERSONNEL

Support services personnel in the 21st century will include those professionals we have known for decades (e.g., counselors, school psychologists, speech correctionists, and social workers), as well as those professionals who might be addressing new or more specific areas. Any prediction of the future is risky at best, especially during times when economic and political changes occur almost daily and when a restructuring and reform movement continues to question and challenge previously unexamined educational assumptions and practices. However, looking at present needs, current movements and trends, and potential support roles, one can suggest other support services professionals. For example, learning diagnosticians could pinpoint reasons for learners not achieving; software specialists might design high-quality software to meet specific learning (and perhaps social and behavioral) needs; legal specialists might define the schools' roles and responsibilities in an increasingly litigious society; and the nation's dropout rate indicates a need for an adult education specialist, a professional trained solely to work with adult learners. Other support roles might develop as the profession's and communities' commitments grow to better meet learner and school needs. This section examines traditional support services professional roles and examines the progress of new support roles to address 21st century challenges and demands.

Who They Are

Examples of traditional support services professionals include counselors, school psychologists, speech correctionists, school nurses/health coordinators, social-based social workers, and in-school suspension workers. While these professionals have served roles in schools for many years, their roles have evolved with learners' changing needs, as well as the nation's and community's expectation of schools and its professionals. As with all professionals, support services personnel cannot become static. They must remain professionally vibrant and competent to meet contemporary demands.

Counselors

For the past two decades the literature has been replete with descriptions, arguments, and debates over the role and function of the counselor. Shertzer and Stone (1980) suggest that the 1970s saw some decline of articles in this area, perhaps because "the issue of who counselors are as professionals had been taken as far as it could be until new forces, ideas, or experiences could be uncovered and brought to bear on the matter" (p. 118). Recent years have brought new directions to counseling in the area of an expanding array of settings in which counselors work. Perhaps this has not affected the notion of the counselor's role and function so much as it has made counselors consider the applicability of previously held beliefs in new settings (Baruth and Robinson, 1987).

The school counselor serves many vital support roles: 1) counsels children and adolescents with academic, social, and personal problems; 2) consults with parents and classroom educators regarding the most appropriate educational experiences for learners; 3) acts as change agents to change educational environments in which learners function and which affect their mental health; 4) serves as an agent for preventing developmental and coping difficulties before they occur; and 5) manages certain administrative functions related to learners' well-being and a multifaceted human services program.

What challenges might counselors in the 21st century expect? Looking at trends and events in the 1990s, one could predict counselors might have to address their intervention toward problems resulting from

- AIDS and other sexually transmitted diseases, which will challenge the nation's doctors and financial resources
- violence (guns, gangs, fights) in schools and communities, which results in pain, sorrow, and disappointment
- changing family structures resulting from divorce, restructured families, and perhaps homosexual marriages
- multicultural populations that continue to immigrate, both legally and illegally, to America—challenging counselors to intervene using strategies appropriate for culturally diverse learners

- economic conditions resulting from major corporations and businesses restructuring to meet economic demands
- educational practices and policy changing due to the restructuring and reform movement

While this list provides only a few topics counselors might be challenged to address as the 21st century nears and begins, the important point is that counselors need to be prepared for change—prepared to accept changes and prepared to provide counseling intervention designed to meet the changes. Counselors cannot plan intervention based upon 20th century perspectives and mind-sets. The effective counselor of the next century will have an understanding of events affecting learners and be able to provide supportive services in team and collaborative settings.

School Psychologists

The school psychologist conducts academic and intellectual assessment and diagnosis (including administration and interpretation of individual intelligence tests); makes behavioral observations and analyses; counsels children and interviews parents, teachers, and others; develops remedial programs for children; and conducts research and evaluation as needed by the school district (Jarolimek and Foster, 1989). Also, school psychologists have various roles in the education of handicapped students. First, psychologists are often involved in the process of diagnosing handicapped students and are sometimes participants in the preparation of Individualized Education Plans. In addition, they may counsel the student or consult with the teacher about behavioral problems (Slavin, 1988).

Several factors will likely change school psychologists' roles in the 21st century: societal changes and expectations affecting our schools, the restructuring and reform movement challenging long-held assumptions about school practices, increased accountability demands, and a greater effort to address the needs of the whole child and adolescent instead of only academic achievement. School psychologists in the rapidly approaching century may be called upon to

- diagnose specific mental health problems
- diagnose special areas of intelligences using the concept of multiple intelligences
- determine a learner's degree of social skills in both small- and large-group settings

- form team approaches with parents, teachers and other support services professionals
- suggest community mental health agencies or social service agencies who have professionals trained to address specific psychological problems

Again, as with school counselors, the effective school psychologist will need to switch from 20th century mind-sets to a 21st century perspective, which affects changing schools, changing attitudes toward schools, and changing perceptions of support services professionals.

Speech Correctionist

A primary role of the speech correctionist is to distinguish between communicative disorders and communicative variations and to convey to classroom educators the differences between the two. Communications disorders include speech disorders (an impairment of voice, articulation of speech sounds, and/or fluency) and language disorders (the impairment, or deviant development, of comprehension and/or a spoken or written symbol system). Other types of abnormal speech include articulation, voice disorders, language disorders, and rhythm disorders. Since communication is such a vital human aspect to learners, speech correctionists play an important role in helping educators distinguish between disorders and variations (McCormick, 1990).

Undoubtedly, speech correctionists will continue to be challenged to address various articulation and rhythm problems; however, speech correctionists in the 21st century will have other challenges. For example, our nation will increasingly experience more language diversity. The speech correctionist working in multicultural settings will need a broad knowledge of communication and will need to understand the unique communication situations of culturally diverse learners—dialects, bilingualism, and TOESL, as well as the differences between home and school language—and various assessment challenges (Baruth and Manning, 1992).

Another contemporary goal of the speech correctionist will be to understand dialectical differences of many culturally diverse learners and learners of the majority culture. Understanding and responding appropriately to the dialect of the learner within a classroom can be a complex and sensitive issue. First, it should be recognized that dialects are not communicative disorders and should not be treated as such by the teacher or the speech correctionist. The American Speech and Hearing Association (ASHA, 1983) has taken a strong position that dialectical varieties do not constitute speech or language disorders. It should be noted, however, that a dialect and a communicative disorder can exist at the same time. For example, if a learner with a Spanish- or African-American dialect also has defective articulation or stutters, the classroom educator should refer the learner to the speech correctionist. The situation grows complex if a teacher is not thoroughly familiar with the features of the dialect; however, both the teacher and the speech correctionist should learn to distinguish accurately between linguistic diversity and disorders. Dialects should not be considered "less than," but only "different from," that which is recognized as standard English. A teacher is in a strategic position to promote understanding and acceptance of a child who has a dialectical difference (Oyer et al., 1987; Baruth and Manning, 1992).

School Nurses/Health Coordinators

The school nurse, a long-accepted support services professional, has played key roles in promoting learners' health and safety and in coordinating health efforts among other professionals.

The school nurse is perhaps the professional with the most well-balanced understanding of the importance of the health status of the student, as well as the medical knowledge to make sound referrals. The nurse is also able to relate to parents and to other medical personnel the specifics of problems found in the schools.

Major responsibilities of the school nurse include (Redican et al., 1986)

(*1*) Constructing and/or maintaining health records of all students
(*2*) Reviewing records periodically to make sure they are accurate and up-to-date
(*3*) Dispensing medication to students in accordance with health policies
(*4*) Providing in-service training on health observation of students to all school personnel
(*5*) Conducting ongoing follow-up on students referred to health professionals for a potential medical problem
(*6*) Participating actively in the development of school health policies

(7) Providing or arranging for health counseling for students
(8) Reporting suspected cases of child abuse and/or neglect
(9) Acting as a medical resource person for health education teachers
(10) Identifying students with special medical problems and educating school personnel in how to deal with the student
(11) Identifying and using community resources for school health services

In order for the nurse to perform assigned tasks, a working relationship with others on the school health team must be established. Basic responsibilities for the school nurse may include (Redican et al., 1986)

(1) Participating in obtaining a health history
(2) Performing physical appraisals
(3) Evaluating developmental status
(4) Advising and counseling children, parents, and others
(5) Helping in the management of technologic, economic, and social influences affecting child health
(6) Participating in appropriate routine immunization programs
(7) Assessing and managing certain minor illnesses and accidents of children
(8) Planning to meet the health needs of children in cooperation with physicians and other members of the health team

The health coordinator plays an important part in the school health program. It is his or her primary responsibility to coordinate the efforts of and act as a liaison between the school, the family, and the community with respect to achieving optimal health for students. The health coordinator is also responsible for arranging in-service instruction for the staff, coordinating health fairs, and planning the health program with the administrator (Redican et al., 1986).

The health coordinator has several other responsibilities and opportunities, which include (Redican et al., 1986)

- promoting the use of community resources and facilities in the health instruction program and aiding in such use by making appropriate contacts and assisting in scheduling speakers, planning field trips, and keeping teachers informed of developments in the community
- providing essential instructional materials, screening new

publications and new materials, and making appropriate ones available to members of the school health team
- fostering interpersonal relationships to promote a closer working relationship of all members of the school health team
- planning ways to create a closer working relationship between teachers and the health service personnel
- encouraging all teachers to inform others of their plans for health teaching and to find out what is being taught by other teachers
- participating in and encouraging curriculum planning for health education and helping develop long-range plans for health instruction

Undoubtedly, the school nurse and health coordinator will continue to play important roles in schools. First, schools' roles are increasing far beyond the academic needs—schools are accepting (as a professional obligation and at society's insistence) responsibility for physical, social, and overall developmental needs. No longer can an educator teach a "subject" without consideration of learners and their needs. Second, learners often do not have access to health and nutritional information at home. While one may debate or question whether the school's roles include health and nutritional needs, educators readily recognize that hungry, tired, and sick students do not learn. Third, AIDS, a national health problem, will continue for years to come: nurses and health coordinators will be faced with teaching about AIDS, informing students about prevention, and working with other educators regarding bleeding resulting from school injuries. Fourth, the high teenage pregnancy rate indicates that school nurses and health coordinators will be called upon to help students at risk of pregnancy, to help classroom educators with developmentally appropriate sex education courses and materials, and to help administrators understand the legalities of school health programs.

In-School Suspension Workers

School, for many years, suspended misbehaving students for a number of days, perhaps three or five days or as much as two weeks. Such a tactic removed the chronic behavior problem from the school and usually required the parent or guardian to visit the school prior to the student's reinstatement.

Some students will need firm disciplinary measures for misbehavior such as constant annoyances, violence, threats to others, or bringing unlawful substances or objects to school. However, educators have realized that suspension for a number of days hurts both the school and the student: the school's role cannot be fulfilled when the student is separated from the learning environment and educational experiences. Therefore, schools are looking for more effective ways to separate misbehaving students from other learners.

Many school systems provide in-school suspension rooms for seriously disruptive students who must be removed from the regular classroom. These support services professionals should be familiar with the school policies regarding suspension and expulsion, alternative facilities, and other avenues available to help them and their students. Many school systems have a systemwide code of student conduct and a list of recommended and even mandatory procedures for dealing with inappropriate and unacceptable conduct. Professionals should always follow school policy in regard to administering disciplinary measures. If they are philosophically opposed to such policies, then they should find a position in a school district where policies are compatible with their own views (McQueen, 1992).

Several indications suggest that placing professionals in in-school suspension positions will continue to grow in popularity.

(*1*) Student misbehavior and violence are increasing in many of the nation's schools.
(*2*) Educators are recognizing the need to keep students in schools (and off the streets) on productive learning tasks.
(*3*) Educators are becoming more aware of students' legal rights to remain in school and to have access to educational experiences.
(*4*) Educators can remove students from situations yet continue classwork, tests, and homework.
(*5*) Students do not have the "enjoyment" of being away from school demands and expectations.

This brief examination of traditional support services professionals does not claim to address all support professionals who have contributed notably to administrators, classroom educators, and learners. Others include special educators, attendance specialists, and media specialists. Efforts of traditional support services professionals have benefitted learners and their educators in many ways, most particularly by providing specialized services for which regular classroom educators were not trained or did not have the time to address. As educational practices change and the restructuring and reform movements continue, these traditional support services professionals will continue to play viable and productive roles. Their roles and responsibilities may change as schools change, but children and adolescents will always need counselors, school nurses, psychologists, speech correctionists, and, unfortunately, in-school suspension specialists.

Who They Could Be during the 21st Century

Predicting support services professionals in the 21st century proves to be as chancy as trying to predict the winner of a Super Bowl Championship a number of years prior to the game. One can only look at current events and needs. For example, support services professionals can consider present learner needs and current events, predict future learner needs and trends, try to predict how events and trends will affect learners, and propose possible ways to address learner needs. One certainty that educators and support services professionals will face is the public's increased expectation for educators to accept more roles and responsibilities, as well as support professionals providing more specialized services. This section looks at possible support services personnel, provides a rationale for each, and suggests possible roles and responsibilities.

Learning Diagnostician

For one reason or another, some students in today's schools do not learn, do not achieve academically, and, generally speaking, do not benefit from educators' efforts. These students, for many years, have been considered lacking in ability, unmotivated, uncooperative, or unwilling to take advantage of educators' efforts. Regardless of the reason, some students underachieve or become school dropouts. The loss to students and to the nation is substantial and deserves to be addressed.

The prospects for a support services professional being responsible for diagnosing learners' problems are favorable. While a few programs have been successful in improving academic achievement, the number of students underachieving and the school dropout rates continue to be high, regardless of curricular materials, instructional materials, and educators' practices. This learning diagnostician could pinpoint reasons for lack of achievement, whether the cause be lack of ability, lack of motivation, or an incompatibility between learners' learning styles and educators' practices. For example, the learning diagnostician will be able to identify abilities or strengths on which educational experiences can be built and also identify weaknesses to be remediated. Reasons for lack of motivation can be identified and addressed, whenever possible. Educators are increasingly recognizing incompatibilities between how students learn and how teachers teach. To address these incompatibilities, the learning diagnostician will examine such aspects as learning types and teaching styles, multiple intelligences, and perceptions of educational success. Other diagnosing roles will obviously surface as support roles are further defined.

Software Specialists and Designers

One only has to look in software and hardware catalogs to locate an abundance of software available for purchase. Many software packages are high quality and designed by experts knowledgeable in content and how children learn; however, candidly speaking, some software serves little useful purpose. The increased technological innovations and recognition of how software can serve as a learning tool suggest the need for a support service professional with the ability to, first, identify well-designed software and, second, design software to address specific learning needs. This support service professional, the software specialist, may have responsibilities similar to the media specialist yet be able to work with educators (i.e., the learning diagnostician) to provide learners with software to meet special needs.

Identifying appropriate software will require knowledge of both available software and students' learning needs. For example, a mathematics teacher might want software for a learner who has a particular learning problem with addition, or a language arts teacher might want to address identifiable spelling problems. In this case, the software specialist will need sufficient knowledge of software to suggest a package which is compatible with the teachers' hardware and the learners' particular need. The knowledge will also include being able to identify strengths, weaknesses, and limitations of the software and also sufficient knowledge of learning theory to suggest developmentally—and instructionally—appropriate software.

What if software is not available to address a particular need? Such a situation requires the support professional to be a software specialist—

one who can actually design software to meet individual learning needs. Again, more expertise is needed than knowledge of hardware and software; the software specialist will also need knowledge of the content areas and learning and motivational theory.

Curriculum Designer

Observers of American educational history can attest to the fact that the school curriculum changes with societal and community expectations. While considerable uniformity exists within states, many differences can also be found from state to state and, in some cases, from system to system within a state. For example, one state and district may want a comprehensive sex education program while another one will not allow such a curriculum. Another may press for strong college preparatory curriculum, yet another offers little concern for what schools teach. In any event, the curriculum usually changes to reflect the interests of some influential group of individuals. Also, states sometimes mandate standards and criteria for systems yet leave actual implementation plans to states or the school systems.

The support service professional serving as a curriculum designer will be a curriculum expert on the philosophical bases, both traditional and contemporary efforts, how to design and implement curriculum changes, the relationship between curriculum and the "real world," and the need for learners to consider the curriculum relevant to their everyday lives. The curriculum designer will also know how curriculum changes affect learners, classroom educators, other support services personnel, and the community. In fact, this support service professional should be a vital link (a spokesperson of sorts) between the school and the community. Such a proposal does not suggest that classroom educators and administrators would not play vital roles in curriculum development. These professionals will play integral roles, especially if the curriculum designer encourages team participation, collaboration, and professional involvement. It is important to emphasize that this support service professional will not design curriculum in isolation but will lead others in the deliberations. In this collaborative effort, the curriculum designer will be the expert who will have objective and knowledgeable perspectives of curriculum and its role in contemporary schools.

Accountability Specialists

The push to hold schools and educators accountable for their efforts and actions grew during the last part of the 20th century. Legislators, taxpayer groups, and the general public call for tighter accountability and documented results for revenues expended. It is a safe prediction that the 21st century will bring an accountability specialist, a professional responsible for documenting results.

This accountability specialist could have responsibilities in several areas such as

(*1*) Preparing accreditation reports for professional associations and state departments of education
(*2*) Preparing summaries of test data (in readable and understandable form) for parents and families to determine their own child's progress and the school's overall progress
(*3*) Determining whether schools have met annual goals collaboratively set by administrators, other professionals in the schools, and parent representatives
(*4*) Determining whether educators are using the most effective practices—not in an administrative capacity but in a consultant role
(*5*) Determining whether the school has met legal mandates established by the state and local school system

It is important to emphasize that the accountability specialist will be a support service professional rather than an administrator. Responsible to key administrators, the accountability specialist will be considered a consultant or leader in accountability efforts. Others, both administrators and classroom educators, will supply this support professional with vital information and documentation. The accountability specialist will then compile and interpret this information, prepare sufficient documentation, and report to interested parties. No longer can accountability be left to chance or be considered a responsibility for some administrator to perform upon completion of duties. A planned and deliberate effort to document "worth" or performance will be necessary in the 21st century. Legislators, taxpayer groups, and the general public will not settle for less.

Mental Health Diagnosticians

Educators once considered themselves responsible only for the academic and moral aspects of students' lives. The three R's were taught along with moral codes of conduct. Later, educators added to this general education effort by adding vocational education and college preparatory curricula. The last half of the 20th century saw the school's role grow significantly. Lunch programs, breakfast programs, health initiatives, after-school programs, and, at least in some areas, condom distribution grew in popularity. Other situations saw closer ties between schools and social service areas, especially in areas of high poverty and high reliance on social services.

Mental health conditions such as anxiety, stress, and depression will likely result in schools assuming greater mental health roles. A support service professional, perhaps called a mental health diagnostician, could detect or screen for mental health problems. Perhaps working closely with the school psychologist and counselor, the mental health diagnostician could be specially trained in mental disorders affecting children and adolescents. This specialist could make referrals, follow up on classroom teachers' referrals, and act on parents' suggestions to determine whether learners' mental health affects their academic progress and overall development. The mental health diagnostician would work with mental health organizations, community agencies, and social service professionals to determine learners' mental health status, as well as the most appropriate action to take.

Expectations placed upon schools in the 21st century will not allow educators to consider themselves responsible only for students' academic achievement and cognitive development. Society is increasingly placing responsibilities on the school—eye examinations and screening for hearing problems will not suffice, especially when people are realizing that detecting mental health problems early is best for the individual and society.

Assessment Specialists—Teacher Competencies and Learner Progress

A support service professional can also serve as an assessment specialist, a professional whose responsibilities lie in assessing teacher competency and learner progress. For years, attempts have been directed toward distinguishing between effective and ineffective teachers, addressing and remediating weak teachers' areas of deficiencies, and, if necessary, providing the documentary evidence to dismiss incompetent teachers. Likewise, classroom educators often need help assessing learner progress, especially in later years when educators have been increasingly aware that tests often do not measure learners' true abilities. This section will, first, suggest how assessment specialists might assess teacher competencies and, second, look at how learners' progress might be most effectively measured.

Four ways assessment specialists might direct teacher assessment include (Porter, 1988)

(1) Selection/certification — Weak teachers can be eliminated either through denying certification or employment.

(2) Clarification of goals — Clear goals can be decided upon so assessment will be directed toward appropriate goals.

(3) Formative evaluation — Assessment experts can provide diagnostic and formative evaluation that can guide teacher self-improvement.

(4) Incentives — These experts can collaboratively decide with teachers appropriate rewards and incentives to motivate teachers to be effective.

Targets of teacher assessment may include (Porter, 1988)

(1) Prior experience — Does the teacher have the correct training?

(2) Knowledge and beliefs — Does the teacher know what he or she needs to know, and does the person have the requisite beliefs and convictions?

(3) Teacher actions — Does the person carry through on his or her potential by actually doing what is needed?

(4) Short-term outcomes — How do students and the teacher react in response to the instruction provided?

(5) Long-term outcomes — What do the students end up knowing, thinking, and doing as a result of the instruction?

Porter's (1988) work suggests an assessment specialist will need the ability to assess teacher competency in several areas: knowledge, skill, and attitude. While testing instruments have been developed to assess basic knowledge, skill and attitudes might be more difficult to measure. Observational forms and scales might be used to measure skills; i.e., the assessment may include observing using an objective scale to assess a teacher's teaching skills.

Teacher attitudes toward teaching, learners, and the profession might be more difficult, especially since these are more intangible. Even with these hurdles, it is likely that an assessment specialist will become a reality. Different from an administrator, the assessment specialist will work with classroom teachers and serve as a liaison between teachers and administrators. This person will work to help teachers become more effective, rather than working in a punitive position. However, if teachers do not demonstrate competency after a reasonable period of time, this person could assume responsibilities for collecting the documentation necessary for teacher dismissal.

The assessment specialists' second likely role will be to assist in the assessment of students' work and behavior. Educators and parents will not be surprised to learn that most tests only measure certain abilities and intelligences and, all too often, fail to measure more abstract aspects of learning. Still, the national trend continues to test any aspect of learning that can be measured and to consider unmeasurable aspects of learning as insignificant or unimportant. For too many years, teachers assessed progress by using paper and pencil tests — a method that did not meet many students' learning and testing styles.

The assessment specialists' roles in assessing learner progress might include:

- warning teachers of the dangers and limitations of testing
- helping teachers design tests that measure more than one type of learning and thinking
- designing tests to measure the various types of intelligences
- suggesting alternative measures of testing such as alternative tests, observational checklists, and portfolio evaluation
- helping teachers to design tests that teach as well as assess
- helping teachers to interpret test results and to plan future instruction based upon test results
- helping parents to understand test results and to have realistic expectations of children and adolescents

This support service professional could serve other educators in several ways. He or she could help administrators determine future school directions and goals, assist teachers in instructional designs and curricular projects, and help formulate a school policy and attitude toward assessment. The national obsession with testing will not go away in the next decade or so. Educators will increasingly be called upon to document their students' progress as well as their own competence. The support service professional working as an assessment specialist can play a major role in this effort.

Staff/Faculty Development Specialist

Several indicators suggest the need for a staff/faculty development specialist, a support service professional with the responsibility of providing or arranging for staff development programs. First, a sense of renewal encompassing the profession is causing professionals to want to be better prepared for daily challenges. Second, new programs appear almost daily to prepare educators to work with children and adolescents. Whether cooperative learning, a behavior management system, or a leadership program, educators are having increased opportunities to improve their professional skills. As previously discussed, the accountability movement is making all educators more aware of the need to demonstrate competencies and to prove their worth.

The staff/faculty development specialist will have responsibilities in several areas:

(1) Maintain familiarity with staff development programs and their various purposes, strengths, and weaknesses.
(2) Provide or arrange for staff development programs that reflect the school's mission statement and annual goals.
(3) Ensure that the staff development program includes themes and topics essential to effective teaching in the 21st century, such as professionalism, accountability, collaboration, technology, and multiculturalism.
(4) Convince staff and faculty members that staff development should not be considered a threatening activity.
(5) Conduct annual or biannual surveys to determine topics of interest to classroom educators and administrators.
(6) Involve administrators and other support services professionals, as well as classroom educators.
(7) Conduct evaluations of each staff development program to determine participants' opinions of the content and the presenter.
(8) Conduct evaluations to determine the long-term effects of staff development so successful programs can be repeated with other educators.

The staff/faculty development specialist must be a forward-looking professional—one who can distinguish between current trends and current fads, one who can encourage yet not coerce participants, and one who can work collaboratively with a wide array of differing professionals.

Legal Specialist

Citizens, and especially parents, are generally more aware of their legal rights and are more inclined to settle disputes through litigation (Sametz et al., 1983). This tendency to initiate lawsuits against schools suggests the need for a legal specialist, a support service professional who can serve as an arbitrator and legal counsel. This professional could assist administrators, classroom educators, and support services personnel with legal matters and could be charged with the responsibility of seeking mutual agreement rather than legal action.

The support specialist could be a legal expert in the areas most likely to involve classroom educators and other school professionals: child abuse, freedom of speech and press, suspension and expulsion from school, corporal punishment, juvenile court hearings, special education, freedom of religion, search and seizure within the school, divorce and child custody, school vandalism, and school attendance (Sametz et al., 1983).

This legal specialist could serve other vital school roles, e.g., ensuring teachers' rights are respected, due process hearings held for teachers facing dismissal, and in fact, any legal issue between the teacher and the school. This specialist would not "represent" either the school or the teacher but would advise parties of their rights and responsibilities. All too often, a lawsuit proves costly and both parties lose in the eyes of the public—this support service professional can work to avoid the bad publicity and extra expense that often result from legal action.

Adult Education Specialist

At least two factors—adults needing to complete their high school educations and adults becoming lifelong learners—suggest schools might need a support specialist trained to plan educational experiences for adults. This specialist will need to know subjects needed for high school graduation, to understand the concept of adults being lifelong learners, and to understand the psychology of adult learners.

It is not possible to know, with precision, what the future will bring, but each day people face problems and issues (employment, political, environmental) that require skillful solutions. Assuming that such problems will become increasingly complex in the future, there are certain problem-solving skills that will be required of all individuals:

(*1*) Knowing how to define problems
(*2*) Knowing how to think up, process, and develop ideas (as individuals and in groups) that will act as possible solutions

(*3*) Knowing how to evaluate solutions

(*4*) Knowing how to develop a plan of action and implement it (as individuals and in groups)

Due to technological advances in information processing, adults are going to be faced with monumental amounts of complex information to absorb. The job of each adult will be to find and translate appropriate information into usable structures. Adults will need to develop skills that allow them to grapple effectively with information overload.

If we are going to develop a lifelong learning society, adults must become more competent at assessing their own learning. Adult students need to ask new questions about their learning experiences as a whole and not just assess them in terms of a grade received or an aptitude or skill learned (Birkey, 1984).

Although roles will vary with school systems, adult education specialists will understand adult learners and their special needs; curricular experiences needed for 21st century living are technology and lifelong learning, legal aspects of educating adult learners, and appropriate methods of evaluation. Likewise, this specialist will need to be knowledgeable in selecting personnel to teach adult learners. Without doubt, educating adult learners can be a challenging activity and also one that can result in rich dividends, both for adult learners and their educators.

Home-Schooling Instruction Designers and Monitors

Some parents and families are deciding to teach their children and adolescents at home rather than entrusting schools with educational responsibilities. Reasons for home schooling include dissatisfaction with school academic achievement records, the amount of time wasted in a given school day, religious objections, and a host of other reasons. Regardless of the reasons, those parents who elect to educate their children and adolescents at home are relying on either the school to provide curricular materials or are purchasing teaching materials from a supplier specializing in home-schooling instruction.

States have rules and regulations for parents wanting to educate their children at home, and, in some cases, the schools even supply the curriculum materials and periodically evaluate learner progress. Little is to be gained from adverse relationships between schools and parents wanting to educate their children. Therefore, it appears that the most professional route would be for schools to take planned and deliberate stances toward the home-schooling movement and in fact, help parents and families in their efforts.

This support service professional, having a home-based instruction and design, will have several roles:

(1) Have sufficient knowledge of accreditation and certification requirements, which will enable one to plan comprehensive and sequential home curricula.
(2) Understand parents' reasons for home schooling, and while one does not have to agree with their reasons, one can accept parents' feelings and reasons.
(3) Help parents obtain curricular materials and understand instructional procedures.
(4) Offer access to counseling and psychological services.
(5) Offer and encourage opportunities for learners to participate in state and system achievement testing programs.
(6) Offer diagnostic evaluation for learners experiencing academic or social difficulties.
(7) Design, with the assistance of the parents, a curriculum that meets physical, psychosocial, and cognitive developmental needs.

Undoubtedly, home-schooling designers and mentors will have other roles: a liaison between the school and the home, a coordinator of services, and an administrator representative, to name a few roles. Individual situations differ with parents' reasons and decisions to educate learners at home. Important keys will include perceiving home schooling as an opportunity for parents, rather than as a threat to the school; avoiding adverse relationships between educators and parents; and helping to provide the best possible educational experiences for children and adolescents being educated at home.

SUPPORT SERVICES IN THE 21ST CENTURY: CHALLENGES AND CHANGING ROLES

Challenges

Restructuring and Reform Movements

The 1990s have been times of examining long-accepted educational practices: school principals and, especially, classroom teachers and support services professionals began making more professional decisions affecting their professional lives; curricula content and instructional practices underwent scrutiny; new methods of preparing teachers were proposed; the possibility of national certification grew in popularity; professionalism among educators expanded; professional practice boards were established, aiming at professional competence above and beyond state certification requirements; and, generally speaking, every aspect of the education profession came under close examination. While perceptive readers realize that educational practices have been examined in the past, the restructuring and reform movements of the 1990s are perhaps the most comprehensive efforts. In addition to the actual changes (e.g., teachers being empowered or having a greater voice in decision-making processes), the movements raised the professional consciousness of educators of all ranks and specialties. These educators knew their profession was being examined and, likewise, exerted efforts to meet new challenges.

Professional Empowerment

Empowerment, simply stated, is educators having the power and responsibility (as well as the professional obligation) to make decisions that affect their personal and professional lives. While some might feel educators should have been empowered decades ago, such was not the case; educators have not experienced opportunities to make professional decisions. In fact, many decisions were made by state departments of education or higher level administrators who undoubtedly considered their decisions to be wise; however, few of the decisions were being reached by educators implementing the decisions or, in fact, by those who actually worked with learners.

Often called site-based management, increasingly more professional decisions are being made at the school level. Teachers, support services professionals, and administrators make decisions directly affecting learners, such as promotion and retention standards, evaluating teacher performance, and making grouping decisions. While these are only a few of the decisions that empowerment and site-based management allow, the important point is educators, both classroom educators and support services professionals, are making decisions that affect their daily routines.

It is important to point out that empowerment calls for professional responsibility and, ultimately, accountability. Educators making decisions must be responsible for those decisions. Professionals not accepting accountability expectations may gradually lose their sense of responsibility and begin blaming circumstances on other people for poor performance. However, when professionals participate in setting exact standards of acceptable performance, they feel a deep sense of responsibility to obtain desired results (Covey, 1991). This accountability, however, should not prevent or discourage educators from engaging in empowered decision making. Accountability demands can be met through collaboration, effective teaming, shared decision making, and acceptance of responsibility.

Empowerment requires several aspects selected as common themes throughout this text such as teamwork, collaboration, professionalism, and accountability. Empowerment should lead to a clear mutual understanding and agreements among professional parties. Covey (1991) calls these agreements "win-win agreements" (p. 192), which result from five areas:

(1) *Specify desired results* — During discussions with team members, identify desired results and establish budgets and schedules. Then, set time lines for achieving the results.
(2) *Set guidelines* — Communicate principles, policies, and procedures that are essential to reaching desired results.
(3) *Identify available resources* — Identify the various financial, human, technical, and organizational resources available to professionals to assist in the reading of desired results. These may include information, communication, and training.
(4) *Define accountability* — Hold professionals accountable for their work and actual results. As previously mentioned, people should have a voice in setting standards and determining results.
(5) *Determine the consequences* — Reach an understanding of all people involved regarding the consequences of achieving or not achieving the desired results. Positive consequences might include financial or intangible rewards such as recognition, appreciation, advancement, new assignments, training, flexible schedules, leave of absence, perks, or other heightened responsibilities. Negative consequences might include retraining or, in rare cases, termination for lack of competencies.

Agents for Change

Support services professionals in the 21st century will see their roles transforming from being a helper to being an agent of change, a professional responsible for taking proactive stances toward restructuring educational thought and practices. Educational institutions do not change alone—change requires agents or leaders who have the knowledge and commitment to develop a plan (perhaps a vision) to improve professional situations and endeavors. Change requires careful planning, effective leadership skills, collaboration, and teamwork. Several factors suggest support services professionals should assume change agent roles:

(*1*) The support service professional is a member of the school team and therefore committed to working toward mutually agreed-upon goals.

(*2*) The support service professional has training and expertise in human relations and problem solving, which contribute to the meeting of team goals.

(*3*) The support service professional works in a prime position to understand both classroom educators' and administrators' positions.

Assuming change agent roles will require change of mind-sets toward what support services professionals do, they (as well as classroom educators and administrators) need to change perspectives of support services professionals from those acting only when called upon, to professionals leading, intervening, and taking proactive positions. The nature of change and some people's reluctance to change suggest that support services professionals' adopting roles of change agents might be a slow process and might also suggest the need for careful and deliberate planning.

Social, Economic, and Political Conditions

Support service personnel working as change agents will be faced with the challenges of changing social, economic, and political conditions. While perhaps such conditions should not affect the daily operation of schools, the reality is the opposite: school decisions and practices are often influenced by outside factors. These conditions, or perhaps challenges, should not be considered obstacles because, while deserving of consideration, they will not prevent support services professionals from becoming change agents, from taking proactive stances, and from advocating teamwork and collaboration. If possible, support services professionals should take advantage of social, economic, and political changes and use these realities as a springboard or impetus to reach goals established by collaborative teams.

Social realities include increasing violence in schools (and throughout society), changing family structures, and increasing multicultural populations. Schools undoubtedly will be called upon to address the problem of violence; e.g., parents and community members justifiably are calling for safe schools where learners can feel physically and psychologically safe. Changing family structures do not allow educators to believe all learners are coming from two-parent homes. Increasingly, learners grow up in one-parent homes or in homes with adults other than the actual mother and father. Educators sending notes to "Mr. and Mrs." risk the possibility of the learner coming from a one-parent home or even the learner's last name not being the same as the parent's. Undoubtedly, much more could be said about changing family structures and their effects on schools; however, it suffices to say at this point that educators need an accurate and realistic perception of homes and families from which students come.

Economic realities include many learners living in poverty, too many people unemployed or underemployed, and social welfare programs experiencing less financial resources. Some learners come to school unfed and undernourished and from substandard housing. Many parents have to work more than one job just for the necessities of life. Educational institutions often have to "make up" for the harsh economic realities of life and often perform services once considered to be the role of the home or community agencies. Educators have to compensate for the effects of poverty on learners' motivation and overall academic achievement, especially in financially strapped school systems.

Political realities include a propensity to hold educators and other professionals accountable for their abilities and skills, as well as for the results of their work. While this sense of accountability should not be viewed as a punitive obstacle, it is important for support services professionals and all educators to be aware of the political atmosphere in which schools and professional educators work.

Other realities could undoubtedly be listed, which will cause support services professionals to reflect upon school practices. However, it is important to note that these examples of social, economic, and political realities might have beneficial effects, especially when support services professionals take positive steps to reduce the effects. Helping students deal with changing family structures, addressing the needs of learners living in poverty, and providing acceptable responses to accountability demands can be excellent contributions for educators to strive toward.

Professionalism

Support services professionals will be affected by professionalism in several ways. First, they will enjoy increased recognition of their abilities, competencies, and roles. Second, they will be called upon to meet higher professional standards and to rise to new heights of professionalism. If one weighs the benefits of increased recognition and the expectation to meet more enacting professional standards, one likely will conclude that the benefits outweigh the efforts.

Increased recognition will result from three primary sources. First, support services professionals will enjoy increased recognition within their profession—both the overall education profession and their specialty areas. Administrators and classroom educators increasingly will recognize how support services personnel's expertise contributes to team endeavors and overall school effectiveness. Similarly, as specialty area certification standards grow more demanding, support services personnel will be better prepared and renewed to meet changing 21st century demands. Second, support services professionals will enjoy increased recognition within their own school situations and communities. Professionals in the school will recognize the talents and abilities support services bring to educational challenges. Similarly, support professionals will be expected to play more significant roles in the community; these roles will demonstrate their professional expertise and commitment to helping others. Third, professionalism will evolve from team approaches and related collaboration and collegiality. Working collegially toward team goals, sharing professional expertise and opinions, sharing accountability expectations, and enjoying the benefits and satisfactions of meeting agreed-upon goals contribute to professionalism and one's desire to engage in professional behaviors.

Accountability

Although there are many definitions of the term *accountability*, in education it means that schools must devise a way of relating the vast expenditure made for education to the educational results. For many years the quality of education was measured by the number of dollars spent or the processes of education used. In other words, a school system that had a relatively high cost per pupil or used educational techniques judged to be effective was considered an excellent system. Seldom was the effectiveness of school systems judged by student outcomes—the educational achievements of students. Now, those outcomes and a clear record of the cost of them must be accounted for (Johnson et al., 1994).

Accountability demands and expectations continued to increase in the late 20th century and, undoubtedly, will continue to grow more acute in the 21st century. Accountability stems from several sources—a litigious society, legislators expecting more results from sometimes fewer dollars, and professional associations and school systems expecting heightened levels of performance.

A meaningful system of accountability for public education should do three things: it should 1) set educationally meaningful and defensible standards for what parents and members of the general public can rightfully expect of a school system, school, or teacher; 2) establish reasonable and feasible means by which these standards can be implemented and upheld; and 3) provide avenues for redress or corrections in practice when these standards are not met, so that, ultimately, students are well served (Darling-Hammond, 1989).

Support services professionals will experience accountability from several sources and will be called upon to

- meet expectations of the community and nation
- meet expectations from the professionals, the education profession, and specialty area organizations
- meet expectations of other professionals in their respective schools
- meet self-expectations for achievement, expertise, and achievement

Much could be written about accountability—its rewards and the personal and professional satisfactions, as well as its frustrations and sometimes seemingly unreasonable demands such as high expectations from school systems and too high workloads. While some aspects of accountability might be perceived as threatening to some individuals, it can result in a sense of initiation, an impetus to reach new professional expectations, and a sense of professional and personal renewal. Increased demands for accountability will be a fact of life during the 21st century. Therefore, it is vital for support services professionals to perceive accountability as a means of renewal—a way to demonstrate competence, expertise, and achievement.

Last, as briefly mentioned, a significant accountability source should be professionals' self-expectations. Support services professionals are better trained than ever before, can enjoy the benefits of working collaboratively and collegially in teams, can take proactive leadership roles, and have technological innovations to contribute to meeting goals. These conditions should provide a new sense of renewal and professionalism and should result in support professionals setting high expectations of commitment, levels of competence, and professional achievement. This sense of high expectations can be the greatest factor in meeting accountability demands. It can lead to the personal motivation and the professional competence to envision goals, formulate carefully planned and deliberate goals, and implement procedures designed to meet goals. High expectations and the accompanying efforts to meet one's expectations can be an effective means to meeting accountability expectations and demands.

Technology

Technology, another challenge facing support services professionals, can promote educators' efforts and learners' academic achievement and overall educational accomplishments. Rapid technological breakthroughs and innovations provide support services professionals with a means of addressing individual learner needs, making work and presentations more interesting and innovative, and reaching higher levels of professional performance. Whether support services professionals want to retrieve information, disseminate information, or provide for educational instruction, technological innovations of recent years can offer notable contributions. Examples of technological innovations and how they can contribute to support services professionals' effectiveness are too numerous to examine in this section. However, the role of technology in support professionals' daily routines will be examined later in this text.

Changing Roles

Support services professionals will undoubtedly experience changing roles in the 21st century. Rather than providing professional services only upon request, support services professionals will assume proactive positions, become team advocates, act as consultants, and take leadership positions. It is unlikely that support professionals will assume these positions in isolation. More likely, they will act in two or more (perhaps all four) simultaneously. For example, support professionals might take a proactive position towards meeting a specific school need. To meet this need, they can advocate collaborative and collegial teaming and, then, serve as consultants and provide leadership expertise. Each of these changing roles requires expertise for which support services professionals need to be prepared to meet.

Proactive Positions

Proactive positions require support services professionals to be active, rather than passive, participants; to be knowledgeable of situations, rather than unprepared; and to be committed, rather than waiting for others to act. Acting in advocacy positions or as change agents, support services professionals need a sense of urgency, a belief that change should be for specific and worthwhile purposes, and a degree of commitment necessary to assume proactive positions. This urgency, belief, and commitment will require an understanding of "what could be" or, as some professionals prefer to say, a vision. Taking a proactive position also requires knowledge of educational situations, the ability to motivate and lead others, the ability to understand how professionalism and accountability relate to the goal, and the ability to use technological innovations to meet desired goals.

Team Advocates

Serving as a team advocate is another changing role of support services professionals. As the chapter on teaming will show, educators have worked in isolation for decades. Classroom educators and support services professionals did not know others' roles and often worked toward similar goals without realizing others' efforts. Support professionals serving as team advocates can complement classroom educators' efforts and vice versa. Skeptics often claim teaming has disadvantages – the extra time, reaching agreements, involving all team members, settling interpersonal conflicts, and evaluating efforts. While these "disadvantages" must be considered, there are numerous benefits – the collegiality resulting from collaborative efforts, mutual understandings, shared decision making, opportunities to lead, heightened responses to educational endeavors, and satisfaction resulting from successful teaming. The benefits definitely outweigh the disadvantages and the time and effort given to the teaming process. Since some educators have not begun addressing problems through teamwork, support services professionals often have to assume team advocacy roles, which require knowledge of effective teaming and a commitment to collegiality and collaborative efforts.

Consultants

Support services professionals will also act as consultants to administrators, classroom educators, other support specialties, and community organizations. Support services professionals have considerable specialized knowledge, an ability to work with both administrators and classroom educators, and usually high levels of motivation and commitment to help others. They can serve in consultant roles to administrators considering educational policy, to teachers making curricular and instructional decisions, and to community agencies needing specialized expertise. Consultants' horizons need to be restructured to include offering consultant services to state departments of education and other state agencies.

Leaders

Assuming leadership roles is probably one of the most challenging and rewarding of support services professionals' changing roles. For many years, the prevailing mind-set held that only administrators could assume leadership roles. To be candid, some administrators lacked leadership ability or lacked the motivation to lead. In these situations, schools did not have the leadership necessary to meet goals. Several factors suggest that the 21st century will be a time for support services professionals to assume significant leadership roles: increased opportunities to participate in site-based management, clearer perspectives of leadership ability and behaviors contributing to effective leadership, and a changing mind-set toward support services professionals taking active leadership roles. However, support professionals must be prepared for leadership challenges. Such preparation can be gained through reading books on leadership, attending leadership seminars, working with effective leaders, and practicing leadership skills. The nation's schools need effective leaders—professionals who can lead others toward collaborative goals and who can motivate other professionals to offer genuine commitments.

SUMMARY

Support services personnel have played significant roles in schools for many decades. Whether counselors, speech correctionists, or professionals serving other support areas, these support specialists provide valuable services that complement classroom educators' efforts. The future will probably see new support service roles—learning diagnosticians, software specialists, staff development experts, and adult education specialists, to suggest a few possibilities. Both traditional and future support services professionals will be challenged by the restructuring and reform movements, professional empowerment, and the expectation to be agents of change. Similarly, they will experience increased professionalism, increased accountability demands, and rapid technological innovations. Support services professionals can meet these changes and challenges through serving as consultants, leaders, and team advocates. The 21st century will be exciting times for support services professionals and, in fact, all educators. Accompanying these changing roles and increased challenges is a sense of professional renewal; the 21st century will be a time when support services professionals can take advantage of this renewal and offer significant contributions to learners and to other educators.

REFERENCES

ASHA Committee on the Status of Racial Minorities. (1983). "Social dialects," *ASHA*, 25(9):23–24.
Baruth, L. G. and Manning, M. L. (1992). *Multicultural Education of Children and Adolescents*. Boston: Allyn and Bacon.
Baruth, L. G. and Robinson, R. N. (1987). *An Introduction to the Counseling Profession*. Englewood Cliffs, NJ: Prentice-Hall.
Birkey, C. J. M. (1984). "Future directions for adult education and adult educators," *Journal of Teacher Education*, 35(3):25–29.
Covey, S. R. (1991). *Principle-Centered Leadership*. New York: Summit.
Darling-Hammond, L. (1989). "Accountability for professional practice," *Teachers College Record*, 91:59–80.
Jarolimek, J. and Foster, C. D. (1989). *Teaching and Learning in the Elementary School* (4th ed.). New York: Macmillan.

Johnson, J. A., Dupuis, V. L., Musial, D., and Hall, G. E. (1994). *Introduction to the Foundations of American Education* (9th ed.). Boston: Allyn and Bacon.

McCormick, L. (1990). "Cultural diversity and exceptionality," in *Exceptional Children and Youth,* N. G. Haring and L. McCormick (Eds.), pp. 47–75, Columbus, OH: Merrill.

McQueen, T. (1992). *Essentials of Classroom Management and Discipline.* New York: HarperCollins.

Oyer, H. J., Crowe, B., and Haas, W. H. (1987). *Speech, Language, and Hearing Disorders.* Boston: Little, Brown, and Company.

Porter, A. C. (1988). "Understanding teaching: A model for assessment," *Journal of Teacher Education,* 39(4): 2–7.

Redican, K. J., Olsen, L. K., and Baffi, C. R. (1986). *Organization of School Health Programs.* New York: Macmillan.

Sametz, L., McLoughlin, C., and Streib, V. (1983). "Legal education for preservice teachers: Basics or remediation," *Journal of Teacher Education,* 34(2): 10–12.

Shertzer, B. and Stone, S. (1980). *Fundamentals of Counseling* (3rd ed.). Boston: Houghton-Mifflin.

Slavin, R. E. (1988). "Cooperative learning and student achievement," *Educational Leadership,* 47(4):31–33.

CHAPTER 2

Renewing Support Services

OVERVIEW

EXCITING POSSIBILITIES FOR professional renewal will challenge support services personnel during the 21st century: rethinking opinions toward the support services mentioned in Chapter 1, professionalism reaching new heights, increasing demands for accountability, technological advances bringing new possibilities to teaching-learning experiences, better understanding of team dynamics and collaboration, and new support services roles necessitated by changing school expectations. Renewing support services includes restructuring thinking to conform with futuristic expectations and committing to an agenda highlighting coordinated efforts, whereby support services professionals and other educators work toward common goals. This chapter focuses on renewing support services to meet changing expectations and suggests possibilities the 21st century might bring.

THE NEED FOR RENEWAL

Several societal, educational, and ethical factors suggest the need for significant changes in the way educators view support services personnel and, in fact, the way support services personnel view their professional roles. First, the United States society is experiencing substantive changes: increasing numbers of culturally diverse learners, a boom in technological advances, increasing numbers of one-parent families, a restructuring of educational efforts, new accountability demands, renewed emphases on professionalism, and innovative methods of making United States schools more competitive with schools in other countries. Second, ethical responsibilities, whether implied or stated, hold educators responsible for fellow education professionals and for helping them reach their maximum effectiveness. Just as the 20th century brought changes and increased demands, the 21st century will also challenge educators to experience a sense of professional renewal and to be prepared and committed to work as a coordinated team toward a common goal.

The need for professional renewal becomes clear when support services personnel examine past and, in many cases, current perceptions of their roles in schools. This sense of professional competence, attitude, and commitment to work with other educators requires support services personnel to consider both their own perceptions of their roles and also to work to change or enlighten perceptions of other educators. For support services' ability and skills to be maximized most effectively during the 21st century, it is imperative that their roles be clarified and reconsidered in light of changing expectations toward schools. This challenge or imperative for significant change requires more than writing a new job description delineating specific roles and responsibilities. A restructuring of thought or mind-set, not only in words but also in actual practice, must take place. For such fundamental changes to occur, educators must understand previous and current attitudes toward support services personnel and strive to envision future roles and possibilities. This section looks at past perceptions of support services personnel, proposes more enlightened perceptions that can enhance schools' efforts, and suggests several mechanisms for professional renewal.

Past Perceptions of Support Personnel

Past perceptions of support services personnel, and perhaps their perceptions as well, have interfered with the effective coordination of educational efforts and the overall educational experiences provided learners. Candidly speaking, several reasons contribute to support services personnel being "left out" of the total education program: misunderstood roles, skills considered too limited to offer significant help, and someone with education and training too different from regular classroom teachers. Overall, educational efforts were further hampered by actual resentment resulting from perceptions that support services personnel threatened the status quo, received special privileges (i.e., not having bus or lunch duty), and had the benefit of working with only a limited number of students. For example, some reading resource teachers worked with fewer than ten students at a time, and counselors did not participate in the more negative aspects of teaching, i.e., the previously mentioned bus duty. Unfairly, regular classroom teachers, not realizing the many responsibilities of support services, felt these professionals did not carry their fair share of the team responsibility.

Such perceptions of support services personnel often handicapped team efforts, thus limiting learners' chances of educational success. For example, situations limiting educational efforts included little coordination between regular classroom teachers and support services personnel, there was duplicated work when groups did not know the others' efforts, and, from a more practical perspective, there was a lack of time for groups to meet as a team, except before and after school. In one relatively small school where coordination and teamwork could have occurred, the speech correctionist and the language arts teacher never met to discuss students' progress in communication skills. The speech correctionist probably realized how the language arts teacher, and vice versa, could reinforce the other's efforts; however, meeting to discuss coordination of services for the overall welfare of students never occurred.

These bleak perceptions of support services personnel and their roles resulted in these professionals working alone or being viewed as a resource person only in times of dire need. Considerable expertise was never tapped and the benefits of team approaches never realized, which handicapped both educational efforts and support services personnel's attempts to reach their maximum potential. Discerning educators and special services personnel clearly perceived a need for improved perceptions, but such substantive changes too often failed to materialize. While team relationships and coordination of efforts showed some improvements during the 1990s due to overall reform movements, educators in the 21st century undoubtedly will have a full agenda focusing on joint efforts to provide the most effective learning experiences.

Changing Perceptions of Support Services Personnel

The emphasis on restructuring education from what has been generally accepted for the past several hundred years has also influenced how educators think about support services personnel and their roles in the educational program. Their expertise and potential contributions are being constantly reconceptualized, and opportunities are provided for their full participation in the total educational program. Likewise, both regular classroom educators and support services personnel are realizing the values and benefits accrued from teamwork and collaborative relationships. These changing perceptions suggest a bright future for support service professionals and their role in contributing to quality educational experiences for all learners.

Several indicators suggest support services personnel of the 21st century will be involved and collaborative team members in the planning and implementation of education programs. First, support services personnel are highly trained and have considerable expertise to offer a team. Rather than a dual situation where classroom teachers and support services personnel worked in their respective directions, educators of all specialties are realizing the benefits of collaboration. Second, educators during the 1990s are beginning to understand how teams work, how teams take on an identity and purpose, and the benefits of collaborative efforts. In other words, the realization is crystallizing that added and enhanced benefits can be achieved through cooperation and collaboration. Third, more administrators are recognizing the benefits of positive and effective teamwork in their schools and are both encouraging collaborative sessions and designing a daily schedule that allows time for teachers, support services personnel, and administrators to work together.

Equally important, support services personnel are being accepted as integral team members. The past perceptions discussed previously are being replaced, due both to a renewed sense of professionalism and increased demands for accountability. Perhaps, also, educators are beginning to realize support services personnel's specialized expertise and potential contributions to learners' education. Another contributing factor is the increase in professional status of all educators and the recognition that professionals work together toward a common goal.

Changing perceptions of administrators and classroom educators have also contributed positively to support services personnel's attitudes toward themselves, both personally and professionally. No longer feeling they work in isolation or are called upon only when other resources have been exhausted, support services personnel can now feel like an integral part of the professional team—helping in the formation of educational goals; suggesting instructional strategies, materials, and assessments; and assessing the overall implementation. Likewise, positive perceptions toward self and others also result from working effectively toward mutually agreed-upon goals, as well as the positive feelings resulting from developing and maintaining positive working relationships.

Increased legal responsibilities resulting from local, state, and federal mandates and increased demands imposed by school districts, parents, and the general public also contribute to educators' changing their perceptions toward support services personnel. The last decade of the 20th century is seeing a flurry of legal battles and mandates in which state legislatures are establishing minimum education programs and minimum achievement scores for grade promotions, and parents are suing school districts for failing to educate children according to legal guidelines. Educators and other professionals undoubtedly want to avoid the hassles and negative publicity of lawsuits; however, the bright side is that professionals, both classroom teachers and support services personnel, are brought together in a collaborative manner to ensure schools meet all legal mandates.

Mechanisms for Renewal and Professional Development

Changing the mind-set toward support services personnel, their opinions toward themselves, and the general attitudes toward working as professional team members will not occur without a specially planned mechanism designed to change role perceptions and to renew professional commitment. Such a mechanism will extend far beyond preparing a new or revised job description that results in only superficial changes. Renewal necessary for the 21st century will require educators to examine and understand the renewal process and to be able to lead others to change long-held opinions. Changes and proposed changes have characterized American education for decades (and even centuries), often to no real avail. Change for the sake of change is not a necessary ingredient to renewing support services personnel in the 21st century. Likewise, educators should recognize that renewal does not automatically mean added work and responsibilities or finding time for additional activities in an already busy day. Instead, renewal can mean looking at situations differently to determine roles and responsibilities, which can be deleted altogether and replaced with more productive tasks, delegated to other professionals, or sometimes, changed to reflect 21st century demands. In other words, renewal does not suggest support services personnel must do everything they always have done and still accept new responsibilities. It means re-examining past and present roles, examining commonly accepted and long-held assumptions, and redesigning mind-sets toward what support service personnel should do. Without doubt, this renewal process must include support services personnel *and* classroom teachers and administrators.

Rather than only superficial and short-lived changes, genuine changes and renewal will include simultaneous and complementary efforts between support services personnel and classroom educators and administrators. Similarly, renewal among support services personnel can and must originate from several mechanisms working in unison: school administrators, district staff, universities, professional associations, and self-renewal.

School Administrators

The role of school administrators in rethinking professional roles and maintaining a school environment conducive to academic achievement and positive impersonal relationships became clear during the last part of the 20th century. No longer a figurehead, school administrators play significant roles in recognizing and promoting the efforts of support services personnel, advocating professional teams, and providing released time for teams to collaborate. Specifically, school administrators can restructure support service roles by

(1) Recognizing both verbally and in actual commitment the need for renewal of support services personnel
(2) Encouraging all professional educators on the school staff to take advantage of the services provided by support personnel
(3) Reducing service responsibilities, i.e., client numbers and extracurricular responsibilities to provide increased release time for professional development and specially designed in-service programs
(4) Encouraging all school professionals to have clear-cut goals, both personal and team, which promote team relationships, utilization of all professional expertise, and coordination of expertise and specialties
(5) Demonstrating and modeling respect for all school professionals and the unique contributions they can offer to the total school program
(6) Accepting responsibility for acting as a catalyst and for providing significant leadership for coordinated efforts
(7) Encouraging and providing support (i.e., monetary funds and leave time) for support services personnel that attend professional conferences and engage in professional development

District Office Staff

Upper-level administrators at the school district office may function in a prime position to provide recognition and renewal opportunities for support services personnel. Rather than leaving efforts and commitments to individual building administrators, officials at the district level may provide equal renewal opportunities for all support services personnel. Opportunities can include

- efforts to ensure comprehensive planning, which includes the efforts of district-level administrators, classroom teachers, school administrators, and support services personnel, and which focuses on genuine renewal in such areas as accountability, technology, and increased professionalism (efforts, however, should not be limited to these areas)
- efforts designed to renew support services personnel, both personally and professionally
- efforts to make support services personnel aware of their accountability responsibilities, technological advances, and the advantages of increased professionalism
- efforts to provide professional opportunities such as grants, fellowships, professional development, and travel opportunities, which may have been directed only to the district office, rather than all individual schools
- efforts to ensure comprehensive evaluation efforts of all professional efforts, especially efforts to renew and prepare support services personnel for the challenges of the 21st century

University

The university, another mechanism for renewing support services personnel, can provide a number of professional opportunities: courses, workshops, speakers, and career counseling, to name a few. When student numbers indicate a need, special curricula can be designed and implemented. Support services personnel can study and update esoteric courses in their areas of specialty or can learn more about current educational issues such as meeting the needs of culturally diverse learners, taking advantage of the latest technological advances, addressing accountability issues, and, generally speaking, seeking renewal opportunities within one's individual area of interest. The 21st century undoubtedly will be a time of increased collaboration between university and school district personnel. Support services personnel can speak to university classes and even teach segments in their areas of specialty. Likewise, university professors will work more closely with school districts, i.e., serving on advisory panels, assisting with instructional and evaluation designs, and helping to promote a sense of renewed commitment and enthusiasm. Such an effort should include considerable "up front" work, during which roles and possibilities are discussed in an attempt to avoid traditional expectations. Without doubt, this effort should focus on rethinking roles, examining mind-sets, and committing to experimentation and innovation.

Professional Organizations

Professional organizations also provide a host of professional opportunities. How many times have educators returned from professional meetings with a new sense of enthusiasm, commitment, and professional outlooks? Scores of well-established professional organizations will provide classroom educators and support services personnel with nearly unlimited opportunities during the 21st century. While the number of professional organizations is far too great to provide a comprehensive description, the following representative examples provide organizations that focus on particular support services areas:

- Council for Exceptional Children, 1920 Association Drive, Reston, VA 22091
- American Library Association, 50 E. Huron St., Chicago, IL 60611
- American Speech and Hearing Association, 10801 Rockville Pike, Rockville, MD 20852
- American School Health Association, 7263 State, P.O. Box 708, Kent, OH 44240
- American Counseling Association (American School Counselor Division), 5999 Stevenson Avenue, Alexandria, VA 22304

Support services personnel will want to explore additional organizations to determine the one or two that best meets their professional needs and interests. Readers wanting a more detailed list and description of professional organizations are encouraged to consult the most current edition of *Encyclopedia of Associations* (Gale Research, Inc., Vols. 1 and 2) located in nearly all public and university libraries.

Self-Renewal

Self-renewal can be among the most powerful means of preparing oneself to meet the challenges of the 21st century, especially since this mechanism requires motivation and determination of the individual support services professional. Self-renewal may occur for any number of reasons: support services personnel may realize classroom educators and administrators are not taking advantage of specialized support services, may recognize that burnout has limited contributions to team efforts, or may realize that additional expertise or renewal is needed to meet the changing demands of the 21st century. Regardless of the reason, it is important to note that the individual reason becomes the actual motivating force and that other educators, as well as the learners, are the beneficiaries.

Self-renewal can take many forms, all of which contribute to the support services professional's effectiveness: additional coursework at the university; guided or suggested readings by a colleague already involved in self-renewal; attending professional conferences in one's areas of interest or expertise; making an effort to hear speakers, both theorists and practitioners; participating in on-site visits to schools, making a commitment to address the changes of the 21st century; and working with other individuals or study groups to gain a better understanding of professional issues facing support services personnel. In all likelihood, choosing a form of self-renewal will not be an "either-or" situation. Instead, support services personnel will choose more than one form of self-renewal — perhaps, several forms with which they are most comfortable or that they feel are most beneficial to individual needs and interests.

Setting Goals for Professional Development

Professional renewal or development, regardless of the means or motivation, includes a rethinking of what the concept actually involves. Rather than being an external requirement imposed by an administrator, successful professional development requires changes in understanding. Participants can begin to see professional renewal as a "rich source of insights, an antidote to burnout, and a pleasurable collegial experience"

(Duke, 1990, p. 74). Another benefit includes a new appreciation for the role of self-awareness in professional renewal, i.e., understanding oneself and accompanying reasons for (or for not) tackling professional development with enthusiasm. Four promising types of activity to help heighten awareness include 1) breaking routine, 2) changing perspectives, 3) examining assumptions, and 4) reading challenging material (Duke, 1990).

Once support services personnel recognize professional development as a genuinely beneficial endeavor, the process of identifying growth goals begins. Goals should not be identified in a twenty-minute conference at the beginning of the year or even in a day-long workshop. Genuine goal setting for improving oneself professionally may take as long as an entire school year so that participants can engage in individual and group activities that lead to the identification of meaningful growth goals and a multiyear professional development plan.

Upon developing an adequate degree of awareness, the participant then engages in a process of goal setting and a plan of professional development designed to reach those goals. The implementation of the plan and the accompanying evaluation can lead to an even heightened awareness and the setting of even more goals (Duke, 1990).

The challenge for support services personnel during the late 1990s and the early 21st century will be twofold. First, rather than basing 21st century ideas on 20th century mind-sets, all educators, including support services personnel, must change perceptions of their respective professional specialties and the responsibilities of each. Second, with these rethought perceptions of what roles can be, then goals and agendas can be established that will enable the person to achieve the goals.

THE POSSIBILITIES FOR THE 21ST CENTURY

The possibilities for the 21st century can be challenging and exciting to professionals wanting to reform education, yet threatening to professionals wanting the security of the status quo. Events such as stricter accountability, increased professionalism, and technological advances will challenge and strengthen the profession. Other catalysts include changing teacher roles, length of the school year, financing practices, school-business and school-university partnerships, and a host of other events that affect educators' practices. Support services personnel will be doubly affected, i.e., changes in their roles as well as changes incurred due to financing dilemmas, changing teacher roles, and increasing expectations for accountability.

This section examines possibilities for the 21st century and their possible effects on support services personnel.

Visions

Anyone offering visions or predictions about events or about what another century, or even decade, will bring, and specifically about the future of American education assumes a difficult and risky task. Many conditions and factors influence American education—economic, political, and social—and can bring changes that either directly or indirectly affect schools' roles and priorities. Events in the 1990s indicate American school systems will undergo changes in the 21st century. The education reform movement, demographic changes, financing dilemmas (i.e., inequities between and within states), technological advances, the public's demand for school productivity, and critics' opinions that American schools are outdated institutions will undoubtedly force educational institutions to reconsider their roles and expectations. As educational institutions change, the roles and expectations of support services personnel will also change to reflect 21st century demands and new expectations of the profession.

Planning American education for the 21st century requires careful interpretation of projections, as well as aspirations for educational systems. What will roles of professionals be? What kinds of information help educational planners in their deliberations? What will tomorrow's students and schools be like? Answering such questions requires considering contemporary trends and events, as well as their influence on the future. Shane (1990), an expert on the future of education, foresees several challenges:

- an increasingly culturally diverse population, both at school and in society at large, which will lead to the Anglo-American population becoming the new minority
- trends in population and aging, which will result in significant percentages of older residents
- environmental problems, which will result in schools teaching that survival might not depend on large military forces and weapons
- changes in the traditional American family, which will lead to

schools addressing problems created by one-parent families, both parents working, and homelessness
* national debt levels, which will influence financial resources allocated to educational institutions

The extent to which educators meet these challenges will depend upon their cooperation, courage, and commitment to collaborative efforts. Hunter (1990) suggests that the American educational system has always maintained an isolationist attitude. In other words, American education concerned itself with serving the goals and the needs of the nation and the people. However, today's contemporary world has become multidimensional and calls for new mind-sets on which to base visions. Educational decisions must reflect cooperative efforts and sensitivity to different cultural, social, and developmental needs of all people (Hunter, 1990).

Events shaping American education as a whole will also affect support services personnel and their roles in educational institutions. For example, counselors will need expertise in multicultural counseling; speech correctionists will need an understanding of dialects; curriculum developers will need to recognize the importance of a culturally responsive curriculum; and technology experts will likely have at their fingertips a wealth of advances, perhaps not even known today. These representative examples suffice to illustrate how support services personnel will be challenged to change perceptions toward their roles and perhaps even to reeducate themselves to meet 21st century demands.

Teachers

The educator of the future will have extensive experience with such topics as brain development, learning environment alternatives, cognitive and psychosomatic evaluation, and affective development. The traditional teaching job will be divided into several parts. After computer-managed courseware has been installed in schools, the information gathered on teachers' performance in a variety of situations will determine which jobs will be delegated to which teachers. School systems will encourage this specialization because they may make money from selling various services to business interests—or teachers may work part-time and sell the services themselves. Some of the new roles may be (Cetron et al., 1985):

* learning diagnostician

- information gatherer for software programs
- courseware writer
- curriculum designer
- mental-health diagnostician
- evaluator of learning performances
- evaluator of social skills
- small-group learning facilitator
- large-group learning facilitator
- media-instruction producer
- home-based instruction designer
- home-based instruction monitor

The previously mentioned isolationist attitude of American education also extends to its teachers. Teachers have often worked behind closed doors, both figuratively and literally, and have not benefitted from other teachers' ideas and methods or the specialized services provided by support services personnel. Teachers' changing attitudes hold a potential for affecting their professional roles with support services personnel; i.e., teachers will see the benefits of closer working relationships, will seek more specialized services, and will seek collaborative efforts to meet the challenges of the new roles listed above.

Length of the School Year

Undoubtedly a factor influencing support services personnel and their roles, the length of the school year will likely change to reflect 21st century economic and societal expectations. The present nine-month school year, an outdated institution, is a product of the 19th century agrarian economy. Young people were needed at home and on the farm from late-spring to mid-fall; thus, educators planned school calendars accordingly. The percentage of people making a living from farming grew small during the last decades of the 20th century and all trends indicate an even smaller number during the 21st century. While lengthening the school year appears inevitable, one might ask how such a move would affect support services personnel.

Year-round education includes three types: single-track, multi-track, and the extended school year. The single-track and the multi-track plans include such calendar plans as 45−15, 60−20, 60−15, and 90−30 (days in school−days on vacation), as well as several other configurations. In addition to better reflecting 21st century economic and social expectations, other distinct advantages become clear (Peltier, 1991):

(1) Problems with overcrowding can be alleviated.
(2) Students can have improved educational opportunities, i.e., continuous progress.
(3) Districts hope to maximize the use of school facilities and, thus, become more cost-effective.
(4) Attendance of both students and teachers can improve due to regularly scheduled vacation periods.
(5) Dropout rates of high school students have been positively influenced.
(6) Students, during their times off, can participate in remedial classes and accelerated classes.
(7) Teachers can benefit from increased salaries due to the increased number of working days.
(8) Vandalism can be reduced since school facilities are open all year.

Glines (1992) makes an important point for implementers of school programs (and support services personnel planning for 21st century expectations): changing educational practices, in this case, the length of the school year, should not be done with a "now" vision. For example, a school district decides to adopt year-round programs because it is overcrowded "now" or a district with low test scores "now" views year round programs as a possible solution. Glines sees a danger in planning future educational practices on "now" expectations, i.e., the decision to extend the school year can be a "catalyst to refocus on every aspect of the educational system—to think philosophy, curriculum, delivery systems, facilities, organizations, vacations, community services, and volunteering—everything pertaining to the enhancement of learning" (Glines, 1992, p. 20).

Glines (1992) emphasizes a point, which this book has sought to highlight. Educators cannot plan educational practice and policy for the next century using 20th century perspectives. Looking specifically at lengthening the school year, how might support services personnel be affected? How might roles change?

Lengthening the school year may impact on support services personnel in several ways. Support services personnel may

- work the full year so their specialized services will always be available to teachers and students

- adopt new roles such as designers of software and testing programs, which address the needs of a diverse student population
- work more as a team member in a collaborative manner rather than working in isolation
- become even more specialized in respective fields and more involved in professional organizations
- receive higher salaries and greater respect due to their longer work year and their increasing specialization
- experience increased demands and expectations for accountability

Regardless of the type of lengthened school year a district adopts, the support service specialist will not be isolated from the decision. Change affecting one group of educators subsequently affects all professionals and, especially, support services personnel whose roles and responsibilities cross student age levels and academic boundaries.

Financing

How best to finance schools was an issue throughout the last decades of the 20th century. Factors contributing to the focus on finance included declining school budgets, realization of severe inequities between and among school districts and states, new demands for ability and the public getting the most for its dollar, and spiraling school budgets. In the 1990s, evidence suggests the concern with school finance will be a major challenge in the 21st century.

Maintaining that teaching is the largest component of school budgets, Odden and Kim (1992, pp. 3–4) feel attention in the future must be directed toward:

- recruitment into the profession, including into preservice training through fellowship or loan programs
- beginning salaries, especially a policy benchmark for beginning teacher salaries, such as the average beginning salary for all college graduates
- base salaries, including whether to provide annual pay increments based on teachers' knowledge and skills
- pay-for-performance that avoids the flaws of individual-based incentive and merit pay programs and that draws on successful private-sector practices that reward all individuals in production units—schools—and foster teamwork and collegiality

- benefits, including switching from a fixed to a flexible benefits schedule
- pensions, by replacing today's defined benefit programs with defined contributions programs that are fairer and less costly, and providing higher pensions

While the professional staff consumes the majority of a district's financial budget and is a challenge with which budget planners must deal, other aspects also affect school finance. First, districts allowing site-based management need to be given responsibility for meeting goals set at national, state, and district levels. Taking site-based management seriously, however, includes allowing site-based budgeting and financing. State school finance policy could take the lead in developing approaches that foster site-based budgeting by stipulating that a fixed percent of base funding be allocated directly to schools as a lump sum or by requiring districts to allocate a fixed percent or all instructional expenditures to schools (Odden and Kim, 1992).

Second, new incentive programs, perhaps to counter the demands for accountability and as a means of becoming more cost-efficient, can take new directions. Nearly all new incentive programs are based on outcomes and schools, not individual teachers. School-based incentives foster cooperation and collegiality among school staffs to accomplish schoolwide student performance objectives. Recent proposals have suggested schools be given greater flexibility in spending funds if certain outcomes are met (Odden and Kim, 1992).

Third, public school choice continues to be a hotly debated topic in the 1990s and will probably continue into the next century. While many supporters contend that parents should be able to choose where their children attend school, others maintain that public school choice would mean the death of the public school system as known today. Likewise, when parents live in one area yet send their children to school in another area, they are less likely to support the school in the neighborhood where they live, i.e., being willing to vote for property tax increases. Also, many states in the 1990s count the child as a pupil in the district attended in calculating financial aid to the district. The effect of this policy is that funding shifts from the resident to the attending district (Odden and Kim, 1992).

The issue of financing education has been a controversial issue for decades and will probably continue to plague and challenge educators. The inequities between and among schools and also the financial problems being faced by many school planners sound an alarm, such that an imperative during the 21st century will be to pinpoint a solution to the financing dilemma.

The financing dilemma may affect support services personnel in several ways. While positions above the number required by local and state mandates may be few in financially strapped school districts, layoffs or massive job shortages should not pose a problem since schools must meet minimum standards defined by law. On a brighter note, support services personnel might benefit due to incentive programs encouraging cooperation, collaboration, and increased productivity. Support services personnel might be challenged to work with less financial resources, equipment, travel allowances, and teaching-learning materials. While these are not ideal circumstances, the goal will be to address accountability and professional demands by getting the most worth from each dollar allocated. At the same time, however, support services personnel can constantly educate administrators, parents, and taxpayers about the role of support services and the legal mandates facing these professionals.

Accountability

While definitions of accountability vary, for most educators, accountability means that students or teachers must exhibit some standard of competency or performance and that schools must devise methods of relating expenditures to outcomes. Several factors have contributed to increases in accountability demands and suggest accountability will be a key challenge in the 21st century (Ornstein, 1988):

(*1*) Increasing numbers of parents realize the importance of schooling and consider their children's education inadequate.

(*2*) The public has the impression that educators are accountable to no one but themselves.

(*3*) School costs continue to rise and taxpayers question how money is being spent.

(*4*) Some educators and policymakers feel an information system needs to identify school effectiveness.

(*5*) The excellence movement, begun in the mid-1980s, continues to interest educators, parents, business people, state legislatures, and governors.

(6) Some educators maintain that modes of proof can be established for assessing outcomes.

(7) Several states have mandated test-driven curriculum standards to assess performance.

The accountability movement appears to be increasing in popularity as the end of the 20th century nears, even though several questions remain unanswered: How do educators measure achievement, especially when varying student abilities are brought into focus? Can tests measure higher order thinking skills and creativity? What action should be taken toward schools with low achievement scores? Can accountability models used by business serve a purpose in schools, and if so, how? What are the psychological effects of constant bombardment of testing on students? The accountability movement will in all likelihood be a powerful force in the 21st century; however, before the movement provides the results many in the United States want, these questions deserve to be discussed and addressed.

Making schools genuinely accountable for students' learning will require involving educators in the development of methods and modes of assessments that measure what students know and can do. In this manner, assessment can be tied to instruction, improvement of practice, and the creation of greater knowledge and shared standards across the educational enterprise as a whole. Many schools, districts, and states have begun to develop alternative forms of assessments based on essays, research projects, exhibitions, and portfolios of students' work (Lieberman, 1991).

One can assert with a degree of certainty that educators will have to deal with the accountability movement in the upcoming century. Similarly, support services personnel will be challenged to prove taxpayers' dollars are being wisely spent. What particular accountability demands might special services personnel face? Since some (but certainly not all) support services personnel might be expendable, it is feasible that, in a district already experiencing financial cutbacks, support staff who could not prove accountability expectations might receive some type of negative treatment. The problem facing the support services personnel might be a quantity versus quality situation. The person might have a large caseload and might be dealing with a record number of referrals, yet the actual quality of services might be quite low. Likewise, the specialists' caseload might be sufficiently large that quality service cannot be provided. A second challenge facing support services personnel is actual assessment. The specialist working cooperatively with another teacher or a team of teachers might be the driving force toward helping a learner; however, documenting performance or contributions on paper might be difficult or impossible.

It is not being implied that the difficulty with accountability and assessing performance should result in support services personnel not being held accountable for their professional responsibilities. The challenge for accountability proponents and support services personnel (who will want a voice in their professional destiny) will be to work cooperatively to determine how most effectively to assess performance, especially considering that roles and responsibilities often cross professional lines.

Technology

Because of recent innovations in technology, some writers suggest that technological advances will totally change schools from what we now know. Others disagree and contend that technology will not penetrate beyond the margins of the school system (Newman, 1992). One could argue for both positions. Technology does, indeed, hold tremendous implications for schools, for helping students learn, for assessment purposes, and for assisting teachers with routine drudgery and paperwork. On the other hand, schools are slow to change, some teachers still feel uncomfortable working with computers, and technological advances can be costly. Still, the technological advances of the last ten to fifteen years provide a strong indication—despite the skeptics—that schools will become much more technologically oriented in the 21st century.

Drucker (1992) contends that schools are not presently using available technology to its maximum potential; however, several factors lead Drucker to suggest that technology will be a more powerful force in schools within ten years. First, many teachers are no longer afraid of computers. They see computers have many uses and no longer view the computer as a means of replacing teachers. Second, children are not afraid to use computers and to experiment with the various forms of technology (Drucker, 1992).

This somewhat cursory glance at possibilities for the 21st century cannot begin to examine recent technological advances, how they have influenced schools, and what the 21st century might bring. However, it does suffice to show that technological advances will continue and will have a dramatic effect on schools. Exciting roles and opportunities include desktop publishing, spreadsheets, and large, easily accessible databases that combine computers with CD-ROM. The extent to which technological advances and tools are used will depend on educators' motivation and the applications they design, plan, and implement.

Like other educators, support services specialists will be challenged to decide how best to use available technological advances. The extent one uses technology will, of course, depend on one's area of specialization, technology designed for one's respective field, and the district's ability and willingness to invest in technology. For example, the school library media specialist should be a master teacher and should be able to work with classroom educators to integrate information management skills into their curriculum and classes. He or she must also be an effective manager of human and material resources because the library media program must be systematically planned, implemented, and evaluated. With shrinking budgets, the library media specialist must be prepared to articulate and defend a budget, as well as seek outside funding when necessary. The library media specialist must also be well versed in the wide range of technologies required to supply the school with information, whether they be traditional reference tools, on-line telecommunications, or carefully selected CD-ROM databases.

School-Business and School-University Partnerships

The last decade or so of the 20th century has seen increased attempts to involve outside agencies into school settings. The two most prevalent, business and universities, provided and continue to provide considerable assistance to schools needing financial resources, equipment, various forms of professional development, and expertise in specialized areas. These partnerships form a logical marriage; businesses have a stake in schools since future employees are being educated and universities realize future students are being prepared in the schools.

Support services personnel in future decades will probably see an increase in these partnerships as schools and outside agencies realize the values of collaboration, helping each other to achieve goals, and sharing resources. Businesses, often blessed with more and better equipment, can share both resources and experts. In any event, the school benefits from business's presence in the school, and the business gains a new perspective of the challenges schools face and the benefits of collaboration.

Universities, especially during the 1990s, began to form collaborative partnerships with public schools. These partnerships usually take one of two forms, either adopting a Professional Development School Model or a model in which the university has a particular skill or expertise to offer the school. In the former, the school actually becomes a teaching training location. Teacher education courses are taught at the school, and in return, university professors and their students help in the classrooms and with other school functions. In the latter, the university addresses a particular school need, i.e., professors plan a program designed to improve test scores or teach teachers particular skills. In both situations, school and university personnel are brought face-to-face and confront issues openly. Both benefit by offering and receiving particular skills and services.

As with other educators, support services personnel need to offer their services when partnerships are formed. Counselors, speech-language specialists, school psychologists, and testing specialists, just to provide representative examples, have skills and expertise that businesses and universities can use. Likewise, businesses and universities can provide resources, materials, equipment, and services that can help support services personnel. Cooperation and collaborative relationships, another benefit accrued from these partnerships, can reach new heights. Factors such as increased accountability, technological advances, and the trend toward increased collaboration will likely result in additional partnerships, whereby support services personnel can offer assistance in specialized areas and receive benefits otherwise unattainable.

Senior Volunteers

Retirees live in every part of the United States and are becoming increasingly active in organizations and communities. Also, the percentages of retirees or citizens over sixty-five will grow significantly between the 1990s and the year 2030. Consider Table 2.1 for a brief overview of ages and percentages.

There are definite advantages in seeking seniors' involvement and assistance. First, they have the resources, experience, and energy to help in schools. These volunteers can assist in classrooms and offices, taking care of tedious routines that dissipate the time and energy of teachers, thereby allowing schools to maximize their potential through the improved management of time, personnel, and money. Teachers who have welcomed senior volunteers into classrooms as aides have been pleasantly surprised to discover a wealth of skills and experiences. Second,

Table 2.1 Individuals Aged 65 – 74.

Year	% Aged 65 – 74
1990s	7.5%
2010	15.0%
2030	20.0%

Source: Compiled from Armengol (1992).

intergenerational programs result, which bring young and old together. At a time when the multigenerational family living under one roof is a rarity, intergenerational programs in the schools give students experiences that they otherwise might have missed (Armengol, 1992).

Highly skilled senior volunteers have made significant contributions: making display cases and bookshelves, tuning pianos, decorating for special events, and repairing cameras and audiovisual equipment. Many senior volunteers can tutor non-English-speaking students and serve as translators for parent-teacher conferences. They can assist with clerical duties in offices and library media centers or act as chaperones on field trips. They have been successful at demonstrating technical skills in industrial arts classes and assisting with typing, computer, and reading labs. A volunteer mentoring program for students in mathematics, reading, and science, as well as programs for disadvantaged students, can have positive results. Senior volunteers are ideal for reading to students and for telling real-life experiences that relate to topics being studied in class (Armengol, 1992).

Looking at the roles that senior volunteers can play in regular classrooms provides indications of how support services specialists can use this valuable resource. Senior volunteers represent a significant resource that support services personnel cannot afford to ignore. Just as senior volunteers help regular classroom educators, they can also assist support services personnel: helping with the paperwork, working with individual children, performing clerical routines, and answering the telephone. In fact, a support service specialist might serve as a contact person or coordinator of senior volunteers. Perhaps, also, the support service specialist, especially an evaluation expert, could design a program to assess senior volunteers' contributions to the school.

Support Services Personnel

The possibilities for support services personnel have no boundaries, limited only by professionals' imagination, commitment, and resources. New roles may result as resources provide more information on learners, as legal mandates require more specialized services, and as present roles expand or change to reflect contemporary educational and societal concerns. As previously suggested, however, support services personnel cannot consider future roles and responsibilities with present perceptions. Just as horses and buggies do not come to mind when people in the 1990s consider transportation, support services personnel cannot think in terms of present perceptions when considering next century roles and responsibilities. Likewise, even with positions that in all likelihood will continue, i.e., counselors, speech and language specialists, and school psychologists, responsibilities within each specialty will likely change. For example, counselors will face increasing challenges resulting from children suffering from crack or other drug addictions, and AIDS; speech and language specialists will be challenged to distinguish between language differences needing to be corrected and those resulting from cultural and geographical differences. Without doubt, support services personnel will carry major responsibilities during the 21st century as schools better address educational and societal needs.

Renewal as a Vitalized Professional

Basic to all new and expanded roles will be renewal as a vitalized professional. Renewal, resulting from any of the mechanisms mentioned earlier in the chapter, can lead to new enthusiasm for one's profession and specialty, the setting of ambitious professional agendas, and raising one's professional consciousness and standards. It is important to note also that support services personnel in the 21st century will benefit from their renewal efforts: increased respect, better salaries, the benefits accrued from collaborative relationships, and the satisfaction one receives from professional commitment. In summary, renewal will be a two-way street, requiring effort and motivation on the one hand, yet on the other hand, paying rich dividends, both for the profession and for the individual.

Technological Leader

The support services specialist is in a prime position to lead other educators toward technological advancements. Able to know technology and its practical uses across academic areas as well as areas of specialty, support services specialists can take the lead in showing others the advantages of technology; making a case to district officials for technological purchases; and, through collaborative relationships, showing educators how technology can serve daily instructional purposes. Future possibilities might include schools being a telecommunications watershed, a place where students and, in fact, all citizens can use schools twenty-four hours a day and 365 days a year. Present arrangements, allowing technology to be used from 8 – 3 only, nine months a year, make little sense and do not contribute to utilization of equipment. Support services personnel can challenge school officials to change perceptions of what the school's role in communities should be.

One might reasonably question whether schools will have the financial resources to support ambitious efforts toward technological advances. If support services personnel want to become technological leaders, will money be available? Will districts see technology as expendable? In tight economic times, will technology take a backseat to other expenditures, perhaps programs mandated by law? While these are excellent questions and deserve consideration, it is likely that school districts will view technology as a wise investment for the future. First, indicators suggest the cost of technology might actually decrease. For example, educators can now purchase calculators at a fraction of their price twenty or so years ago. Through mass production and competitive markets, manufacturers can produce, and subsequently sell, calculators for only a few dollars. As computers and software packages continue to be produced in markets similar to what manufacturers of calculators experienced, prices might actually fall, thus giving school districts a technological edge. Second, unlike many so-called advances, technology and especially computers have spread throughout society. Students see computers virtually everywhere – businesses, doctors' offices, and in many homes. It is unlikely that schools will be able to dismiss technology and computers in a world so dependent upon these advances. Support services personnel serve in a prime position to lead school districts and individual educators toward technological literacy.

Multi-Support Area Qualified

A trend in the mid-1990s is to become qualified in more than one area of specialty. Such a trend might have resulted from personnel seeking multiple specialties to improve employment possibilities, districts realizing that personnel qualified in more than one area is a viable means of saving money, and the belief that many learners need multiple services rather than the service of only one area.

Integration, another trend during the 1990s, focused on several areas: teaching across subject area lines; having educators trained in more than one area so relationships could be studied; and the combining of experts, each sharing their areas of expertise. This trend, along with the understanding of the value of collaborative relationships, contributes to educators being able to contribute in multiple ways. Often, educators, due to state certification requirements, might experience difficulty developing more than one area of specialty. Support services personnel, however, work across subject area lines, with a number of teachers simultaneously, and with administrators and other specialists. Therefore, support services personnel serve in an excellent position to seek multiple qualifications.

Curricular and Instructional Specialists

Usually classroom educators are considered to be most knowledgeable about curricular and instructional issues, i.e., what should be taught and what instructional methods should be used. This assumption appears logical and valid, especially since these educators work with students on a daily basis and are the actual planners of everyday instruction. Support services personnel also need to become curricular and instructional specialists since collaborative teams of specialists and classroom educators are becoming the norm, rather than the exception. Such a suggestion broadens the roles and realms of expertise for support services personnel. Rather than having expertise in only one area, i.e., speech and language, the specialists would know how to weave speech and language remediation into curricular and instructional areas. For example, the speech and language specialist, when working with the language arts teacher, needs to understand what content is being addressed, what instructional methods are being employed, and, also, how speech and language activities can be integrated in daily lesson plans. These levels of expertise will allow support services personnel to see the ''whole picture'' surrounding a learner and also contribute to maximum assistance being given.

Testing and Evaluation Specialists

Educators during the last decades of the 20th century learned the harsh realities of testing: tests often result in psychological damage, and also, faulty test results too often become the basis for crucial educational decisions (Lieberman, 1991). While school psychologists and sometimes counselors have major responsibilities for school testing programs, educators in the 21st century need a testing and evaluation specialist. Such a support service specialist will have training in testing and evaluation, understand the dangers and limitations of testing, recognize the psychological effects, and be prepared to work with other educators needing assistance in designing tests and understanding test results. Even in the 1990s, testing is considered to be a problem for both educators and learners, yet with the increased demands for accountability, testing will likely continue to grow in popularity, especially among those not understanding its fallacies and dangers. A testing and evaluation specialist can play a major role in helping students, teachers, and parents understand the necessity and limitations of testing.

Culture and Gender Specialists

The rapidly increasing cultural diversity enriching the United States and the recognition of gender differences among learners call for support services specialists capable of relating teaching-learning experiences to culture and gender. An area much too complex to explore in detail here (see Chapter 7) culture and gender influences on learning deserve to be explored and understood. Extensive work (Manning, 1993) has focused on previously unrecognized cultural and gender differences and has shown that these differences, do, indeed, affect learning, overall achievement, motivation, and attitudes toward learning. A major shortcoming of the American education system has been its tendency to provide the same teaching-learning experiences for all learners, regardless of culture, social class, or gender. The 21st century, without doubt, will see growing cultural diversity and increasing recognition of cultural differences; however, frankly speaking, most school districts do not have support services personnel trained in cultural and gender differences. Such a support service professional could work with individual learners and help other educators recognize the dangers of relying too heavily on one instructional mode and similar achievement expectations.

Accreditation/Certification Specialists

Most corporations have some type of production or quality control manager, a person trained in how to maintain quality, how to obtain more production, and how to present understandable evidence, showing others the corporation's accomplishments. Yet schools often rely on a number of professionals such as the principal, assistant principal, or district office personnel to show that the school is accomplishing its goals. With the increasing demands for accountability, schools in the 21st century will need an accreditation or certification specialist. This new support service specialist will be responsible for leading others in the gathering of information for the accreditation process, compiling the information in a readable and understandable form, and, generally speaking, accepting responsibility for the accreditation process.

Accreditation and certification organizations might include local, regional, or national accrediting agencies, as well as state departments of education. Other roles might include preparing an annual report to teachers and parents, in which updates on progress toward goals are provided. The accreditation and certification specialist will need an overall understanding of the entire school program, curricular and instructional approaches, and, of course, the accreditation and certification requirements facing schools. As previously mentioned, a number of people in the past accepted responsibility for various aspects of the process and while involving a number of people allowed a collaborative effort, all too often, such roles were "add-on" to an already busy day and, also, were accomplished by people who were novices to the accreditation and certification processes. Having one support service professional responsible for the entire operation will provide a knowledgeable expert capable of leading others into collaborative efforts toward a common goal.

SUMMARY

Several indications suggest the 21st century will be a prime time for support services personnel to make valuable contributions: perceptions toward support services personnel are changing from a person working in isolation to an active team member; many opportunities are providing means of professional renewal, both renewing previous skills and regearing for new roles; and roles and responsibilities are evolving, which make specialists even more important members of the school team. Committed support services personnel striving to meet the challenges of a changing education professional (such as increased accountability, technological advances, and a renewed sense of professionalism) and understanding the value of collaborative working relationships will provide a sense of renewal and recommitment to meet 21st century demands.

REFERENCES

Armengol, R. (1992). "Getting older and getting better," *Phi Delta Kappan*, 73:467–470.
Cetron, M. J., Soriano, B. and Gayle, M. (1985). "Schools of the future," *The Futurist*, 19(8):18–23.
Drucker, P. F. (1992). "Performance, accountability, and results," *American School Board Journal*, 179(3):A4–A11.
Duke, D. L. (1990). "Setting goals for professional development," *Educational Leadership*, 47(8):71–75.
Glines, D. (1992). "Year-round education: What lies ahead?" *Thrust for Educational Leadership*, 21(6):19–21.
Hunter, E. (1990). "A vision of the future: Cooperation and courage," *NASSP Bulletin*, 74(522):6–11.
Lieberman, A. (1991). "Accountability as a reform strategy," *Phi Delta Kappan*, 73(3):219–220.
Manning, M. L. (1993). "Cultural and gender differences in young adolescents," *Middle School Journal*, 25(1):13–17.
Newman D. (1992). "Technology as support for school structure and school restructuring," *Phi Delta Kappan*, 74(4):308–315.
Odden, A. and Kim, L. (1992). "Changing school finance: Imperative for the 90s," *The Education Digest*, 57(8):3–6.
Ornstein, A. C. (1988). "The evolving accountability movement," *Peabody Journal of Education*, 65(3):12–20.
Peltier, G. L. (1991). "Year-round education: The controversy and research evidence," *NASSP Bulletin*, 75(536):120–129.
Shane, H. (1990). "Improving education for the twenty-first century," *Educational Horizons*, 69(1):10–15.

PART II

Forming Professional Teams and Empowering Individuals

CHAPTER 3

Empowering Teams and the Teaming Process

OVERVIEW

EDUCATORS DURING THE late 1980s and early 1990s began to realize that significant education reform and change required teamwork, an understanding of team dynamics, and effective team leadership. While individuals could contribute to change efforts, teams working effectively toward common goals could have far more dramatic effects — more motivated professionals, the advantage of a number of educators offering suggestions for meeting agreed-upon goals, and the powerful effects of teamwork. This understanding of how teams could contribute to significant educational changes came at a time when leadership skills were being better defined and also when support services personnel were being better trained and seeking to become integral members of the school effort. This chapter examines teams, team building, effective team leadership, the added benefits of teams, and support services professionals' roles in team efforts.

EMPOWERMENT AND BEYOND: SUPPORT SERVICES INITIATIVES

Support services professionals' initiatives can be directed in several directions: advocating team approaches, acting as agents of change, empowering change and providing leadership, and deciding on an agenda to meet team goals. Again, it is important to note that support services personnel must take active leadership roles on teams, rather than accepting the traditional "wait to be asked" attitude.

Advocating Teams as a Means toward Significant Change

Perceptive support services personnel advocate team approaches to address the needs of learners and the overall school program. Rather than working in competition with regular classroom teachers and administrators or working in isolation, perhaps toward similar goals, support services personnel can initiate team approaches to meet clearly designated goals. Support professionals can take several initiatives: ensuring a team approach, whereby many professionals' expertise can be utilized; identifying school problems and needs; identifying appropriate strategies; showing how support services professionals' specialized expertise can support the team's initiatives; and helping to design and implement evaluative strategies for evaluating progress toward the team agenda.

Many educators already realize the benefits of working in teams, especially those working in interdisciplinary teams; however, other educators might not realize the benefits that working in teams can offer. Educators, for many years, have planned and implemented instruction alone, without the benefit of other educators' expertise. With these educators, support services personnel may have to make a special effort to explain the team approach and to show the professional and personal benefits of working with others. Support services personnel in these situations play advocacy roles as they encourage other educators to give teaming a chance, especially when leadership will be provided by the support service professional.

Acting as Agents of Change

Change does not come easy for many people, particularly educators who believe traditional instructional approaches work. Likewise, working alone is "a way of life" for educators. Change often appears unnecessary or threatening and has the potential for causing considerable stress. People often avoid the stress of change by denying that change will occur or failing to recognize the need for change. Also, some people find living with the status quo easier and more acceptable (even when they do not like the status quo) than accepting the uncertainty associated with change.

Such situations, perhaps more probable than many educators care to admit, will challenge support services personnel to use advocacy roles, to act as a catalyst, to lead rather than coerce or threaten. Perceptive support services personnel realize the delicate nature of their roles in these situations; it is imperative that other educators feel change agent roles are being directed toward the welfare of the team and the overall school. Special care must be taken to avoid regular classroom educators and administrators feeling that support services personnel are trying to "take over" the school program or trying to push a personal agenda. Thus, effective support services specialists lead by example, rather than manage by coercion.

Hackman (1990) thinks it is a serious mistake to call a performing unit a team and yet really manage members as individuals (p. 493). If teams are to be effective, thinking must be realigned to reward teamwork rather than competition. To redirect educators' thinking toward this end, support services personnel need to consider several questions (Kain, 1993):

(1) Are teams and team functioning considered in evaluation or does evaluation always return to the individual's performance?
(2) Are teams publicized as success stories of our schools or are only individual stars praised?
(3) Are team members sent together to conferences and workshops and do other factors (such as seniority) determine who goes where?

Acting as agents of change requires support services personnel to initiate the change process in several ways (Maeroff, 1993):

- Teams can set priorities so that all of the team's ideas are not just dumped on the school with no sense of what is most important.
- Teams can model the kinds of behavior that they would like to elicit from colleagues.
- Teams can try to anticipate objections so that the answers are provided before some of the negative reactions are registered.
- Teams should remember that each member is only part of the team.
- New relationships with business, with foundations, and with higher education can help build a network of support for professional development that is largely based in the school.
- Closer links can be formed between professional development and the needs of the learners in school.

Deciding on a Team Agenda

The agenda for the team of support services personnel, other educators, perhaps administrators, and sometimes learners calls for support services personnel to take several specific roles:

(*1*) Providing the leadership to form the team and convince individual members of the need for change and to address a particular problem

(*2*) Leading through encouragement, praise, and adequate guidance, rather than managing in a comfortable atmosphere

(*3*) Providing all team members with worthwhile roles that prove both personally and professionally rewarding

(*4*) Planning a clear agenda with challenging yet attainable goals and, if necessary, convincing other team members of the necessity of attaining the goals

(*5*) Making sure all roles and responsibilities complement others, i.e., team members' roles tap their particular expertise and assist the total team effort

(*6*) Establishing a realistic time line for meeting a particular challenge, with the help of other team members

Planning the agenda, with the leadership of the support services personnel, should be a cooperative endeavor. Such leadership requires that all participants feel their input was recognized, considered, and valued, and if possible, they become a part of the overall agenda and effort. Care is in order to ensure that all participants feel they have integral roles and that the goals of the agenda depend upon their participation and willingness to work as a vital team member.

Hackman (1990) and Kain (1993) warned against specifying challenging team objectives yet skimping on organizational supports. Four areas Hackman (1990) identifies for organizational support include a reward system that honors teams, an educational system that allows teams to initiate learning, an informational system that gives teams access to the data they need, and material resources to reach team objectives. Support services personnel, accepting leadership roles in team efforts, need to consider Hackman's warning. Hackman (1990) feels that lack of organizational support is the saddest way for a group to fail. When a team becomes excited about its mission, failing because of the lack of organizational support can be a difficult experience.

Support services personnel also need to recognize the importance of preplanning and preorganization. Too often, team leaders concentrate on the end results or the goals the team hopes to accomplish. While these important aspects should be considered, it is also imperative to focus on the beginning of the team effort. These preliminary initiatives include setting clear expectations, maximizing feelings of ownership, and building a common knowledge base. Concentration on these components will establish the skeletal structure, which contributes to effective teaming development and develops a common focus, common understanding, and a common commitment to teaming (Smith, 1991).

TEAMS, TEAMWORK, THE TEAM PROCESS, AND SUPPORT SERVICES PERSONNEL

Support services personnel can play a major role in team approaches: convincing others of a rationale for teaming, explaining roles and functions, looking to business and industry for tips, overcoming barriers, resolving conflicts, and evaluating team effectiveness. Effective support services personnel will not wait for an invitation to participate or wait until a situation calls for their specialized expertise. Rather than being limited by these traditional approaches, support services professionals will take more active leadership positions and actually initiate team approaches to addressing or correcting school situations.

Rationale for Team Approaches

Some administrators and educators might not be accustomed to team approaches and might be reluctant to work with other school professionals. In such situations, the support service specialist initiating the team might need to explain the reasons for educators working on teams. A convincing rationale might take several directions (or some combination):

(1) Using the old adage, "Two heads are better than one," team members should understand the increased thinking power of teams. One individual, regardless of his or her intelligence, cannot match the combined intelligence, thinking power, and diverse perceptions that teams can offer.

(2) Team members feel an "increased sense of ownership"—efforts, challenges, problems, and accomplishments belong to a team; team members share the realization that these aspects could not have been addressed or accomplished by one person's singular efforts.

(3) Team members can experience increased power to make a difference. While a team might not be able to conquer some obstacles, a team has a better chance than one person. This increased power might include a team's insistence for materials, in-service oppor-

tunities, special programs, or anything that complements the team effort.

Support services personnel, presenting a rationale for team approaches, must use considerable tact to keep other educators from feeling they are being coerced or being forced to work cooperatively. This task will be increasingly less of a problem as educators better understand the teaming process and the benefits accrued from working on teams.

Forming Teams

A serious mistake when forming teams is to assume all team members share a common vision of the teaming process. In addition, they might be unwilling to change old habits and to adopt a common vision. Support services personnel forming teams must remember two essential points. First, team members already have the social skills needed for survival and might be unwilling to change their social skills to meet the challenges of teaming. Second, being a team member means giving up some ego—members have to accept the dynamics of a team and realize the professional ''give and take'' necessary for effective team decision making (Dickinson, 1989).

Support services professionals will see various behaviors beginning to emerge during the first meeting. Some members will enter the team and wait to see what unfolds; others will look for alliances among other group members; still others may take charge and try to control the group (Schein, 1990). Roles for support services specialists will include (Golner and Powell, 1992):

(1) Easing members into the structure of the group so they will feel comfortable and at ease

(2) Providing a vision of how an effective group should operate

(3) Providing or arranging for staff development designed to teach or improve communication, trust building, decision making, and conflict management

(4) Choosing a leader, accepting responsibility for leadership roles, or allowing a leader to develop

Acceptance of responsibility for forming teams also includes recognizing when a member wants off the team. Allowing a person to remove himself or herself from a team should not be perceived as a failure on the leader's part. For any number of reasons, some people might not work well on teams, and, realistically speaking, both the person and the team would be better off with the person off the team. Little will be accomplished, either for the person or the team, when a leader or other team member forces an unwilling person to remain on a team.

Shaping the Development, Dynamics, and Performance of Work Groups

Regardless of the goals facing the team or the composition of the team, several questions can influence the development and performance of work groups. While the following questions and considerations are worth the support service professional's attention, they will also want to develop other questions for considering individual situations (Hackman, 1990, p. 2):

- What can leaders do to help groups be more productive and satisfying?
- Why do groups that appear to be similar often vary so much in effectiveness?
- Why do things that happen the first time a group meets so strongly affect how the group operates throughout its life?
- Why is the way a group relates to other groups sometimes more important to its effectiveness than the way members relate to each other?
- How do the types of work a group has to perform affect the way members interact and the kinds of problems they typically encounter?
- Why do people so often have love-hate reactions to groups of which they are members?

As one of the questions suggests, group dynamics will be significantly influenced by the atmosphere, dynamics, verbal and nonverbal communication, and the attitudes during the first meeting. In fact, a tone will be established that might influence the outcome of the team's efforts or at least relationships during all meetings. The support service professional, arranging the organization meeting, needs to move with great caution to ensure all members feel both personally and professionally involved with the proceedings and outcome of the first meeting.

Roles of Teams

Prior to advocating that educators try team approaches or delving into the actual workings of a team, support services personnel need to understand the roles and functions of teams, as well as develop an agenda to clarify roles and functions to other team members. Equally important, the team advocate has a responsibility to convey what teams can and cannot do, their limitations, whether they can take deliberate action or whether they act only in an advisory capacity, and their location in the school chain of command.

Regardless of what the team attempts to achieve, all teams have basically the same goal: to plan an agenda for reaching a goal, conduct team meetings in such a manner that all participants' expertise is utilized, and conduct team dynamics in a cooperative and harmonious fashion. Therefore, it is essential that all team members learn how to work well with each other on a daily basis.

While the role of the team might vary with the school or from situation to situation, several roles underlie all team operations. Support services personnel should encourage at least three team roles (Merenbloom, 1991):

(*1*) Examine their identity as a team since individuals will be working toward a common goal.
(*2*) Explore commitment to the selected tasks, how responsibilities will be shared, and how they will work to support each other and the team.
(*3*) Consider the time commitment that working on a team will require to determine whether one can effectively work on the team.

As previously suggested, support services personnel, acting as advocates or leaders, will need to consider individual situations in an attempt to determine any special roles. Leaders or advocates should not assume that members know roles—such an assumption that can lead to frustration later in the team experience. During the first or no later than the second meeting, specific roles of the team should be discussed so that all members will know what they should or should not do.

Establishing Team Goals

Establishing team goals may be one of the most important activities in which a team can engage. Team members must feel like they had input into the team's goals, must feel goals are realistic and attainable, and must feel their and other team members' expertise contribute to reaching the goals. Examples of team goals might include

(*1*) Designing a campaign to garner community support for a particular program or the overall school program
(*2*) Designing a technology plan that includes proposed hardware and software to purchase and that includes a proposed budget
(*3*) Designing an accountability program for evaluating the efforts of administrators, classroom teachers, and support services personnel
(*4*) Designing a program for orientating new students (and teachers) to the school

While these four are only representative, they still serve as examples of goal setting and projects that teams might choose.

Support services personnel should give some thought to the length of time the team will operate. Some teams operate on a permanent and ongoing basis; others may be temporary and exist only until their work is completed. Before committing to working on a team, educators should be told the approximate length of time they will serve on the team. Admittedly, predicting the time to complete a task might be difficult; however, after careful consideration of the goals, some estimate of time commitments should be given.

Directions from Business and Industry

Support services professionals can look to business and industry to take advantage of several directions that hold promise for team process and productivity. Business and industry have allowed self-managed teams to give employees control over everything – from work schedules to how to perform the work and from hiring to firing. These teams can increase efficiency, effectiveness, and motivation at the work site. These assumptions or directions include (Maeroff, 1993):

- Those closest to the work know best how to perform and improve their jobs.
- Most employees want to feel that they "own" their jobs and are making meaningful contributions to the effectiveness of their organizations.

- Teams provide possibilities for empowerment that are not available to individual employees.

These three directions or assumptions could apply to schools, yet teamwork is often foreign to most teachers. Support services personnel may face a special challenge with teamwork because, traditionally, most teachers' success has been measured by their adeptness at working alone. Not only do teachers seldom collaborate, they are not expected to be either leaders or followers of other teachers (Maeroff, 1993). Using the assumption from business and industry that teams provide unique possibilities for empowerment, support services personnel need to prod, albeit gently, teachers to look toward successful directions of the business world.

Characteristics of Effective Teams

What characteristics should support services personnel strive to have in teams? What characteristics hold the potential for making teams successful? What characteristics particularly correlate with successful completion of projects? Several characteristics of effective teams include

(1) Team members work for the benefit of other team members and for the team as a whole.
(2) Team members explore their roles and functions from both personal and professional perspectives.
(3) Team members receive the support, financial and otherwise, of the school and district administration.
(4) Team members consider the effects of their actions on parents and learners.
(5) Team members have adequate time for planning deliberations.
(6) Team members meet in an atmosphere where they feel free to share thoughts, ideas, and responsibilities.
(7) Team members received adequate in-service training to conduct their activities.
(8) Team members practice effective human relations skills.
(9) Team members believe in the teaming concept and process.
(10) Team members include all available resource professionals in both planning and implementing.

Developing a team with these characteristics should be considered an ongoing process, whereby improvements and progress are continually made. A team may never have all these characteristics, yet it can still be an effective team; however, effective leaders should not be satisfied with four or five of these characteristics — efforts should be continuous to make the team more effective. Likewise, effective teams should not become "an end to themselves." Teams should have a clear purpose, and leaders should strive to make teams more effective with the expressed intent to meet the stated purpose.

Carl Larson and Frank LaFasto (1989) conclude that teams that succeed have eight characteristics in common: 1) a clear, elevating goal; 2) a results-driven structure; 3) competent members; 4) a unified commitment; 5) a collaborative climate; 6) standards of excellence; 7) external support and recognition; and 8) principled leadership.

Attributes of Team Building

The team-building process and the team itself need to have several attributes that contribute to working effectively. Just as an effective book has particular attributes and effective teaching can be described, specific attributes can be ascribed to the teams, both the concept and the process. Also, as opinions vary on attributes of most entities capable of being described, opinions vary somewhat on attributes of teams and teaming. However, sufficient agreement exists for support services personnel to develop a clear idea of attributes to work toward.

Hackman (1990) considers three attributes to be essential: groups are real, groups have specific tasks, and groups work in an organizational context. While Hackman refers to a number of people working toward a group rather than a team, support services personnel can still benefit from his conclusions.

1) Groups are real groups; that is, they are intact social systems, complete with boundaries, interdependence among members, and differentiated member roles. It is possible to reliably distinguish members of real groups from nonmembers, even if members do not have regular face-to-face interaction and even if membership changes frequently. Moreover, members are dependent upon one another for some shared purpose, and they invariably develop specialized roles within the group as that purpose is pursued. 2) Groups have one or more tasks to perform. The group produces some outcome for which members have collective responsibility and whose acceptability is potentially assessable. The kind of outcome produced is not critical; it could be a physical product, a

service, a decision, a performance, or a written recommendation. Nor is it necessary that the outcome actually be assessed; all that is required is that the group produce an outcome that can be identified as its product and that it be theoretically possible to measure and evaluate that product. 3) Groups operate in an organizational context. This means that the group, as a collective, manages relations with other individuals or groups in the larger social system in which the group operates. Frequently, this social system is the parent organization that created the group, but on occasion the salient context is outside the group's own organization—such as the opposing team and spectators for an athletic team. The critical elements are that the group as a whole has consequential transactions with outside entities and that members manage these transactions collectively (Hackman, 1990, pp. 4–5).

Maeroff (1993) also offers several attributes that provide support services personnel with insight into teams and the teaming process. 1) Teams of teachers gather for an extended period, altogether free from routines and from the demands of regular duties. 2) Participation is voluntary, and no one is compelled to be part of a team. Each team is introduced to a process for analyzing conditions in the school and for devising strategies for improvement. 3) Each team thinks about how to involve the rest of the school community in the change process (Maeroff, 1993, p. 515).

While Hackman (1990) and Maeroff (1993) offer insightful suggestions for attributes of teams and teaming, support services professionals need to consider individual situations to determine attributes for which to strive. These situations might include the number of people on the team, the number of tasks to be addressed, the nature of the tasks, members' previous experiences working on teams, the team's power or level in the chain of command, or whether members' dispositions contribute or hinder group dynamics processes.

Effective Leadership at the Team Level

Support service personnel can play vital leadership roles in setting up teams and conducting the team's agenda. Effective leadership is essential at the team level in order for it to reach its full potential. In deciding leadership techniques to use, one must consider the uniqueness of teams. Teachers differ from team to team and teams react in different ways to challenges. The leadership should include its own structure to accomplish its goals and purposes. For maximum success in meeting its tasks, teams should have a significant degree of autonomy. Without doubt, regulations and guidelines direct and, in some cases, dictate many decisions, but teams should still have the autonomy and authority to make decisions within the framework of the guidelines (Merenbloom, 1991).

As previously suggested, support services personnel accepting leadership positions need to consider individual situations and, then, make leadership decisions. Merenbloom (1991) speaks in a general manner as he suggests roles of team leaders:

(*1*) Presiding over meetings
(*2*) Involving all members in team discussions
(*3*) Dealing with differences of opinion or divisiveness among team members when problems arise
(*4*) Accepting other group members
(*5*) Developing an agenda for each meeting
(*6*) Handling the paperwork for the team or delegating the responsibility
(*7*) Facilitating the evaluation of the team's functioning
(*8*) Monitoring time limits during the team meeting
(*9*) Serving as the liaison between the administration and the team
(*10*) Monitoring the achievement of the team's goals
(*11*) Submitting reports and receiving communication for the team
(*12*) Establishing consensus needed for decisions
(*13*) Coordinating the involvement of resource personnel
(*14*) Monitoring the effectiveness of decision-making processes within the team
(*15*) Helping team members realize opportunities for professional growth and for contributing to the team's agenda

Since the specifics of leadership are addressed in other parts of this book, it will suffice here to say that support services personnel will need to take significant leadership roles. For those uncomfortable with leadership roles, leadership skills can be developed through study and practice. The change schools will need in the 21st century and the changing perception of the roles support services personnel play in the school process suggest the latter should take the lead in addressing the challenges facing schools.

Identifying and Overcoming Barriers

Support services personnel need to be aware of several barriers that detrimentally affect the teaming process and the outcome of the team's work. These barriers may include (but are certainly not limited to) reluctance of educators to work on teams, lack of team cohesiveness, insufficient effort, lack of knowledge of the agenda being pursued, inappropriate task strategies, and lack of leadership. It is important to emphasize that support services personnel must maintain a keen sense of scrutiny so other barriers do not interfere with the progress of the team.

First, reluctance to participate can limit an individual team member's performance, as well as the outcome of the team's work. Reluctance may result from lack of teaming experience, feeling threatened by the teaming process, feeling another job has been placed in an already full schedule, or a myriad of other individual reasons. The role of the support service professional will be to detect reluctance, to attempt to identify its causes, and to address the problem. For example, one could speak with the reluctant person to make him or her feel comfortable. Another approach, when all else fails, is to allow the reluctant member to leave the team. Leaders, whether support services personnel or other professionals, cannot solve all problems.

Second, lack of team cohesiveness can result in members working individually toward personal agendas, rather than working for the welfare of the team. Cliques or factions might develop within the people, which further complicates the teaming process and fails to take advantage of a team working in unison toward a common goal. Support services personnel must spot cliques and factions and realize their effects on team unity and potential. Appropriate action might include conversing with individual members to explain the need for group unity, attempting to solve problems getting in the way of cohesiveness, working with each faction and subtly modeling effective skills, and identifying particular problems and trying to find a solution.

Third, insufficient effort on the parts of one or two members can create problems for other team members. Whether preoccupied with other interests or personal or professional problems, some members simply may not do their share of the work. The support services specialists' efforts in this case can be directed toward talking with the person to determine the cause and to helping the person, if possible. Such a situation requires careful and gentle intervention. The person might not want to reveal the reasons for insufficient effort or might not feel efforts have been acceptable.

Fourth, members' lack of clear understanding of the team's agenda can also be a barrier with serious consequences. Goals often change, communication often confuses, and people often fail to understand the indirect results of goal changes. Support services personnel can address this problem with a significant degree of success by clearly stating the goals that the team decided to pursue, having sufficient discussion for all members to understand the goals as well as implications, and mailing a written statement of the team's goals (and the accompanying minutes of the meeting) to all team members. Understanding and accepting of team goals can be a deciding factor in the team's success because members not sold on the goals will not work individually toward the goals or support the overall team effort.

Fifth, inappropriate task strategies can lead to frustration; i.e., tasks may be addressed by entire team efforts while other tasks might be done by an ad hoc committee. Inappropriate strategies include expecting members to vote on decisions before sufficient discussion has occurred, assuming team members have adequate background knowledge for fruitful discussions to occur, and allowing one or two team members to speak for the entire team. While appropriate strategies vary with the individual situation, leaders with a keen awareness or insight are the most effective.

Sixth, another barrier might be an actual lack of leadership—teams may simply fail to meet the challenge, take too long for deliberations, fail to reach a consensus, and, generally speaking, falter as an effective team. Such a situation can be an ideal time for support services personnel to offer leadership, to help and encourage the leader, and to demonstrate effective leadership skills. This assistance should be offered subtly and in such a manner that resentment and additional loss of time and effort will not result.

Factors Contributing to Team Effectiveness

Several factors contribute to teams being more effective and, overall, educators experiencing a more enjoyable team endeavor. First, team effectiveness increases when interpersonal relations on the team allow members to learn from one another, allow improved personal and professional communication, and foster professional growth. Second, team effectiveness and commitment grow as educators feel less isolated;

more of a working team; and more willing to provide assistance, guidance, and insight from peers. A third factor contributing to team effectiveness is administrative support. While administrators may lack the power to make some decisions, other decisions may complement the team's efforts. In essence, regardless of whether the administration can provide direct assistance (i.e., financial, released time, and in-service opportunities), the administration can support teaming, both as a concept and as a process. Fourth, team effectiveness can be enhanced when team members demonstrate harmonious relationships and, in fact, socialize outside team meetings. Fifth, members developing an evaluation or accountability system recognize professional responsibility for helping each other grow and improve (Chrisco, 1989).

Resolving Conflict among Team Members

Without doubt, conflicts will occur among team members. Conflicts are virtually inevitable because team approaches require educators to work closely with one another in situations calling for extensive communication, interaction, and cooperation. Also, most educators have not been professionally trained to work in teams and to handle conflicts and disagreements. As educators work in teams and voice differing opinions, conflicts will undoubtedly arise. Resolving conflict should be viewed as positive, developmental, and as a productive means to an end.

(*1*) *Conflict avoidance-conflict involvement* — Conflict avoidance is expressed in denial, repression, suppression, and continuing postponement of facing the conflict. The tension associated with conflict avoidance is expressed in fatigue, irritability, muscular tension, and a sense of malaise. Excessive involvement in conflict is expressed in a "macho" attitude, a chip on one's shoulder, or a tendency to seek out conflict to demonstrate that one is not afraid of conflict. It is also commonly manifested in obsessive thoughts about fights and disputes, with much rehearsing of moves and countermoves between oneself and one's adversaries.

(*2*) *Hard-soft* — Some people take an aggressive, unyielding response to conflict, fearing that otherwise they will be taken advantage of. Others fear they will be considered to be hostile or presumptuous and, as a consequence, are excessively gentle and unassertive. They often expect the other to "read their minds." A more appropriate stance is a firm support of one's own interests combined with a ready responsiveness to the interests of the other.

(3) *Rigid-loose*—Some people immediately seek to organize and to control the situation by setting the agenda. As a consequence of feeling threatened by the unexpected, they push for rigid arrangements and rules and get upset by even minor deviations. At the other extreme are people who like a loose, improvisational arrangement in which rules and procedures are implicit rather than overt. An approach that allows for both orderliness and flexibility in dealing with the conflict is more constructive than one that is either compulsive in its organizing or in its rejection of orderliness.

(4) *Intellectual-emotional*—At one extreme, no relevant emotion is felt or expressed as one communicates one's thoughts. Frequently, beneath the calm, detached surface is the fear that if one feels or expresses one's emotions, one will do something destructive or humiliating. However, the lack of appropriate emotional expressiveness may convey to the other a lack of commitment to one's interests and a lack of genuine concern for the other's interests. At the other extreme are people who believe that only feelings are real and that words and ideas are not to be taken seriously unless they are thoroughly soaked in emotion. The emotional intensity of such people impairs the ability to mutually explore ideas and to develop creative solutions; it also makes it difficult to distinguish the significant from the insignificant or even trivial.

(5) *Escalating-minimizing*—At one extreme, some people experience any given conflict in the largest possible terms. The issues are cast so that what is at stake involves one's self, one's family, one's ethnic group, and precedence for all time. Escalation of the conflict makes it more difficult to resolve, except when the escalation proceeds so rapidly that its absurdity becomes self-apparent. At the other extreme are people who minimize their conflicts. Yet, by minimizing the seriousness of the differences between the self and the other, they can produce serious misunderstandings and may not devote enough effort to resolving the conflict constructively.

(6) *Compulsively revealing-compulsively concealing*—At one extreme, some people feel compelled to reveal whatever they think and feel about the other, including their hostilities and fears, in the most blunt, irrational manner. Or they may feel they have to communicate every doubt or weakness they have about themselves. At the other

extreme are those who feel they cannot reveal any of their feelings or thoughts without seriously damaging their relationship to the other. Either extreme can impair the development of a constructive relationship (Deutsch, 1992).

Conflicts during the teaming process need to be resolved in a highly professional, nurturing level. Resolving conflict includes a focus on group dynamics, communication skills, respect, acceptance, professionalism, a belief in the team process, and time (Merenbloom, 1991).

Evaluating Team Effectiveness

As with any individual or group endeavor, a team's effectiveness should be evaluated to determine its overall success, its strengths and weaknesses, and areas on which to focus attention. As a prerequisite to this section, it is important to point out that evaluating teams should be a positive experience rather than a fault-finding mission.

Several professionals or agencies may evaluate teams and their efforts:

(*1*) Administrators
(*2*) Regional accrediting groups
(*3*) State accrediting groups
(*4*) Other teams from the school or other schools
(*5*) Self-evaluation

While the authors appreciate the need for external review from objective sources, they also firmly believe in the self-evaluation process. Team members need an opportunity to evaluate their individual efforts, as well as team efforts. Self-evaluation may be the most appropriate form of evaluation because it involves close introspection by team members using an evaluation form that parallels the philosophy, practices, and uniqueness of the particular team. A self-evaluation involves an open sharing of feelings about the activities of a team and facilitates channeling this discussion into constructive goal-setting activities. Also, self-evaluation serves as a means of getting team members together to examine what they are doing, how they could improve, and how some priorities for improvement would be established (Merenbloom, 1991). Just like other team endeavors, team members should have the opportunity and responsibility to design the means of evaluation and to design specific evaluation items.

Support services personnel have several resources to consider when designing self-evaluation instruments and procedures. Hackman (1990) proposes evaluating outputs, members' capability to work interdependently, and the degree of growth and personal well-being of team members. Russell et al. (1992) propose evaluating the team's ability to implement shared decision making. Merenbloom (1991) suggests including more specific evaluative items that relate specifically to what members did. While support services personnel should consider all three sources, the actual evaluation form for a particular team should reflect an individual team's goals, priorities, strengths, weaknesses, limitations, tasks, and other individual factors.

Hackman's (1990) specific proposals include the following: 1) evaluate the degree to which the group's productive output (that is, its product, service, or decision) meets the standards of quantity, quality, and timeliness of the people who receive, review, and/or use that output. If, for example, a group generated a product that was wholly unacceptable, it would be hard to argue that the group was effective—no matter what the group's own evaluation of its product was or how the product scored on some objective performance index. 2) Evaluate the degree to which the process of carrying out the work enhances the capability of members to work together interdependently in the future. Some groups operate in ways that make it impossible for members to work together again; for example, mutual antagonism could become so high that members would choose to accept collective failure, rather than to share knowledge and information with one another. In other groups, members become highly skilled at working together, resulting in a performing unit that becomes increasingly capable over time. 3) Evaluate the degree to which the group experience contributes to the growth and personal well-being of team members. Some groups operate in ways that block the development of individual members and frustrate satisfaction of their personal needs. Other groups provide their members with many opportunities for learning and needs satisfaction.

In summary, Hackman (1990) feels that determining a team's performance involves much more than simply counting outputs—it is also necessary to consider social and personal dimensions.

Russell et al. (1992) suggest evaluating a team's degree of shared decision making and offer eight dimensions to be considered: 1) *Goals/vision/mission:* the degree to which teachers are involved in framing the goals and mission of the school; 2) *Facilitating procedures and structures:* the degree to which teachers have adequate time, reduced teaching loads, waivers from contracts and regulations, and changed schedules to permit collegial work to occur; 3) *Curriculum/instruction:* the degree to which teachers participate in determining the school program, curriculum goals, textbook selection, educational materials, and classroom pedagogy; 4) *Budgeting:* the degree to which teachers participate in matters related to designing and implementing the school budget; 5) *Staffing:* the degree to which teachers are involved with the administration in making decisions such as recruiting, interviewing, hiring, and assigning staff; 6) *Staff development:* the degree to which teachers can design and implement staff development activities that meet their own needs; 7) *Operations:* the degree to which teachers are involved in managing the building (its use, improvement, and maintenance); and 8) *Standards:* the degree to which teachers share in setting standards for their own performance and for student performance and discipline.

Merenbloom (1991) looks at more specific items, such as the following:

(*1*) Do team members commit to the teams and teaming both as a concept and a process?

(*2*) Do team members explore their role and functions as a team?

(*3*) Do team members make an effort to get to know one another?

(*4*) Do team members discuss their expectations with others?

(*5*) Do team members work effectively with all school personnel?

(*6*) Do team members support the efforts of the team leader?

(*7*) Do team members make efforts to resolve conflicts?

(*8*) Do team members share leadership responsibilities?

(*9*) Do team members participate equally in making decisions?

(*10*) Do team members adopt and use guidelines for gaining consensus for decision making?

(*11*) Do team members specify specific goals and objectives each year?

(*12*) Do team members evaluate goals and objectives each year?

(*13*) Do team members have an agenda for each meeting?

(*14*) Do team members consider the concerns of parents, students, and community people?

(*15*) Do team members demonstrate sensitivity to group dynamics at team meetings?

In designing evaluative instruments, support services personnel may choose either of these three sources as an instrument or might elect to devise an original instrument based upon Hackman's (1990), Russell et al.'s (1992), or Merenbloom's (1991) work. Regardless of the direction taken, team evaluation should focus on the individual team and should be positive and ongoing.

Providing Effective Staff Development

Another trend toward greater professionalism involves staff development. Staff development refers to the further education and training of professional educators, whether classroom teachers, administrators, or support services personnel. These training experiences may focus on subject matter, teaching skills, or any area that increases educators' effectiveness. Most staff development opportunities consist of one- or two-day workshops at the school site or a special off-campus university course. While staff development has been criticized as not relating to educators' actual roles and responsibilities, staff development during the past few years has increasingly been considered as an important aspect of teacher education and career enhancement (Ornstein and Levine, 1989).

Support services personnel can play vital roles in designing and implementing staff development programs. Often, classroom educators are too isolated to see problems other than their own and do not realize other educators experience similar problems, challenges, and frustrations. Administrators might also have a limited perspective of school problems and might only be aware of problems brought to their attention. Support services professionals work in an ideal position to know areas needing staff development, especially when they work with both classroom educators and administrators. Support services personnel can document the need for staff development in several ways:

(*1*) Educators better understanding an educational concept or program will be better able to implement the program and provide appropriate educational experiences.
(*2*) Educators often need staff development opportunities that teacher education institutions are unable or unwilling to provide (Merenbloom, 1991).
(*3*) Educators working on teams are often expected to deal with and make decisions about unfamiliar educational concepts and programs.

Support services personnel during the 21st century might serve in a prime position to identify staff development needs and opportunities. Therefore, whether they actually provide or make arrangements for the staff development opportunity, support services personnel need to know characteristics of effective programs.

Characteristics of effective staff development programs include (Merenbloom, 1991).

(1) Thorough understanding of teams and teaming, both as a concept and a process
(2) Definite goals, objectives, and an organizational plan
(3) Sufficient lead time prior to implementation
(4) Sustained, sequential, continuous efforts
(5) Sensitivity to the needs of all educators
(6) Provisions for motivating participants
(7) Safe, trusting, and positive environments
(8) Involvement of all participants
(9) Strong leadership of professionals responsible for the program
(10) Opportunities to add new dimensions to the program for future professional growth

SUPPORT SERVICES PROFESSIONALS AS TEAM AGENTS

Support services professionals' changing roles during the late 1990s and early 21st century will include several specific dimensions, all related to the role of active team agents—to lead rather than manage, to instill motivation, and to show and model the benefits of working toward common goals. Likewise, support services personnel, cognizant of their changing roles, will show how demonstrating professional behavior, being held accountable, and taking advantage of technological advances can contribute to effective teaming.

Dimension: Leadership Rather than Management

Too often, leaders do more managing than leading. Consequently, too many schools and school districts are overmanaged and underled. Such a condition leads to an emphasis on doing things right rather than doing right things and on following directions rather than solving problems (Sergiovanni, 1990).

Providing effective leadership can be a major contribution of support services personnel. First, support services personnel can improve leadership abilities through courses, workshops, and specialized readings. Second, working as neither a classroom educator nor an administrator, support services personnel can take advantage of both allegiances and build upon the strengths of both groups. Third, being careful to lead rather than manage, these professionals can model effective leadership techniques and skills.

Perceptive support services personnel will quickly recognize the challenges of leadership—patience, a degree of collegiality, a clear sense of direction, a willingness to offer and accept constructive suggestions, and the ability to detect when a team feels frustration. Also, some attention might need to be given to building interpersonal relationships that might be detrimentally affected by support services personnel's changing roles. Classroom educators and administrators might need to be educated about changing professional roles and support service personnels' active stances toward leadership and effective teaming.

Dimension: Motivation

Support services personnel's roles as team agents also include instilling motivation in the team motivation to work as a team, to work toward specific goals, and to work for the self-satisfaction of meeting goals through teamwork.

Busy professionals often have a full agenda of classes; workshops; planning sessions; and meetings with parents, individual learners, and other team members on an individual basis. The invitation to work on a team toward one or more goals might be considered as additional work or another meeting to add to an already too busy schedule.

In such cases, support services personnel will need to show understanding for others' time predicaments and try to arrange team meetings conducive to as many members' schedules as possible. Along the same line, extra efforts to motivate members might include calling upon their sense of professionalism, arranging for release of selected other duties, or, if financial budgets allow, offering an honorarium for participation.

Dimension: Work toward Common Goals

Perhaps the support services professionals' major role will be leading the team toward common goals. Likewise, leaders should make clear that a hidden agenda will not influence the team's deliberations or decisions. Effective leadership requires letting team members know that their input, suggestions, and criticisms are being considered by the team. While dissension during the discussion of goals may be expected and encouraged, the final goals reached by the team should receive the team's dedication and commitment. To do otherwise will mean team members might be pursuing personal agendas and, while not intentionally, might sabotage the team's efforts.

Team Dimensions: Professionalism, Accountability, and Technology

Teams and teamwork should reflect three other dimensions:

(*1*) Professionalism among team members should be evident in all deliberations.
(*2*) Accountability should be a key essential, with all team members and the overall team being objectively evaluated.
(*3*) Technology should be evident in the team's work and should be employed to ease workloads and to make team members more knowledgeable.

Professionalism

Several advantages result from educators exercising professionalism in all team endeavors. All educators should undoubtedly strive for professionalism and demonstrate professional behavior in all academic and social situations; however, demonstrating a sense of professionalism might be even more important for team members since the team process requires members to respect the rights of others and to meet one's obligations.

First, professionalism contributes to improved interpersonal and working relationships. Anyone who has worked in a hostile situation with quarreling and bickering knows the problems: people failing to agree on issues that should be quickly resolved; time wasted on points that do not significantly affect the outcome; people working toward a personal agenda rather than toward team goals; and, generally speaking, the stress and uncomfortableness of working in hostile situations. Committing to a sense of professionalism can significantly change how teams work (and ultimately their success). In essence, more can be accomplished in a more satisfying environment.

Second, professionalism can contribute to an increased chance of meeting team goals. A team, working productively toward an agreed-upon goal, can commit far more mental power and commitment toward reaching goals. Likewise, professionalism can enhance motivation in team members that lack commitment to complete tasks. Modeling professionalism can provide a subtle, yet highly effective, means of changing other team members' behaviors.

Third, professionalism can contribute to an enhanced sense of team accomplishment made possible by working collegially. Just as most educators feel a sense of accomplishment and pride upon finishing an individual task, teams can experience similar feelings. A team that has worked professionally and collegially towards a common goal can attest to the benefits of professionalism in teaming situations and the resulting sense of accomplishment.

Accountability

Team efforts, just as individual efforts, must be evaluated and held accountable for its actions, accomplishments, and shortcomings. As previously stated, evaluations, at least the preliminary evaluative efforts, should be of an internal nature because team members are most aware of the team's goals, strengths, weaknesses, and actual deliberations. Acting in a professional manner, teams can objectively evaluate and point out accomplishments as well as shortcomings.

Accountability also includes evaluation by professionals outside the team. This liaison between the team and the administration, whether individual school or school district, needs to be acquainted with the team's goals and actual accomplishments. This external evaluator should be provided with either team minutes or a summary of its work, so an objective evaluation can be conducted. Likewise, the evaluator should evaluate with an approved evaluation form, which team members have previously seen. In fact, team members should be notified during the first meeting that team efforts and the leader's performance will be evaluated upon completion of the team's work. Rather than posing a threat, accountability should be viewed as a means of documenting effectiveness, determining strengths, and pointing out areas needing improvement.

Technology

Today and increasingly into the 21st century, the United States will be an information-based society. Educators preparing learners for this society need to help students acquire and retain more and better information than ever before. While several technology breakthroughs will affect schools, the computer will continue to be the heart of technological innovation. Nothing can equal computers' capacity to deliver information, particularly when linked with other technologies, such as video disks, software banks, and satellite communication networks (Ryan and Cooper, 1988).

A team's effectiveness can be significantly enhanced when members take advantage of technological advances. First, and perhaps simplest, the team's minutes or dialogues can be processed and maintained as a record. Second, networking with other teams deliberating similar goals can provide insight and, perhaps, a means to success. Third, team members needing additional information on a particular subject can learn through video disks and other technological means. Teams in the 1990s and the 21st century should not work with antiquated means. Technology and the most technological advances should be reflected in the teaming process, as well as support services personnel's changing roles.

SUMMARY

Without doubt, the education profession and educators' daily routines have changed and will continue to change: teams replacing individual efforts; dimensions such as professionalism, accountability, and technology being considered; and changing support services personnel roles. Team efforts are (and will continue) to replace educators working in isolation and calling upon support services personnel only when needed. However, educators accustomed to traditional expectations of working alone might need encouragement and active assistance as they work in teams toward team-set goals. Support services personnel can play major roles in initiating positive change through teams. Rather than assuming others will take leadership steps toward teaming, effective support services professionals can take deliberate steps toward promoting the team concept and assisting with the teaming process.

REFERENCES

Chrisco, I. M. (1989). "Peer assistance works," *Educational Leadership*, 46(8): 31–32.

Deutsch, M. (1992). "Typical responses to conflict," *Educational Leadership*, 50(1):33.

Dickinson, T. S. (1989). "Creating a humane environment: Teaming in the middle school," *In Focus* 17:16–19.

Golner, S. J. and Powell, J. H. (1992). "Ready for teaming? Ten questions to ask before you jump in," *Middle School Journal*, 24(1):28–32.

Hackman, J. R. (Ed.). (1990). *Groups That Work (and Those That Don't): Creating Conditions for Effective Teamwork*. San Francisco: Jossey-Bass.

Kain, D. L. (1993). "Helping teams succeed: An essay review of *Groups That Work (and Those That Don't): Creating Conditions for Effective Teamwork*," *Middle School Journal*, 24(4):25–31.

Larson, C. E. and LaFasto, M. J. (1989). *Teamwork*. Newbury Park, CA: Sage.

Maeroff, G. I. (1993). "Building teams to rebuild schools," *Phi Delta Kappan*, 74:513–519.

Merenbloom, E. Y. (1991). *The Team Process: A Handbook for Teachers*. Columbus, OH: National Middle School Association.

Ornstein, A. C. and Levine, D. U. (1989). *Foundations of Education* (4th ed.). Boston: Houghton Mifflin.

Russell J. J., Cooper, B. S. and Greenblatt, R. B. (1992). "How do you measure shared decision making?" *Educational Leadership*, 50:39–40.

Ryan, K. and Cooper, J. M. (1988). *Those Who Can Teach*. Boston: Houghton Mifflin.

Schein, E. (1990). *Organizational Culture and Leadership*. San Francisco: Jossey-Bass.

Sergiovanni, T. J. (1990). *Value-Added Leadership: How to Get Extraordinary Performance in Schools*. New York: Harcourt Brace Jovanovich.

Smith, H. W. (1991) "Guide teaming development," *Middle School Journal*, 22(5):21–23.

CHAPTER 4

Advocacy Agents

OVERVIEW

SERVING AS ADVOCACY agents can be a prime contribution of support services personnel in the 21st century. Moving away from the tradition of working in isolation to provide professional services, support services personnel can take an advocate role toward helping educators move beyond the status quo. Roles may include being an advocate for team approaches, ensuring each student feels well known by a significant adult in the school, assisting in providing developmentally appropriate curricular experiences, initiating community outreach programs, taking new and significant professional roles in addressing accountability demands, and helping teachers to take advantage of technological advances. While these represent only a few advocacy roles, this chapter examines support services personnel's advocacy roles in more detail and then offers possibilities for future advocacy roles.

ADVOCACY ROLES: PAST AND PRESENT

Deciding on advocacy roles for the 21st century requires understanding past and present roles. Realistically speaking, few schools had support services personnel years ago because specialized training did not exist, learners' problems and special needs went unaddressed, and classroom teachers assumed nearly all educational roles. More recently, schools employed support services personnel who worked in isolation with learners with special needs or responded to learners recommended by teachers. Present perceptions have a more enlightened view of support services personnel's contributions, yet maximum potential might be lost when support services personnel do not contribute to teacher teams. Scenarios of future roles suggest advocacy roles, whereby support services personnel take the lead toward helping learners, rather than waiting for classroom educators to initiate an agenda.

ADVOCACY ROLES: BEYOND THE STATUS QUO

Progressing beyond the status quo will require changing longheld mind-sets toward education, redesigning job roles and responsibilities, collaborating toward new possibilities, and, generally speaking, rethinking and restructuring education as previously and presently known. Such a task will require a reconsideration (and, in some cases, an initial consideration) of professional roles and responsibilities, financial allocations, accountability expectations, technological innovations, leadership roles, and a host of other possibilities. A crucial aspect will be to perceive "what could be" and "how can it be accomplished," rather than planning 21st support services with 19th or 20th century perspectives.

Specialists

First and foremost, support services professionals should receive the professional respect they rightly deserve. Professional training and teacher education institutions have progressed to a point where support services personnel receive excellent professional training and clinical experiences and then benefit from in-service training and workshops sponsored by universities, the state department of education, and professional associations. The result: support services personnel are among the best educated and trained professionals serving learners today. The challenge for the late 1990s and early 21st century will be for support services personnel's specialized services to be recognized and utilized. Likewise, support services personnel taking advocacy roles help educators and improve the quantity and quality of services provided to children and adolescents.

Once educators and administrators recognize specialists' expertise and talents, team approaches can occur in which services of all professionals complement one another. Support services personnel can serve as advocates for learners, provide a fresh and objective perspective of learners, show parents and learners the total commitment given by educators, coordinate services between schools and social service organizations, and address learners' psychological and social needs, in addition to the academic needs traditionally addressed by educators.

A more advocative role will eliminate or at least reduce classroom teachers and support services specialists duplicating services, will contribute to more effective team approaches, and will result in learners having a more individualized educational program and teams having an agenda that reflects learners' educational plans. Such an advocacy role can become a reality when classroom educators and support services specialists reconsider roles and develop a professional relationship that allows learners to benefit from complementary expertise and talents.

Increased Professionalism

For decades, administrators at the district office level and, in some cases, legislators made decisions that affected the teachers' and students' daily lives. The previous mind-set held that these people had an overall perspective of educational goals and achievements and served in the best position to formulate educational policy. Opinions of teachers and support services professionals, working daily with learners, were too often ignored or considered unimportant to the overall educational plan.

Responsibility for education has now shifted from legislatures and policymakers to administrators, educators, and support services professionals making decisions that affect their lives. Increasingly, educators decide what students need to learn and how they should be taught. Educators given this responsibility feel a greater sense of professional responsibility for teaching, and if successful, learning occurs. This process includes assessments to determine whether educational plans worked and to indicate appropriate future directions. Other changes in the professional environment and, subsequently, affecting educators' professionalism include collecting and comparing student achievement statewide and nationally, assessing and comparing teachers through newly developed instruments, professional educational boards moving to develop education standards, and focusing on helping poor and underachieving students (Myers and Myers, 1990). Other professional changes include teachers being empowered to make major educational decisions about the curriculum, their students, and their working environment (Clark and Cutler, 1990).

This new sense of responsibility for educational decisions has led to enhanced professionalism, which, in turn, provides support services professionals with new advocacy opportunities. Since support services professionals have specializations crossing curricular lines, they can provide valuable services. For example, testing and assessment specialists can assist in testing programs, both of students and teachers. Those with curriculum backgrounds can help with specific subject area challenges or attempts to achieve cross-curricular units. Specialists with expertise in growth and development can assist teachers planning developmentally appropriate instruction. Those working in inner cities can design educational plans addressing the needs of poor, urban learners.

In years past, support services specialists, generally speaking, provided services only when needed. The new sense of professionalism includes educators and support services specialists taking greater responsibility for their professional lives. Also, rather than waiting patiently to be called upon, support services personnel increasingly adopt advocacy and leadership roles, taking strong stands for the overall welfare of learners and the education profession.

Friend and Significant Adult

The Carnegie Council on Adolescent Development (1989), in its renowned *Turning Points: Preparing American Youth for the 21st Century*, focusing primarily on middle school youth, suggests all learners should be well known by at least one significant adult in the school. Without doubt, this belief also holds true for elementary and secondary schools. All children and adolescents should feel that at least one adult in the school knows and understands them.

Another advocacy role for support services personnel can be to serve as a mentor, friend, confidante, or just an adult willing to listen to learners' concerns. Social interaction may occur before, during, or after school; at lunch; or, perhaps, during a period of the day set aside for learner-adult interaction. While the primary goal is simply to be available for a student when needed, a secondary goal might be to serve as an ombudsman between learners and other educators in the school. This adult should attempt to be objective and should avoid preaching, castigating, or condemning students' actions or behaviors. Advice may be given; however, students should feel comfortable with the social interaction and should feel the adult is looking after their (the student's) best interests.

The support services specialist serves in a unique position to assume this significant advocacy role. First, support services personnel have specialized training in dealing with esoteric problems, i.e., counselors who know intervention techniques and also have made commitments to ethical responsibilities such as confidentiality. Second, due to the nature of their training and job descriptions, support services personnel often work with small groups or on a one-on-one basis, which contributes to their ability to relate to students on a first-hand basis. Third, educators often judge learners by comparing other students in the class. John may be compared to Bill because both are ten years old and live in the same neighborhood—one may "shine" and the other may come up short, often on the basis of false perceptions. Jessica might be compared to her older brother, Joshua, who compiled a straight A record during the previous year. Support services personnel can often play significant advocacy roles by providing a sense of objectivity, a professional commitment to see students as individuals, and help for classroom educators to realize the dangers of faulty judgments.

Schools for too long have become institutions where some students feel lost in the crowd—too many students, too few opportunities for learner-adult interaction, and too many educators believing that job descriptions do not include being a significant and caring adult or friend to learners. Learners need an advocate, someone who knows them and respects them as human beings. The support services specialist accepting this advocacy role can take two directions. The learner sees a caring adult in the school, and other educators' attitudes may change when they have an advocate model to consider.

Assurer of Legal Rights

The public's recognition of its legal rights in school matters can be seen in the increasing litigation facing school systems. Clark and Cutler (1990) wrote,

> Superintendents, principals, and teachers are all pausing these days, eyeing possible "legal ramifications" of their actions. As a result, there is a growing tentativeness among some teachers and administrators, a reluctance—even an unwillingness—to engage in actions that have been routine for many years. (p. 179)

Having long been required to abide by legal mandates, schools now increasingly face legal demands; i.e., organizational and grouping patterns must not result in segregation, placement decisions must be objective and result from group consensus, counselors must consider students' disclosures confidential, and learners requiring specialized education services must receive correct diagnosis and placement and have the right to an individual educational plan. In other words, students' rights do not cease when they enter classrooms. The 1990s and the 21st century will likely be times of increasing litigation, especially because people appear increasingly prone to legal actions, parents and families expect schools to meet legal obligations, and the complexity of school and society has the potential for resulting in litigation. Undoubtedly, a support service specialist trained to ensure all schools meet legal obligations may become the norm during the next century.

What legal obligations might this support specialist have the responsibility to monitor? The 21st century might very well see a support service person responsible for legal matters. Legal issues might include students' speech and expression, dress and grooming, physical protection, privacy, suspension, equal opportunity, and perhaps, teachers' rights of expression, privacy, and employment. This specialist might not be a board-approved attorney, but he or she still would have the knowledge to interpret the law as it relates to students and teachers.

The proposal to have a support service specialist with legal expertise should not be taken lightly. If the 21st century reflects the tendency to litigation, which characterized the 1980s and 1990s, educators and their students will benefit from having a support service staff member with knowledge of the law. Both teachers and students (as well as students' parents) should understand their rights and responsibilities in an educational situation. As Clark and Cutler (1990) aptly pointed out, teachers have the right to express themselves, to make decisions about students and the curriculum taught, and to enjoy privacy in their professional life. Students have rights in schools just as they do in the community. The support service professional, serving as an assurer of legal rights, can play a valuable role in schools by helping educators know their rights and responsibilities and by helping students receive the benefits of the law.

Contribution to Developmentally Appropriate School Practices

Researchers and writers have suggested for several decades that the school curriculum, instructional practices, and the overall teaching-learning environment should reflect learners' developmental levels.

While developmental psychologists have offered insightful theories regarding physical, psychosocial, and cognitive development, the process of translating theories into practice has been somewhat slow, especially beyond the early childhood years. The recognition of development as a potential basis for educational decisions and the current emphasis on reforming education to meet the developmental needs of learners provide evidence that the 1990s and 21st century will be prime times to base school practices on learners' developmental levels.

A future support service specialist, trained in learner growth and development, can serve in an excellent position to ensure curriculum content and instructional practices reflect learner development. One might ask, "Since educators have preparation in learner growth and development, why is another professional needed to address learners' needs?" On the surface, such an argument appears to have validity; however, in the reality of everyday classrooms, little evidence suggests educators base learning expectations and practices on learner development. Several reasons might exist for failing to use development as an indication of teaching and learning practices. First, educators, traditionally taking only one growth and development course, might not have a sound knowledge of development, especially educators in grade levels other than their original levels of certification. Second, educators trained only a few years ago might not be knowledgeable in contemporary research on learner development. Third, the typical school day of taking care of learners, providing educational experiences, and performing clerical duties might result in little time for reflective thought and planning of what constitutes developmentally appropriate instruction.

The support service professional, expertly trained in human growth and development, can serve a valuable function, not as a supervisor or administrator but as a resource person capable of making specific suggestions for making educational experiences reflective of development. For example, this support service specialist can have a solid knowledge of physical, psychosocial, and cognitive development of children, young adolescents and adolescents. Accompanying this solid background in development will be a genuine commitment to developmentally appropriate educational experiences. This support service specialist will help educators plan educational goals and specific learning objectives as well as select curricular content, materials, instructional practices, and assessment techniques. Again, this specialist would serve in a resource capacity, rather than as an administrative supervisor.

Equal Access Advocate

Much has been written about schools providing learners with equal access to all educational programs, extracurricular activities, and educators' attention. The equal access concept sounds legitimate and like an honorable goal, especially since the American concept of education embraces equal opportunity for all learners. The gap between exclusivity and equal access has narrowed somewhat during the last decade, predominantly in areas required by legal mandates. Unfortunately, however, some school experiences continue to be denied to all learners, making equal access only a "buzzword" and a concept that schools, unknowingly or unwillingly, fail to provide.

Three episodes illustrate how schools deny equal access. First, an eighth grade girl "tried out" for cheerleading with over a hundred other girls, even though only fourteen would be selected. While she memorized the cheers, learned the required jumps, and gave four days to pursuit, the girl failed to "make the team." The school completely failed to provide equal access to over eighty-six young girls, including the girl who practiced diligently to become a member of the team.

The second situation, just as serious as the first, involved another seventh grade girl trying out for the school play. She remained after school and faithfully participated in the tryouts. Again, nearly a hundred students tried out for the eleven parts, yet this time, even worse odds faced female would-be participants: of the eleven parts, the teachers only needed four girls! Not only did the school violate the concept of equal access to participating in the play, girls faced even more difficult obstacles to equal access.

Third, another school required seventh grade students to choose between art, music, and band. A young learner, showing talent and interest in both art and music, faced a difficult decision because the school schedule did not allow students to participate in all three areas or even two areas (Manning, 1993).

Such blatant denial of equal access raises several questions: Does the concept of equal access apply to extracurricular activities, as well as educational programs prescribed by state or local mandates? Do all learners, regardless of gender, culture, and developmental level, deserve equal access to participation in activities provided for some learners yet not required by law? Do schools have an ethical and professional responsibility to provide all learners with equal access? Without doubt, these questions can be answered in the affirmative. A learner should not be denied any educational program or extracurricular activity because educators fail to provide sufficient opportunities. No longer can schools espouse the advantage of competition or blame scheduling dilemmas for students being "selected" or "weeded-out" or being placed in no-win situations of having to make "either-or" choices (Manning, 1993).

While all three situations may be legal and perhaps within the bounds of professional ethics, the consequences do not change: learners, wanting to be active participants in the educational program or extracurricular activities, faced denial and rejection and realized that equal access applied only to selected students. The positives associated with providing equal access for all learners greatly outweigh educators' efforts. For example, learners feeling anonymous in large schools begin to feel known and recognized; learners with low self-esteem, resulting from being denied participation, experience increased self-worth; and students realize the advantages of equal access and the disadvantages inherent with competing for a limited number of participatory opportunities. These possibilities can become a reality when educators take definite steps to ensure all students have equal access to all school programs and activities.

Support services personnel can play valuable advocacy roles in helping to ensure equal access for all learners. Classroom educators often are not in the position to view the inequality students often face. Or perhaps they are "too close to the situation" to realize the ill effects of students not being provided equal access opportunities. The support service specialist responsible for ensuring equal access would serve as a resource person, rather than in an administrative or legal role. Serving in an oversight capacity, this person would recognize the importance of equal access and alert teachers when students failed to have opportunities. Specific areas might include athletic teams, plays, cheerleading squads, computer facilities, band opportunities, and other opportunities for extracurricular activities.

Why, after all these years, do schools need a support service person to ensure equal access? Because equal access has not become a reality in United States schools. Whether educators do not recognize the importance of equal access or the dangers of students being left out, the result remains the same: students have been "weeded out" or excluded from participation in both academic and extracurricular activities. Equal opportunity is the law and whether or not equal access can be equated with equal opportunity, schools have a responsibility to give all learners an opportunity to grow, to develop, to excel, and to realize their potential. The support service specialist can be the person responsible for ensuring that all educational programs reflect the equal access concept.

Outreach Coordinator

Learners and their educators have a significant advocate when support services personnel serve as outreach coordinators to bring educators and the community together for learners' overall welfare. All too often, teachers work in isolation, administrators deal with the daily demands of school operation, parents and families hurry through daily schedules, and community members fail to realize how their many talents and resources can be assets to schools. People often fail to recognize the dynamics and power of group action. Working as a group toward an educational goal can have multiple advantages over working alone. However, people often do not recognize problems and possible solutions, sometimes wait for others to take action, and, generally speaking, lack the leadership ability to initiate coordinated action. Support services specialists, appropriately trained in outreach efforts, can play valuable roles working as coordinators and liaisons between educators and the general community.

What might support services specialists in this advocacy role actually do? Possible roles might include

(*1*) Coordinating school-community efforts to help the school and its learners
(*2*) Involving parents and families in the education of their children
(*3*) Compiling a list of strengths and resources that community members might be willing to share with the school
(*4*) Coordinating efforts and programs, whereby educators actually provide services to community members in special areas of interest
(*5*) Promoting school-business partnerships, whereby schools receive much needed assistance (i.e., financial resources, equipment, or workers sharing areas of expertise)
(*6*) Coordinating the assistance of social service organizations
(*7*) Accepting responsibility for scheduling parent-teacher conferences when parents want to meet with more than one teacher at a time
(*8*) Coordinating efforts between individual school administrators, district offices, and individual teachers

(9) Seeking outside funding for special projects, which the school district cannot afford

(10) Working with and communicating with school board members — educating them about the various aspects of the school operation and communicating to teachers and administrators board rulings and policies and the reasoning for board actions

A crucial aspect of this advocacy role is to provide leadership for outreach. While leadership will be discussed later as an advocate role itself, providing effective leadership is an essential for outreach activities to be successful. Rather than waiting for community members and businesses to volunteer resources and expertise, support services professionals, acting in advocacy roles, can initiate deliberate action to involve people and organizations outside the school. Either due to lack of time or lack of commitment, some community resources are not made available to schools because people and organizations do not know school needs. In one large urban area, a national corporation came to a school's rescue with financial resources, equipment, and personnel when it realized the school's needs. Considerable time passed and, ultimately, was wasted until the corporation realized the school needed its resources. A support service professional, employed as an outreach specialist and advocate, could have offered the leadership to coordinate the efforts of the school and the organization.

Leadership Efforts

Sergiovanni (1990) wrote, ". . . Too many schools, school districts and state systems of schooling are overmanaged and underled" (p. 17). Whether one agrees with this statement, nearly all educators and community people agree that effective schools need strong leadership—not someone who arbitrarily makes decisions and tells others what to do, but people who know how to lead others and who do not fear others making suggestions for improvement. Many principals and other administrators undoubtedly have effective leadership skills and lead their schools to great heights. Suggesting a support service specialist with responsibility for leadership and teaching these skills to others in no way negates the leadership skills of others. Instead, the proposal holds the support service specialist might be in a better or less threatening position to encourage others to take a particular direction. In fact, the proposed direction or initiative might be the principal's idea. The support service professional complements the work of the administration by leading others toward an established goal.

Support services professionals providing leadership can develop or enhance several behaviors such as (Sergiovanni, 1990)

- being driven by deep commitment to ideas and ideals
- speaking often of perseverance and persistence
- holding the course and continuing to try in the pursuit of one's convictions
- communicating to others the need for excellence and pushing themselves and others forward by words, behaviors, and deeds

Relating Sergiovanni's list to educational situations, a support service specialist responsible for leadership or committed to teaching leadership to others might encourage other educators to strive for academic achievement and the previously mentioned equal access; continue on task even when criticism from educators, parents, and learners create doubt; and encourage others to demonstrate or achieve specified behaviors or goals. It is impossible to tell support services professionals a specific plan of action. Such an attempt would insult the leadership specialist and would take away from her or his chances of success.

Another main role for support services personnel is to teach leadership skills to other educators and learners. Leadership became an important focus during the late 1980s and early 1990s. Specific leadership behaviors and skills were identified, defined, and taught. It might appear that some people are "born leaders," but, in reality, leaders can be trained and improved. The support service person can become a leadership advocate and, as a result, provide valuable services for both educators and learners.

Technology Advocates

The increasing recognition of how technology can contribute to teaching-learning situations suggests teachers should be taking advantage of this valuable resource. Such use, however, is not the case. Either due to hesitancy toward change or lack of equipment or computer skills, many teachers do not use technology in their classrooms. The support service person can serve as an advocate for technology and for helping educators design lesson plans utilizing computer technology.

Since technology is a major topic throughout this book, this section only addresses support services personnel being advocates for technology use in schools. Support services personnel can take several advocacy roles, including but not limited to

(*1*) Assisting in preparing classroom educators to incorporate technology in classrooms
(*2*) Providing an environment wherein both educators and students learn and develop skills
(*3*) Modeling for educators how computers make a difference in teaching-learning situations (Harrington, 1993)
(*4*) Working as a liaison person between teachers and administrators to encourage districts to purchase both hardware and software
(*5*) Continuing to stay technologically literate so as to be able to help and support classroom teachers and administrators

Sometimes, when classroom teachers and administrators feel threatened or overwhelmed by technology, support services personnel's encouraging remarks and patience explaining a procedure can be a major contribution. Advocacy roles do not mean forcing educators to use technology or making educators feel inept or less of a teacher for not using technology. Instead, support services personnel need to assume advocacy and support roles in which educators are encouraged and helped in specific situations. Also, many times the support service specialist serves in the best position to provide sound and effective leadership toward helping other school faculty and staff members utilize technology.

Specialists Addressing Specific Issues

The 21st century holds the potential for support services personnel addressing specific issues such as multiple intelligences, learning styles, cultural and gender differences, and perhaps issues or areas not evident in the 1990s. This section examines three possibilities that might require a support service specialist for each area or perhaps only one specialist responsible for responding to "learner differences," an area receiving significant attention as educators better understand learners and their differences.

Multiple Intelligences

The theory of multiple intelligences (Walters and Gardner, 1985; Gardner, 1987a; Hatch and Gardner, 1988; Blythe and Gardner, 1990) deserves consideration when planning and implementing educational experiences and when assessing students' potential. Multiple intelligences can provide alternatives to current educational practice in several areas. The seven intelligences have implications for educators, for the ways we regard human capacities, and for curriculum development. They consist of the following: 1) linguistic, 2) logical-mathematical, 3) musical, 4) spatial, 5) bodily kinesthetic, 6) interpersonal, and 7) intrapersonal. Gardner (1987a) maintains that the schools place a very high premium on linguistic and logical-mathematical intelligences because they promote performance in the essential subject areas of language, mathematics, and science. In light of his theory of multiple intelligence, Gardner (1987a) suggested a new set of roles for educators. First, educators might become "assessment specialists" (Gardner, 1987a, p. 191) who would try to understand as sensitively as possible the abilities and interests of students. These specialists could use "intelligence-fair" (p. 191) tests to look specifically at spatial and other individual abilities, rather than measuring only traditional forms of intelligence. Second, Gardner recommends the teaching of arts and humanities, which includes revealing and building upon students' latent abilities in these areas. Third, the teacher's role can include matching students' profiles, goals, and interests to particular curricula and to particular styles of learning. Fourth, Gardner suggested educators (or perhaps one designated educator) being responsible for matching students to learning opportunities in the wider community. Whether working in apprenticeship roles or as interns in organizations, learners can work to secure a feeling for the different roles of society (Gardner, 1987b).

The support service specialist working to address multiple intelligences and helping classroom educators plan learning experiences appropriate for each intelligence can take several directions (Campbell, 1992):

(1) Encourage classroom educators to plan educational experiences for a variety of human abilities and talents rather than the commonly addressed linguistic and mathematical intelligences.

(2) Plan assessment that objectively measures areas of intelligences usually not taught or assessed.
(3) Provide in-service activities or appropriate experiences that show classroom educators that multiple intelligences require different teaching skills than those needed for more traditional, whole-group lecturing.
(4) Encourage students to work with students rather than for them, explaining what they explore, discovering what they discover, and often learning what they learn.
(5) Encourage teachers to become more creative and multimodal in their own thinking and learning.

Prior to helping classroom educators, support services specialists might need to consider their own thinking about their concept of intelligences and, if necessary, reforge thinking to reflect more contemporary thought on learners' various intelligences. Since multiple intelligences is a relatively new concept, many educators and support services personnel may not be acquainted with this more contemporary perspective of intelligence. In this case, readers are referred to Gardner's seminal work on multiple intelligences published in the *Harvard Education Review* in 1987.

Learning Styles

Learning styles have been defined in several ways. First, Cornett (1983) believed that learning styles are consistent patterns of behavior defined in terms of cognitive, affective, and physiological dimensions. To some degree, learning styles are indicators of how individuals process information and respond to affective, sensory, and environmental dimensions of the instruction process. A second definition came from the NASSP (1979): learning styles are characteristic, cognitive, affective, and physiological behaviors that serve as relatively stable indicators of how learners perceive, interact with, and respond to the learning environment. The implications of learning styles, however, extend beyond mere definitions. Style characteristics are derived from genetic coding, personality, development, motivation, and cultural and environmental influences, which are relatively persistent qualities in the behavior of individual learners (Keefe, 1990a). A steadily increasing body of research suggests that equating learning styles and teaching-learning activities contributes to meeting an individual's unique needs (Dunn and Dunn, 1979; NASSP, 1979; Cornett, 1983; Keefe, 1990b; Stewart, 1990). Unlike multiple intelligences, educators have had access to the research and writings on learning styles for a number of years. However, candidly speaking, few educators have matched learning styles and educational experiences to any significant extent. The support service specialist with knowledge of learning styles can provide valuable advocacy roles through encouraging educators to recognize learning styles and assisting in the planning and implementation of appropriate instruction. Special considerations include an understanding of learning styles, differences among learners with similar learning styles, and assessment issues. Support services personnel can assess students' learning styles, assist in locating appropriate curricular materials, help teachers with lesson plans and instructional activities, help with assessment, and help parents understand learning styles.

Cultural and Gender Differences

Educators acquainted with children and adolescents can suggest examples of extreme differences in physical, psychosocial, and cognitive development. Recent research, however, indicates learners also have cultural and gender differences, which further contribute to their overall diversity. While educators can easily recognize developmental differences, cultural and gender differences may not be as obvious and, thus, might not be reflected in educational practice. Research on culture and its effects have focused primarily on friendships, identity development, social expectations, self-esteem, and learning styles. Understanding the relationship between culture and these crucial developmental areas allows educators to plan teaching-learning experiences that build upon the strengths of cultural diversity. The time has long passed for learners to be considered as individuals and to have their cultural and gender differences reflected in their educational experiences.

ADVOCACY ROLES THE FUTURE MIGHT BRING

Several factors suggest support services personnel will plan more lucrative roles in the 21st century: the increased emphasis on the value of teamwork, especially when educators have complementary strengths and expertise; the trend toward specialists accepting responsibility for roles previously accepted by classroom educators; the effort in the 1990s to include all children and adolescents in the American dream; and the increasing acceptance of support services personnel as vital members of a professional team. While predicting future roles is limited by 20th century perspectives and one's imagination of what education can be, several other roles can be suggested. Roles other than those suggested will depend upon schools' and support services specialists' imagination and commitment to children and adolescents.

Diagnosing Learning and Social Problems

Too many educators plan instruction for whole classes, with little regard for individual factors such as learning and social problems. With educators working with increasing numbers of students (and students with increasingly complex needs), support services personnel can play vital roles in diagnosing learning and social problems. Learning problems might include various disabilities, teachers not addressing students' learning styles, teaching toward the "wrong" intelligence, and educators failing to understand learners' motivation and perceptions of success. Social problems might include withdrawal resulting from shyness or other problems, feeling friendless or disliked, being pressured to make cross-sex friends before students are ready, and the many problems associated with peer pressure. Regardless of whether a learner's problems are academic or social, the result remains the same – learners need help, and support services specialists can play important roles in diagnosing the problem and planning an agenda for remediation.

Designing Appropriate Curricular Experiences

In some grades, curriculum has taken a back seat to instruction; i.e., educators have recently recognized the need to focus new energy toward improving curricular experiences. Too often, state department of education certification requirements have resulted in educators knowing their curriculum areas yet knowing little of other curriculum areas. The support service specialist, while perhaps not a specialist in all curricular areas, is in a prime position to encourage cross-curricular approaches. Support services personnel attending team meetings consisting of science, mathematics, language arts, and social studies (and ideally, art, music, and physical education) teachers might be in a prime position to encourage cross-curricular approaches, thematic units, and other integrated curricular approaches. Likewise, the support services professionals might be in a prime position to recommend (and perhaps make arrangements for) guest speakers, school-business partnerships, senior citizen volunteers, parent volunteers, and other community people willing to share areas of expertise. The complex nature of contemporary curriculum and the increasing demands placed upon schools call for team approaches to curriculum design. The support service specialist of the future can play integral roles in such curricular endeavors.

Addressing the Need for Mental Health Intervention

Schools have long been considered as "identifiers," i.e., identifiers of child abuse, emotional problems, social maladjustments, various handicaps, and other problems that interfere with social and academic progress. Today, more than ever, the public continues to place responsibilities on educators to accept nonteaching roles, i.e., determining students in need of mental health intervention. Considering educators' already full day and learners' problems resulting from contemporary society's seeming urge to make children grow up too fast, a support service advocacy role can be to assess the need for mental health intervention. This specialist, trained in assessment and identification techniques, can either identify students, meet with students on a referral basis, or speak with students that indicate an interest in talking. It would be essential that this person's qualifications include a knowledge of cultural and ethnic backgrounds, gender concerns, social class problems, and situations requiring an understanding of familiar backgrounds. While training in identification and counseling procedures would be necessary, this support service specialist role would be limited to identification and making referrals to a more qualified and specially trained specialist. Such a support service specialist can play roles in today's schools where personal problems often go unnoticed and increase in severity as learners grow older.

Evaluation and Testing Specialists

The need for support services personnel assuming evaluation and testing roles has been previously suggested; however, an advocacy role in this area, is without doubt, needed and a distinct possibility. This proposed support service role will require: training in testing and evaluation practices, knowledge of various testing instruments, understanding the dangers and pitfalls of testing, recognizing that testing should reflect multiple intelligences, helping parents and families understand testing, recognizing how culture affects testing and vice versa, testing for diagnostic purposes, and a host of other issues. Another role can be to help teachers design appropriate tests, both formative and summative. The emphasis on testing in our contemporary society has resulted in extreme criticism of the testing movement. While United States school children will likely be tested for years to come, testing will probably continue to be under scrutiny. Likewise, both educators and child-advocacy groups will continue to state the dangers of testing and push for reform. The support service specialist, acting as a testing specialist and an advocate for responsible testing, needs to understand the pros and cons of testing and also needs to plan an agenda for both testing appropriately and addressing the dangers and limitations of testing.

Providing Media Instruction

Multimedia in a technology center should be considered a valuable resource that can be utilized by teachers to motivate learners. Multimedia includes chalkboards, television, film, overhead projectors, tape players, record players, videotape recorders, cameras, computers, CD-ROMS, and video laser disks. Multimedia also should include video disks, photographs, software, bulletin boards, maps, and video and software programs developed by students. Integration of multimedia, including computers, holds promise for challenging learners. Teachers need to be trained to utilize multimedia and computers effectively in their classroom instruction. Learners will need teachers to help facilitate their understanding of computers and multimedia. Because computers and media are being utilized in society and they are interactive, they have an important role in business and education. The difficulty is to make sure that computer and multimedia programs are based on sound educational principles (Allen et al., 1993).

Support services personnel assuming advocacy roles has been a significant thrust of this text. Teachers need a support service specialist who can "bring technology into the classroom." As previously mentioned, this advocacy role can include both producing media instruction and helping classroom teachers in the production of educational media. The effective classroom of the 21st century will reflect the technological advances evident in our society. A support service specialist, accepting an advocacy role in promoting technology and media-based instruction, can play a valuable role in helping schools reflect media and technological advances.

Designing and Monitoring Home-Based Instruction

The home-schooling movement has grown substantially during the last decade of the 20th century. Parents are increasingly dissatisfied with the public school, for example, some considered the public school as bureaucratic, stifling of creativity and individuality, a place where violence was too common, an institution promoting secular values, a place where time wasting was the norm, and an environment too factory-like. Feeling that public schools were unable (or unwilling) to change, some parents and families began to educate their children at home. School districts, at first, perceived home schooling as a threat to their commonly accepted roles, but, during the later years of the 20th century, many schools have accepted the inevitable and have begun to help parents in home-schooling efforts. Schools began to supply textbooks upon parents' request, to test students' progress, and, generally speaking, to help parents in their efforts. In many situations, adverse relations turned into positive working relationships – the overall welfare of the child or adolescent was at stake as educators recognized the benefits of helping parents to educate children.

As the number of home-schooling parents increases, an advocacy role of support services personnel can be to assist with home-schooling efforts. This advocate could be the liaison professional between the school and the parents. Responsibilities might include ensuring learners' rights are met, ensuring parents have the proper textbooks and curricular materials, ensuring learners have opportunities to be tested, and any other issues that might arise in home-schooling efforts. Representing both the school's administrative policy and the educator's commitment to excellence, this support service professional can be the contact person when a parent decides to educate learners at home. Objectivity would be the key – the support service specialist would neither condemn or recommend home schooling. He or she will, however, advocate parents' and children's rights, fair treatment, opportunities to educate learners in the most conclusive environment, and instructional excellence for all learners.

Providing Accountability Measures

Accountability, another thread throughout this book, will continue to challenge educators during the 21st century. Evidence during the 1990s indicates numerous accountability demands, i.e., teachers being held accountable for learners' academic achievement and overall welfare, as well as teachers being held accountable for their own achievement being measured by competency tests and other measures. Support services specialists can play significant roles in helping classroom teachers understand and meet accountability demands, as well as helping teachers and other support services personnel respond to accountability issues such as teacher testing. Rather than accountability being a passing fad, this issue will continue to challenge educators in the 21st century. Having a support service specialist responsible for interpreting accountability demands, completing the required paperwork for documentation, and selecting valid and reliable accountability methods can be a major advocacy role for support services personnel to assume.

Advocates for Team Approaches

While team approaches were addressed in Chapter 3, this section looks only at support services personnel working as advocates for team approaches. Classroom educators' tendency to work in isolation sometimes prohibits team approaches. Support services specialists can play valuable roles in encouraging classroom educators to try team approaches and in helping teachers understand the importance of team dynamics. Support services personnel serving as advocates for team approaches need to work toward changing the mind-set as to what effective teachers do. The concept of teachers working alone needs to be replaced with the philosophy of working together and utilizing complementary expertises. The support services specialists can provide significant leadership in this restructuring of thought: teaching the values of team approaches, understanding the powerful effect of team spirit, promoting professionalism among team members, working to maximize the benefits accrued from team approaches, handling conflicts and interpersonal relationships, convincing administrators to give up long-held authority, and modeling effective team approaches. This advocacy role will take enthusiasm, commitment, and considerable tact or ability to promote positive interpersonal relationships. The United States school system has long expected teachers to work alone and to be self-sufficient—the time has come for team approaches to what individuals once did. The time has also come for support services specialists charged with the responsibility to provide leadership in team approaches.

SUMMARY

Serving as advocacy agents will be among the support services personnel's most important roles during the 21st century. Schools need to assume advocacy agents to move beyond the status quo and to provide leadership toward meeting future educational challenges. A prerequisite challenge for support services personnel will be to change attitudes and mind-sets toward what education can become. A multitude of roles will challenge support services personnel, some perhaps even unheard of today. Working either as an individual professional or as an integral team member, another challenge will be for support services personnel to accept advocacy roles and work toward significant changes in the educational system. Specific benefits of support services personnel acting as advocacy agents are too numerous to name; however, generally speaking, the learners and the entire education profession will be beneficiaries when these professionals assume more advocacy and leadership roles.

REFERENCES

Allen, H. A., Splittgerber, F. L. and Manning, M. L. (1993). *Teaching and Learning in the Middle Level School*. Columbus, OH: Merrill.

Blythe, T. and Gardner, H. (1990). "A school for all intelligences," *Educational Leadership*, 47(7):33–36.

Campbell, B. (1992). "Multiple intelligences in action," *Childhood Education*, 68:197–201.

Carnegie Council on Adolescent Development. (1989). *Turning Points: Preparing American Youth for the 21st Century*. Washington, DC: Carnegie Council on Adolescent Development.

Clark, D. C. and Cutler, B. R. (1990). *Teaching: An Introduction*. New York: Harcourt Brace Jovanovich.

Cornett, C. E. (1983). *What You Should Know about Teaching and Learning Styles*. Bloomington, IN: Phi Delta Kappa Education Foundation.

Dunn, R. S. and Dunn, K. J. (1979). "Learning/teaching styles: Should they . . . can they . . . be matched?" *Educational Leadership*, 36(4):238–244.

Gardner, H. (1987a). "Developing the spectrum of human intelligence," *Harvard Education Review*, 57:187–193.

Gardner, H. (1987b). "An individual-centered curriculum," in *The Schools We've Got, the Schools We Need*, Council of Chief State School Officer and the American

Association of Teacher Educators (Eds.), Washington, DC: Council of Chief State School Officer and the American Association of Teacher Educators.

Harrington, H. L. (1993). "The essence of technology and the education of teachers," *Journal of Teacher Education*, 44(1):5–15.

Hatch, T. and Gardner, H. (1988). "New research on intelligence," *Learning 88*, 17(4):36–39.

Keefe, J. W. (1990a). "Learning style: Where are we going?" *Momentum*, 21(1):44–48.

Keefe, J. W. (1990b). *Learning Styles: Theory and Practice*. Reston, VA: NASSP.

Manning, M. L. (1993). "Making equal access a middle school priority," *Focus on Later Childhood/Early Adolescence*, 5(4):1–2.

Myers, C. B. and Myers, L. K. (1990). *An Introduction to Teaching and Learning*. Fort Worth: Holt, Rinehart and Winston.

National Association of Secondary School Principals. (1979). *Student Learning Styles – Diagnosing and Prescribing Programs*. Reston, VA: NASSP.

Sergiovanni, T. J. (1990). *Value-Added Leadership: How to Get Extraordinary Performance in Schools*. New York: Harcourt Brace Jovanovich.

Stewart, W. J. (1990). "Learning-styles-appropriate instruction: Planning, implementing, evaluation," *The Clearing House*, 63:371–374.

Walters, J. M. and Gardner, H. (1985). "The development and education of intelligences," in *Essays on the Intellect*. F. R. Link (Ed.), pp. 1–21, Washington, DC: ASCD.

CHAPTER 5

Training and Educating Support Services Personnel

OVERVIEW

THE PROFESSIONAL PREPARATION of support services personnel in the 21st century must reflect many changes: our increasingly culturally diverse society, rapid technological advances, the creation of service roles designed to meet needs not presently being addressed, and a greater sense of professionalism among support services personnel. In addition, the profession will increasingly be held accountable for its actions by state and national accrediting agencies, as well as by professional associations representing the respective support professions. The increased demands placed on educators of support services personnel warrant examination of pedagogical experiences to determine their effectiveness in the 21st century. Programmatic designs, as well as actual coursework and field experiences, must provide support services personnel with the competencies needed for successful collaboration with other educators, as well as meeting the educational needs of learners needing specialized assistance. This chapter focuses on support services personnel's professional preparation and on competencies needed for the upcoming century.

PROFESSIONAL PREPARATION

Rapid changes in society and technology have led to revolutionary changes in public expectations of schools in general and professionals in particular. Many training institutions have been accused of preparing educators for schools and students that no longer exist. These institutions have lost contact with their constituency and continue to prepare educators as they did twenty years ago (Friedman et al., 1980). To make the situation more acute, changes during the last fifteen years such as rapid technological advances and adamant demands for accountability place even greater challenges on the training and educating of professional educators.

Professional preparation in the 1990s and 21st century cannot be more of the same experiences designed for educators of yesteryear. The professional educator who could not be trained to address the needs of learners in 120 semester or quarter hours cannot be trained in 150. The amount of formal educational experiences needs to be a consideration, however, because more consideration needs to be directed toward designing actual experiences needed. The changing nature of society suggests preparation programs should not be "set in concrete" but should be sufficiently flexible to meet changing expectations. Even with this proposed flexibility, specific competencies should underlie all programs and courses. Educational experiences for support services personnel cannot be left to chance or whim—educated and certified support services personnel need specific experiences that contribute to specific competencies.

Coursework

Coursework for providing support services personnel with professional preparation includes general education components and professional components. Each plays a major role in the preparation of support services professionals. Likewise, each is dictated by institutional governance structures and state and national accrediting associations. The first part of this section examines the general education component, while the second section looks at professional education components. Next, requirements as suggested dictates of several accrediting organizations representing specific support organizations are examined.

General Education

The general education component of the professional education program has the purpose of developing a well-educated professional. As one can imagine, deciding the qualities or characteristics of a well-educated professional can result in considerable disagreement. In fact, little consensus exists to suggest the program or courses a college or university should offer to facilitate the individual's development of needed characteristics. Evaluating and certifying knowledge, attitudes, and skills prove difficult for colleges and universities.

Generally speaking, the general education component develops the sensitivities, appreciation, and knowledge that determine the degree to which a person is educated. This "education" includes becoming acquainted with one's heritage and acquiring the intellectual skills allowing one to continue learning after graduation. Sometimes called "liberal education," this component theoretically liberates a person from narrow perspectives, ideas, and values. Also, the component also supposedly opens the mind to the complexities of the world, to foster development of sophisticated intellectual and personal skills, and promotes the formulation of an individual philosophy of life (Friedman et al., 1980).

The state accrediting association, National Association of State Directors of Teacher Education and Certification (NASDTEC), bases general education requirements on several studies: humanities, mathematics, the biological and physical sciences, and the social and behavioral sciences. Specifically, NASDTEC standards suggest accomplishment in the following:

(*1*) Stimulate scholarship that will give understanding to concepts not now extant and help prepare people for rapid adjustment to essential change.
(*2*) Foster individual fulfillment and nurture free, rational, and responsible adults.
(*3*) Cultivate appreciation for the values associated with life in a free society and for responsible citizenship.
(*4*) Develop leaders who are intellectually competent, imaginative, and vigorous.
(*5*) Contribute fundamentally to and give direction to the use of professional knowledge.
(*6*) Encourage discernment in examining the values inherent in foreign cultures to the end that a clearer understanding of other peoples will reduce world tensions.

According to NASDTEC, the following broad areas of study should be addressed in the general education component (Friedman et al., 1980):

(*1*) Language skills as essential tools in communication
(*2*) World literature with emphasis on, but not limited to, the writings of English and American authors
(*3*) The aesthetic values in human experience expressed through the fine arts

(4) The scientific and mathematical concepts upon which contemporary civilization depends
(5) Contemporary world culture
(6) Social, geographic, political, and economic conditions and their impacts on current problems in the nation and the world
(7) The growth and development of the United States as a nation and its place in world affairs
(8) The principles of physical and mental health as they apply to the individual and to the community
(9) America's pluralistic culture and heritage

The National Council for Accreditation of Teacher Education (NCATE) recognizes that programs of general education vary widely among different institutions and suggests that general education be individualized according to the needs and interests of the student. According to NCATE, general education should include the studies most widely generalizable.

The NCATE standard for the general education component states that there should be a planned general studies component requiring that at least one-third of each curriculum for prospective teachers consists of studies in the symbolics of information, natural and behavioral sciences, and humanities (Friedman et al., 1980).

Professional Education

All professional education programs are based on established educational research and essential knowledge of sound professional practice. The professional education unit supports an integrated approach to general education, professional studies, and specialty studies. Each program in the unit reflects a systematic design with an explicitly stated philosophy and objectives. The curriculum encompasses the knowledge domains represented in academic study, professional research and practice, and professional ethics. It demonstrates an understanding and application of instruction for individual learning needs (NCATE, 1986).

The professional core seeks to provide prospective teachers with the knowledge, attitudes, and skills needed to teach in elementary, middle, and secondary schools. While the general education component provides the foundation that supposedly all educators need, the professional education component provides expertise to understand learners and to provide appropriate teaching experiences. Such experiences include human growth and development, educational philosophy and history, pedagogical courses, and, in the case of support services personnel, training in specialized areas. Professional core courses may vary from institution to institution as attempts are made to provide appropriate educational experiences. Likewise, educational experiences vary among support services personnel; i.e., counselors and media specialists may share general education requirements yet have vastly different professional education cores.

It is unrealistic and beyond the limits of this text to comment on the knowledge base (the skills, information, and attitudes that professionals need) that all support services professionals need; however, to make the point that the knowledge base and professional education core differ according to professional specialty, the authors selected three professional specialties for more extensive elaboration.

First, the Council for Accreditation of Counseling and Related Educational Programs (CACREP, 1988), The National Association of School Psychologists, and the previously mentioned NCATE (1986) have developed and implemented standards designed to aid in the process of developing programs (Thomas, 1990). Four essential elements in counseling and school psychologist programs include philosophy and assumptions, outcomes and evaluation processes, a model or an organizing theme, and knowledge base source documents. CACREP (1988) outlines a core curriculum for all counselor education programs that includes human growth and development, social and cultural foundations, helping relationships, groups, lifestyles and career development, appraisal, research and evaluation, and professional orientation. In addition, school counselors must complete work in specialized environmental studies related to the school setting and specialized studies that enhance a delivery model for counseling services in the schools. This core can be used to develop a program philosophy and specific program outcomes and to establish an organizing theme around which to build the program (Thomas, 1990).

Second, school library media specialists handle all commonly expected roles of librarians but also act as resource persons to faculty members by aiding in expanding the curriculum and developing in-service programs for teachers. In the past fifteen years, the role of the typical school librarian has shifted dramatically from a primary responsibility of circulating books and helping students to a responsibility that might require the individual to become a curriculum consultant, media specialist, computer expert, and public relations officer (Ayers and Pratt, 1990).

Systematic planned evaluation is necessary to make changes and to keep up with the ever-changing role of the school library media specialist. The knowledge base supporting the program for preparing school library media specialists provides a basis for curricular and other programmatic decisions and also serves as a basis for developing a system of evaluation and accountability (Ayers and Pratt, 1990).

Martin (1986) suggests several questions that professionals designing curricular experiences for school library media specialists might ask:

- What are the on-the-job expectations of a school library media specialist?
- What are the expectations of the school library/media center?
- What changes can be expected in the next decade in the school library/media center and the role of the school media specialist?
- What types of communication links are needed between school library media specialists and the clients served?
- What is the substance of the program designed to prepare school library media specialists?

Several informational sources serve valuable roles as teacher training institutions develop knowledge bases for the various specialized services. The American Library Association (ALA), American Association of School Librarians (AASL), and the Association for Educational Communications and Technology (AECT) have developed guidelines for school library media programs. School media specialists must be prepared in the roles of information specialist, teacher, and instructional consultant.

Serving as an information specialist, the school media specialist

- provides access to the library media center
- provides adequate resources
- provides assistance in locating information
- guides users in the selection of appropriate resources
- develops policies for the use of resources
- operates accurate retrieval systems

The role of teacher includes instructing students, other educators, and parents in the use of the school library media center. The school librarian, serving in the role of instructional consultant, provides assistance to teachers on matters of curriculum and instructional development (Ayers and Pratt, 1990).

Third, vocational education has changed throughout history as demands for workers changed and, in all likelihood, will continue to change in the 21st century, especially as technology opens new frontiers requiring specialized training. Vocational educators received a new impetus when the Vocational Education Act was passed in 1963. The Act required each state to establish a state advisory committee for vocational education (Wentling and Lawson, 1975).

Examples of vocational education programs include home economics education, business education, marketing education, technology education, and trade and industrial education. Vocational education poses some unique problems for the program planner, the students, the faculty, and those who would evaluate the programs. The lack of a national certification standard for vocational education (let alone the separate disciplines of which "vocational education" is comprised) and the lack of clarity as to where vocational programs are administratively located are but two of those problems. Literature on vocational education teacher preparation programs is scanty, indicating a need for sound research about such programs (Ritz, 1990).

The knowledge base for vocational educators depends on the respective programs. Likewise, the specific content or areas of study that contribute to the knowledge base also differ. Several examples of knowledge bases and supporting areas of study are stated next.

The knowledge base of *home economics education* is the work of the family and occupations based on home economics skills. As this description indicates, home economics has two roles, family and the world of work. Consequently, the preparation of home economics teachers must investigate the work of the family unit and then encourage the development of additional technical skills in the preservice teachers so that they can prepare students for home economics occupations such as cooks, child care workers, restaurant managers, and fashion designers. The areas of study that come from this knowledge base include consumer and resource management; housing and living environments; individual, child, and family development; nutrition and food; and textiles and clothing.

The knowledge base for *business education* is business concepts. Education for business provides students with the necessary skills to allow them to assume employment roles within the business community. Education about business provides general education to all students to allow them to understand the business affairs of our global society. To help students attain the goals of business education, programs are structured around the content areas of keyboarding, computer applications, personal finance, economic systems, and employability skills (Ritz, 1990).

The knowledge base for *marketing education* is the marketing enterprise. Marketing education extends its mission from the preparation of skilled personnel to include a general studies component that provides a knowledge of marketing and its role in the context of public, private, and nonprofit enterprises. This is accomplished through instruction in economics, management, and the various marketing specialty areas such as sales, advertising, buying, and channels of distribution.

The knowledge base for *technology education* is technology. Formerly referred to as industrial arts, technology has taken on the new mission of providing technological literacy in the general studies curriculum component. The goal is to provide all students with a general knowledge of technology and how technology affects individuals, groups, and the environment. The areas of study involved in technology education include communication, mass transportation systems, construction, and manufacturing.

The knowledge base for *trade and industrial education* includes competencies required for students to become skilled trade workers. This area does not often require degreed personnel but does require some 2,000 hours of on-the-job experience for certification. It is possible to earn credit for work experience or by successfully passing the National Occupational Competency Testing Institute (NOCTI) examinations. The knowledge base is derived from the specific skills the worker must demonstrate. Trade and industrial programs prepare students to work in such areas as auto body repair, automotive technology, robotics, media production, and cosmetology (Ritz, 1990).

Field/Clinical Experiences

The curriculum for the preparation of professional educators includes clinical and field-based experiences to provide sufficient opportunities for the application and evaluation of the theories that are being taught. These experiences are sequenced and occur concurrently with the professional education curriculum. They provide opportunities for analysis, application, and evaluation so that theories and practice in schools are related. This sequence enables prospective educators to move through stages of increased responsibility for classroom instruction or other professional roles in schools (NCATE, 1990). Field-based and clinical experiences are systematically selected to provide opportunities for education students to observe, plan, and practice in a variety of settings appropriate to the professional roles for which they are preparing. These experiences are accompanied by professional feedback to education students to encourage the most effective practice. Clinical and field-based experiences provide the education student with individual cases or problems, the diagnosis and solution of which involve the application of the principles and theories from the knowledge bases of the particular professional program. Education students participate in field-based and/or clinical experiences with culturally diverse and exceptional populations to allow them to understand the unique contributions, needs, similarities, differences, and interdependencies of students from varying racial, cultural, linguistic, religious, and socioeconomic backgrounds. Clinical and field-based experiences enable the education student to develop skills for providing quality instruction or services prior to entering a student teaching assignment or other professional internship. Clinical and field-based experiences may include, but are not limited to, observations, micro teaching, developing case studies of individual students, tutoring, assisting school administrators, translating theory into practice, curriculum development, use of instructional technology including the computer, and participation in school- and community wide activities (NCATE, 1990).

This section looks at efforts to improve field experiences for professional educators and then examines field experiences in several specialized support areas. Generalizations can prove helpful as teacher educators plan field experiences; however, local and state needs and national accrediting association standards must also be considered vital to programs.

Speaking generally, the following suggestions or guidelines hold potential for improving field experiences (Henry, 1989).

(*1*) Field experiences should be early and continuing.
(*2*) Specific learning tasks should be identified and developed at all levels.
(*3*) Select superior teachers as role models for field participants.
(*4*) Prepare supervisors for their tasks.
(*5*) Examine the basic concepts and assumptions about internships and extended field experiences.
(*6*) Limit the number of schools that have field participants.
(*7*) Increase and improve the university-public school linkage.

(*8*) Minimum competencies should be identified and demonstrated by field participants.
(*9*) Establish an internship as the culminating field experience.

Rather than attempting to describe field experiences in all support areas and possible areas during the 21st century, the authors will select several representative areas for examination.

The first support service area addressed will be *school counselors*. Taken either before or during field experiences, a common core of learning should prepare prospective counselors for field experiences: human growth and development, social and cultural foundations, knowledge of helping relationships, knowledge of group processes and working with groups, lifestyle and career development, techniques of individual appraisal, research and evaluation, and professional orientations. The field experience should provide students opportunities to realize the relevance of and actually use the above common core areas (Baruth and Robinson, 1987).

Knoff (1986) advocates the supervision process in laboratory experiences and includes five supervision components: 1) knowledge, 2) skill, 3) confidence, 4) objectivity, and 5) interpersonal relationships. This model also encompasses five statuses relative to school psychology: 1) practicum, 2) internship, 3) entry level, 4) independent practice, and 5) supervision. Finally, three school psychological functions, 1) assessment, 2) indirect services, and 3) direct services, complete the model. Knoff (1986) further notes that supervision should have an empirical base and remarks that the supervision components can be used as a basis for the evaluation of field experiences.

Such a model or any other model should provide opportunities for prospective counselors to translate classroom theory into practice and should be based on clearly defined goals and objectives; relate to contextual issues; and be purposeful, articulated, and reflective (Griffin, 1986).

Field experiences in counseling programs include practicum and internship experiences that provide for the integration and application of knowledge and skills gained in didactic study. These experiences should be in settings compatible with students' career goals and should include both observation and participation in specific activities. This might include role playing, listening to tapes, viewing video playbacks, testing, organizing and using personnel records, interviewing field practitioners, preparing and examining case studies, and using career information materials. These supervised counseling practicum experiences should provide interaction with individuals and groups actually seeking counseling services. The student provides these services under the supervision of a faculty member by means of direct observation or recorded audio- and/or videotape. The internship serves as a postpracticum experience that provides an actual on-the-job experience and includes all activities that a regularly employed staff member would be expected to perform. Supervision should be performed by qualified staff in the field placement setting and also by a member of the counselor training faculty (Baruth and Robinson, 1987).

Field-based experiences for *school library media specialists* usually spend 135 clock hours in the field, working directly with a school library media specialist (Ayers and Pratt, 1990; AASL/ALA, 1989; Burks, 1988). Like other specializations, library media specialists must take an array of core courses that complement the field experiences and vice versa. Examples of expected competencies resulting from field experiences include

(*1*) Planning for instruction in the library media center
(*2*) Developing teaching strategies
(*3*) Evaluating materials and equipment
(*4*) Evaluating library media center programs
(*5*) Managing the school library media center
(*6*) Developing professional and leadership skills
(*7*) Developing basic communication skills

In addition to these seven competencies, school library media specialists must also demonstrate basic skills relative to cataloging, handling reference materials, and using bibliographic techniques (Ayers and Pratt, 1990).

Likewise, field experiences should occur in an actual school library media center, should be under the direction of a qualified school library media specialist, and should provide evaluations of the library media specialists. Coursework and field experiences should complement each other to produce a school library media specialist who can (Barron and Bergen, 1992):

- serve as a master teacher
- work with classroom teachers to integrate information management skills into curriculum and classes

- work as a good manager of human and material resources
- plan, implement, and evaluate the library media program
- articulate and defend a budget, as well as seek outside funding through grants and business partnerships
- possess an excellent knowledge of the wide range of technologies required to supply the school with information—reference books, online telecommunications, or carefully selected CD-ROM databases
- play vital partnership roles with other members of the instructional team

Increasingly in the 21st century, library media specialists will be expected to make maximum use of technology and technological advances. Librarians have been instrumental in the use of information technology from clay tablets and papyrus to CD-ROM databases and satellite communication. The profession has seen itself as providing teachers and students access to and assistance with the available technology. Too often, the library is associated solely with books. The book will continue to be a critical technology to which students and teachers need access, but the book is only one of the technologies needed in order to manage effectively the information necessary for teaching and learning. One of the reasons for the use of the label *school library media specialist* is to help people bridge the conceptual gap between a librarian whose function is to deal with information transferred via the book and a librarian whose function is to deal with information transferred via the most appropriate medium (Barron and Bergen, 1992).

For field experiences for *vocational education* support professionals to be effective, students need demonstrated competence in their respective knowledge bases, as well as well-planned experiences in their vocational area. Many hours of laboratory experiences are required to prepare vocational teachers for a world of work. Field experiences in vocational education areas will be enhanced when students observe those vocational classes they plan to teach; maintain a journal of their observations such as actual occurrences and reflections; plan and assist with specific lessons; and self-evaluate teaching performances, including what went well during instruction and where improvement is needed (Ritz, 1990).

Field experiences for vocational educational support services professionals should include opportunities for observation, practica, and student teaching. In observation experiences, students merely observe learners and teachers in an attempt to gain a better understanding of what vocational education teachers do and what learners are like. The practica include actual work in which the student takes responsibility for classes and teaches classes under the close supervision of the cooperating teacher. Students may attend only two or three times per week and will probably maintain a journal or log. The third experience, student teaching, usually occurs during the senior year and usually lasts an entire semester. The student teaching experience should provide a wide array of experiences; e.g., students should have two placements, one at the middle school level and one at the high school level, each of which should also be divided into an urban and a suburban area (Ritz, 1990).

Several characteristics of effective field experiences for prospective vocational education professionals include (Ritz, 1990)

- placements that are representative of the occupations that the student will seek after graduation
- opportunities to work on the job under the direct supervision of a manager with the organization
- rotation of vocational education students to provide the greatest occupational exposure
- students maintaining a journal or weekly log describing their experiences, skills developed, and the relationship of the work experiences to the overall professional preparation program
- specific and detailed forms for collecting, reporting, and documenting data
- university supervision including actual visitation to work sites to communicate with employers and to assess the technical competence gained through the experience

While this has not been an exhaustive examination of field experiences, the discussion does show the importance of prospective support services personnel having first-hand experiences with learners and practicing teachers in actual school situations. Several criteria contribute to field experiences (regardless of specialty) being effective, e.g., the field experience (Mead, 1991)

- requires a formal commitment on the part of schools and school systems, as well as professional preparation institutions
- occurs in a school that serves a demographically representative population
- occurs in schools that are devoted to both the development of teachers and the instruction of students
- requires a sustained period of time, preferably long enough so that students can develop accurate perspectives

- involves cadres of interns large enough to reinforce the role of the school as a clinical site
- allows educators in the schools to accept major responsibility for training prospective educators
- includes seminars, preferably at the school sites, for reflection upon experiences
- gives interns or prospective professionals the status of membership in the school's instructional team

INCREASED PROFESSIONALISM

Professionalism affects the education of support services personnel in at least two ways. First, preparatory institutions better understand the knowledge, attitudes, and skills needed for support services personnel to be effective and to make valuable contributions to school systems. Several factors contribute to this belief: research indicating directions for effective programmatic decisions; institutions' internal reviews to improve general education, professional education, and field experiences; NASDTEC and NCATE accrediting agencies' efforts to promote state and national excellence, respectively; and professional associations representing specific specialties such as National Association for Schools of Music (NASM), Council for the Accreditation of Counseling and Related Educational Programs (CACREP), American Library Association (ALA), National Association of Schools of Art and Design (NASAD), and National Association of School Psychologists (NASP).

What professional characteristics should institutions preparing support services personnel seek to instill? Howsam et al. (1985) offer several characteristics of a profession, such as professionals

- providing essential services to individuals and society
- working with an identified area of need or function, e.g., maintenance of physical and emotional health, preservation of rights and freedom, and enhancing opportunities to learn
- possessing a body of knowledge and a repertoire of behaviors and skills needed in the practice or the profession
- participating in decision-making processes in the service of a client, the decisions being made with the most valid knowledge available, a background of principles and theories, and within the context of possible impact on other related conditions or decisions
- basing decisions on one or more undergirding disciplines from which basic insights, applied knowledge, and skills are derived

- organizing members into one or more professional associations, which, within broad limits of accountability, are granted autonomy in control of the profession, e.g., admissions, educational standards, examination and licensing, career line, ethical and performance standards, and professional discipline
- agreeing to performance standards for admission to the profession and for continuing practice
- receiving a high level of public trust and confidence in the profession and in individual practitioners, based upon the profession's demonstrated capacity to provide service markedly beyond that which would otherwise be available
- accepting responsibility in the name of his or her profession and being accountable through his or her profession to society

Regardless of the professional specialty, support services personnel have a responsibility to work collaboratively with other professionals toward common goals, to work for the betterment of the profession, and to commit to lifelong learning in order to become an effective professional, one who has kept up with current trends in the profession and with issues affecting professional practice.

ACCOUNTABILITY DEMANDS

The demands for accountability, popular in the 1990s, will continue to be a reality and trend during the 21st century. Media articles have spotlighted the alleged incompetence of professional educators and have affected the images of educators and the teacher educators responsible for their preparation (Henry, 1989). Professionals continue to be challenged to prove their "worth," to prove their competence, and, generally speaking, to document their effectiveness.

While most support services personnel can attest to the accountability demands of the general public, the education profession and its various specialties are also subject to the constant scrutiny of their own accrediting associations. NASDTEC, NCATE, and all the associations representing individual specialties hold professionals accountable for behaviors, competencies, attitudes, and overall effectiveness. This scrutiny and accountability should not be perceived as "evils" or "obstacles" to overcome or to work around. Instead, support services professionals should view accountability as a means of improving behaviors and performance. One aspect related to accountability holds true: if professions do not hold themselves accountable and do not scrutinize their behaviors and performance, outside organizational bodies, perhaps with little knowledge of challenges faced by various professionals, will assume the task.

Institutions preparing support services personnel also periodically conduct internal reviews to evaluate effectiveness—to the student, to the profession, and to the institution. While each institution needs to examine its mission statement as well as geographical challenges, criteria examined may include

- *Centrality:* Does the professional preparation program contribute the overall mission of the institution?
- *Student Credit Hour Production:* Does student credit hour production indicate a sufficient number of students are in the program to provide a feeling of "collegiality" or "community of learners" among prospective professionals?
- *Quality of Teaching among the Faculty:* Do faculties' student ratings and evaluations, course development and improvement, and involvement with other college and university faculty indicate quality or excellence in teaching?
- *Quality of the Faculty in Research:* Do faculties' research, publications, and presentations indicate quality or excellence?
- *Adequate Staffing for the Program:* Do data indicate the program is sufficiently staffed to conduct daily operations?
- *Quality of Program as Perceived by External Groups:* How do data suggest external groups (other institutional faculty, state constituents, regional groups, national groups, or other constituent groups) perceive the program?
- *Accreditation:* Is the program accredited by its respective association?

These few criteria provide only representative examples of aspects to evaluate. As previously mentioned, institutions need to consider their own individual programs and overall mission statements and then formulate an evaluational document. Conducting an internal program review as a means of responding to accountability demands can be an excellent mechanism for identifying strengths and weaknesses.

Learning Diagnostician

A reality confronting educators is that many children and adolescents do not learn, perhaps due to lack of motivation, lack of ability, incompatibilities between teaching and learning styles, some specific disability, or one or more of many other factors. While American education practices have worked and contributed to the success of many students, a sad fact is that many other learners did not succeed and either dropped out or graduated with minimal skills. The need is being increasingly recognized to have a trained specialist—perhaps called a learning diagnostician or learning strategist—who determines actual causes of students not learning and then devises an educational plan to build upon students' weaknesses and to address the actual learning problem or reason for lack of academic achievement.

Competencies of learning diagnosticians will include the ability to

- diagnose specific learning problems
- plan individual instructional experiences designed to address a specific problem
- recognize and plan for developmental, social class, cultural, and gender differences
- suggest appropriate teaching materials and learning resources
- work collaboratively, collegially, and professionally with classroom educators and other support services professional
- meet accountability measures—both for addressing learners' needs, as well as other professional responsibilities
- utilize technological advances to meet learning problems

This support service professional will need the general education, professional education, and field experiences required of other education professionals, as well as specialization programs and experiences designed to address these competencies. Also, training should include knowledge of the growth and development characteristics of the age learner that the learning diagnostician plans to assist.

Software Specialists

The increasing use of technology in schools, without doubt, will continue as technological advances become more available and, educators probably hope, become less expensive. Undoubtedly, the upcoming decade will bring a need for a support service professional trained in the design, evaluation, and use of software. Three reasons suggest this person will be responsible for the actual design of software. First, educators working daily with learners need software designed to address specific learning needs. Software developers often design products to meet the learner needs of a wide variety of learners and, subsequently, fail to help individual learners. Second, the problem of bad software continues to plague school systems. Third, while educators have warned of the dangers of worksheets for years, some software packages offer few alternative to worksheets. In some cases, the only difference is that poorly designed exercises are on the monitor rather than a desk (Callister and Dunne, 1992). These three reasons convincingly suggest the need for a profession working in the school who can design effective and worthwhile software. Likewise, this professional would be responsible for helping regular classroom teachers and other support services personnel utilize the software in the most effective manner.

Examples of competencies that software specialists might include are the ability to

- prepare evaluation guidelines for selecting software
- select quality software that meets learners' academic needs
- provide in-service sessions that show classroom educators and school administrators how technology can contribute to learners' academic success
- work with classroom educators, school administrators, and other support services personnel to use technological advances to save time and to handle bookkeeping tasks
- devise a system whereby software can be catalogued and its location identified when needed
- prepare a plan to make the school's use of technology reflect society's and businesses' increasing use
- form an advisory committee that monitors software purchases and actual usage

Developing these selected competencies will require a strong specialization in technological advances and, especially, in computer usage and software design. This professional preparation cannot be a hodge-podge of computer courses and experiences; rather, training must prepare experts capable of making maximum use of computers and the actual design of software that addresses a particular school's needs.

Curriculum Designers

The curriculum designer of the 21st century will need to include curricular aspects considered contemporary (or perhaps unheard of) today. The school curriculum must change to reflect the needs of a changing society. Our curriculum in the 1990s does not teach sheepherding, fitting horseshoes, or repairing wagon wheels. Instead, the curriculum addresses contemporary concerns such as an understanding and prevention of AIDS, the idea of a global village or economy, and, of course, the basics of learning how to read and write. Therefore, the curriculum designer must prepare for the present and the future, rather than rely too heavily on the past.

What might the curriculum in the late 1990s and the early 21st century be like? What aspects must designers consider to make the curriculum relevant, purposeful, and useful? What will the designer include, regardless of how our changing society affects the curriculum? Those aspects and other dimensions will be considered and addressed in the next section.

First, the curriculum in the 21st century will likely be interdisciplinary in nature, where students see and study relationships. For example, rather than studying science, mathematics, and social studies in isolation, common themes cross subject area lines and contribute to students learning the whole picture rather than isolated fragments.

Second, perhaps there will be greater efforts to provide curricular experiences for slower and faster students. In the mid-1990s, educators have realized that gifted and talented learners are bored and underchallenged, and, for maximum potential to be achieved, the curriculum, as well as everyday school practice, needs to challenge these learners.

Third, curriculum designers (as Chapter 7 examines in considerable detail) will need to incorporate multicultural aspects into the curriculum. Our increasing multicultural populations, as well as our nation's role in a changing global village and economy, requires change in the curriculum and school practices.

Fourth, a 21st century curriculum will probably reflect a concern for world welfare, the prevention for and cure of AIDS, the strain of our growing world population on our environment and the world's food supply, and, the authors hope, an equitable treatment of all races, cultures, and social classes living in the United States.

Fifth, as this book has previously mentioned, technology will play a major role in the school's and nation's future. Curriculum designers must incorporate technology in both the content and skills the schools teach. The school curriculum must not prepare learners to use paper and pencil and typewriters when, in all likelihood, they will be working with laptops, CD-ROMs, and laser printers.

Institutions providing professional preparation for curriculum designers should work toward specific competencies. The curriculum designer should have competencies that allow him/her to

(*1*) Understand and offer an appropriate response to intellectual, social, and cultural dimensions affecting the curriculum
(*2*) Understand concerns and influences of the community and the absolute necessity of community members and organizations considering their input valued
(*3*) Design a curriculum that reflects and meets all state and other accrediting agencies
(*4*) Design a curriculum that reflects the increasing cultural diversity enriching our nation, society, and schools
(*5*) Incorporate technology as content and as a tool to be utilized, both in and out of school
(*6*) Provide a curriculum relevant to all cultures, races, and social classes, as well as both genders
(*7*) Design a curriculum that prepares learners to function successfully in a democratic society
(*8*) Involve committees, teams, classroom educators, other support services professionals, and administrators in the curriculum design process

The curriculum, viewed as all experiences that learners encounter in a school day, plays powerful roles. Its design must be a collaborative effort led by a professionally trained expert capable of understanding contemporary forces affecting the school and its curriculum.

Assessment Specialists—Learners

The overemphasis on testing and the often extreme reliance on test scores to categorize learners' abilities and to determine student achievement pose a dilemma for students, educators, and parents. Educators and parents will not be surprised to learn that most tests only measure certain abilities and intelligences and, all too often, fail to measure more abstract aspects of learning. Still, the national trend continues to test any aspect of learning that can be measured and to consider unmeasurable aspects as insignificant or unimportant. To compound the seriousness of the situation, states and school districts have used test scores as a means of holding educators accountable and as a means of justifying monetary expenditures (Allen et al., 1993).

Since the overemphasis on testing will probably continue during the 1990s and beyond, what specific steps can educators take to reduce the ill effects created by misuse of tests? First, it is important to point out that not all testing is misused. Diagnostic testing to determine learners' developmental or achievement levels can lead to better placement and improved instruction. Such testing is needed and should play an integral role in all schools; however, the situation quickly changes when testing is misused, overemphasized, or serves only to justify grouping patterns or as a means of holding teachers accountable for situations often beyond their control. In these cases, educators need to reassure learners of their self-worth and explain that, while tests measure valuable information, other abilities and skills are not measured. Second, educators should work through professional organizations to bring the testing dilemma to the attention of the public. Third, educators should insist that their districts selectively choose tests such as the Sternberg Triarchic Abilities Test (STAT), which can be group-administered and provides scores for analytic, creative, and practical abilities (Allen et al., 1993).

An assessment specialist, working in a diagnostic role (diagnosing learning problems and whether learners have left- or right-brain orientations and determining learners' areas of multiple intelligences), can provide enormous assistance to both learners and teachers. These assessment specialists should be able to design assessment tasks that are worthy problems or questions of importance, are realistic in terms of real-life assessments of adult life, are genuine problems rather than routine and staged, are fair in the sense that students can prepare for assessment as well as self-evaluation (Wiggins, 1993), and are objectively prepared to reduce bias against diverse cultures and social classes.

Other competencies of the assessment specialists include realization that classroom teachers sometimes need help preparing both formative and summative tests and need help interpreting results and explaining results to parents. Also, this support service professional will need expertise in planning and implementing schoolwide assessment programs designed to determine specific accomplishments, strengths, and weaknesses. Last, and vital to the mental health of students, this assessment specialist needs to understand the detrimental effects of testing on learners and needs to help learners cope with the demands of testing.

Assessment Specialists—Teacher Effectiveness

The steady trend to evaluate teachers' content knowledge and teaching skills gained momentum during the late 19th century. Rumors of teachers not knowing subject areas they were hired to teach, not having adequate teaching skills, and not being committed to the profession aroused the interest and downright ire of parents' groups, educators themselves, school boards, and lawmakers. The result was increased testing of teachers at both preservice and in-service levels. The interest in holding teachers accountable for their knowledge and actions will undoubtedly continue (and in all likelihood will increase) during the 21st century.

Presently, educators' competence and performance are assessed in various ways. The National Teachers Examination measures teachers' knowledge of content and teaching skills, and many states have developed instruments for measuring teacher effectiveness at either the preservice or in-service levels or both. Three factors continue to impede the assessment of teachers. First, considerable discrepancy exists in these state instruments; there is little agreement on factors to be assessed. Second, considerable confusion exists as to appropriate action for teachers not demonstrating minimal competencies. Third, most districts do not have a qualified, professionally trained assessment specialist working to evaluate teachers' effectiveness and for planning specific programs for helping teachers succeed in the classroom.

The professional preparation program for the assessment specialist working to determine teachers' content knowledge and teaching effectiveness should include the approved curriculum for professional education, as well as a strong background of test construction, testing procedures, and methods of remediating teachers' weaknesses. Suggested competencies of an assessment specialist may include being able to

- design assessment instruments to determine content knowledge and teacher effectiveness
- select "the best" from instruments prepared by other states and professional associations
- design instruments for support services personnel represented in the school
- know how culture, race, gender, and social class may affect teachers' evaluations
- explain test results to principals and other administrators interested in the outcomes of testing
- provide programs and experiences to remediate teachers' weaknesses
- know the legal factors associated with teacher evaluation
- insist on teachers' input (from individuals, committees of

teacher-representatives), so their concerns and suggestions about their evaluation can be heard and considered

This assessment specialist will not be an administrator but, rather, a school-based support service professional trained to help teachers, and as a result, help learners. Likewise, this person's "school position" (that is, in relation to classroom teachers and administrators) should be as a support service professional helping teachers rather than collecting information for a teacher dismissal or a lawsuit. Teacher evaluation is a given—during the next century, our society and lawmakers will demand our teachers be evaluated—and the assessment specialist can play a major role in this effort.

Media Producer

Educators' increasing use of media suggests that schools need a support service professional trained to design and produce media. It is important to note that this specialist's roles will differ from those of the librarian/media specialist. This person will be more of a "producer," "maker," and "designer" than the traditional media specialist. As the librarian/media specialist needs a library/media center, the media producer needs a lab with proper equipment to make media productions of various forms.

The media producer needs knowledge and skills in producing media through and for computers and other technological advances. This support service professional also must be aware of legal responsibilities, e.g., copyrights and infringements; capable of producing media to complement special productions and situations; capable of crossing subject area lines to produce interdisciplinary media; willing to help other support services personnel in their presentations to other educators and parents; capable of working closely with librarian/media specialists; and knowledgeable of current trends and issues. This professional, more than a maker of transparencies, needs a solid background in how media contributes to motivation and learning, methods of media production, and computer and educational technology.

As with other support services personnel, training for media producers will require a carefully planned program of experiences, including both curriculum content and field experiences, in which the professional media producer can gain first-hand experiences working under the direct close supervision of a media producer. For field experiences to be most worthwhile, this supervisor should have interest in and experiences working with children and adolescents.

Home-Schooling Instruction Designer and Monitor

Historically, compulsory school attendance laws have been justified in a variety of ways—parental inability or unwillingness to educate their offspring, a social need to elevate the level of moral behavior, the need to maintain the social and economic machinery, the desire to widen opportunities for social mobility, the need to acculturate an immigrant population, and the need to pass on the cultural heritage and "civilize" the young. Compulsory attendance laws in the United States date back to 1852, and only in recent decades have they come under serious attack (Noll, 1993).

The first barrage of criticism of schools came primarily from the radical reformers of the 1960s and 1970s. Critics of American education contended the government monopolized education and created educational environments where educators treat knowledge as a commodity, deadened the individual's will to learn, and established an artificial "success" that damages learners unable to take advantage of the system. The second assault came primarily from the Christian fundamentalists who viewed the secularism of the public schools as a threat to values taught at home (Noll, 1993).

The home-schooling movement in the 21st century will likely grow in popularity. Even if the growth is small and percentages remain low, educational institutions will be expected to work with parents planning home-schooling experiences. While school systems will be expected to allow parents this opportunity, educators will still want some control over learners' educational experiences, as well as some evidence of learners' academic progress.

A support service professional, perhaps called a "home-schooling instruction designer and monitor," can plan appropriate curricular experiences and, in some cases, offer parents evaluational services. This support person needs professional competencies (e.g., knowledge, attitudes, and skills) that contribute to working with parent educators and to contributing to children's overall welfare. First, this support professional will need *knowledge* of the home-schooling movement (its origins, goals, and philosophies) and appropriate home-schooling curricular experiences. Second, it is important that this professional have *attitudes* conducive to home schooling and view home schooling as a positive and worthwhile endeavor, rather than a threat to the school and its established practices. Last, this support professional needs *skills* necessary to work with parents and also to suggest appropriate instructional and evaluational methods.

Adult Education Specialists

The significant school dropout role in the United States and the increasing recognition that learning should be a lifelong process suggest that adult education will continue to grow in popularity. Adult education can be defined "as any organized, sustained activity engaged in by adult individuals for the purposes of changing their knowledge, skills, or values in any area" (Cranton, 1989, p. 4). While educating adults has been a practice for a number of decades, the emergence of a support service specialist especially trained to design educational experiences for adults is a distinct possibility. This professional will support other educators with an array of service roles. For example, competencies of the adult education specialist include

- demonstrating abilities to help adult educators to work with adult learners
- knowing learner characteristics, e.g., reasons for seeking adult education; age, gender, and educational backgrounds; and characteristics contributing to educational success
- designing appropriate instructional strategies for cognitive, affective, and psychomotor development
- selecting materials and resources appropriate for adult learners
- evaluating both adult learners and instructional designs

These adult education specialists face several professional challenges. First, many adult literacy education programs were added to existing public education systems, and these programs have often been viewed as "poor stepchildren" without legitimacy. Today, adult literacy education, much more than an add-on, is meritorious in its own right and, therefore, no longer needs to be tied exclusively to primary provider education systems (Foucar-Szocki and Mitchell, 1993).

Second, support services personnel will need professional training especially designed to prepare them to teach adult learners and to teach others to work with adult learners. Their effectiveness will depend upon their knowledge of the psychology of adult learners and their ability to lead other educators to work with adult learners. In essence, successful adult education programs cannot be slightly modified programs designed for educators of children and adolescents. These professionals will need high-quality graduate programs that have been accredited by appropriate professional associations and that focus educational experiences solely toward adult learners.

Staff Development Experts

The phrase *staff development activities* includes all of the several efforts to improve professional practice at the local level. Traditionally, the term *in-service education* has been used for this purpose, too, although staff development seems to be a more inclusive concept.

The idea of school district-sponsored staff development activities is rooted in the belief that the district and the teacher share in the responsibility to keep teaching and curriculum practice in tune with emerging trends in education and society. These may be activities related in a general way to education, such as preschool inspirational presentations by a leading educator or by the superintendent. Or they may be courses or workshops intended to enable teachers to fulfill a job-specific requirement. For example, a district has adopted a reading program that differs significantly from the conventional approach. Teachers who are unfamiliar with it will not know how to implement it in their classrooms. Accordingly, the school district arranges for a series of workshops for teachers that will prepare them to use the new reading approach. As an inducement for teachers to attend, in-service credits may be awarded for the completion of such courses (Jarolimek and Foster, 1989).

A staff development expert and his/her support service person can play valuable roles in a school. It is important to note that this expert will not be an administrator responsible for making crucial personnel decisions. This person, as the title implies, will be responsible for designing staff development programs that meet educators' specific needs and for demonstrating knowledge of how professional educators think and learn.

OTHER EFFORTS TO EDUCATE SUPPORT SERVICES PROFESSIONALS

Professionals' education and training do not end at graduation day or when employment begins. The concept of education being a lifelong process holds true for the professional education of support services personnel. Efforts to improve or upgrade support services professionals include continuing education programs, professional associations' efforts, mentoring programs, and trends toward national certification.

Continuing Education

Nearly all professionals embrace the concept of continuing professional development and engage in a wide variety of learning experiences throughout their careers. These experiences include professional publications, individual and group discussions with colleagues, self-assessments, internships, and on-the-job practice/reflection, as well as face-to-face and technology-mediated formal educational programs. The potential beneficiaries of professionals engaging in these experiences, in addition to the individual practitioner, are their clientele, employing organization, profession, and the general public.

Within the last thirty years, there has been an increased emphasis and investment in continuing professional education, particularly in formal educational programs, on the part of various institutional providers such as employing organizations, professional associations, and college/universities. As a result, continuing professional education is emerging as a highly dynamic and unique field of educational practice. Currently, continuing professional educators are beginning to reassess, discuss, and give consideration to expanding the concept and focus of this field of practice. Such dimensions include the following (Scheneman, 1993):

- scientific to practical knowledge
- information acquisition and competency maintenance to performance enhancement
- educator-centered instruction to self-directed or collaborative learning
- formal classroom instruction to experiential-based learning in the context of work and life
- professional to whole person or human development
- short-term to long-term growth and development of professionals
- standardized principles to ethical analysis and decision making
- institutional sponsorship to interorganizational and interprofessional collaboration

Professional Associations

Professional associations contribute to support services professionals in several ways. A wide array of professional organizations function in the United States and abroad. It is recommended that support services personnel seek active participation in an organization supporting the overall welfare of children and adolescents and an organization representing their specialization. Examples of professional organizations working toward the welfare of learners include (Manning, 1993)

- Association for Childhood Education International (ACEI), 11501 Georgia Ave., Ste. 315, Wheaton, MD 20902-1924 (301-942-2443, 800-423-3563). Publishes *Childhood Education* and *ACEI Exchange* (five times annually), *Journal of Research in Childhood Education* (biannually), three division newsletters (quarterly), books, pamphlets, and position papers. Conducts topic workshops and annual study conferences that focus on timely issues and concerns.
- Association for Supervision and Curriculum (ASCD), 125 N. West Street, Alexandria, VA 22314 (703-549-9110). Publishes *Educational Leadership* with special articles (eight times annually), books, and booklets. Several publications deal with areas of interest to educators (e.g., urban education, collaboration, empowerment of teachers, motivation, and cooperative learning).
- National Association of Elementary School Principals (NAESP), 1015 Duke St., Alexandria, VA 22314 (703-684-3345). Publishes *Principal* (five times annually) and various books and handbooks. While NAESP focuses mainly on the elementary level, the middle level is also addressed. *Principal* regularly includes ''Middle School Notes'' and occasionally features special themes.
- National Association of Secondary School Principals (NASSP), Council on Middle Level Education, 1904 Association Dr., Reston, VA 22091 (703-860-0200). Publishes *NASSP Bulletin* (nine times annually) and various monographs and books (e.g., *An Agenda for Excellence at the Middle Level: Middle Level Education's Responsibility for Intellectual Development*).
- National Middle School Association (NMSA), 4807 Evanswood Dr., Columbus, OH 43229 (614-848-8211).

Publishes *Middle School Journal* (five times annually), newspaper *Middle Ground* (quarterly), newsletter *Target* (quarterly), occasional papers Midpoints, various monographs, and position papers. Monograph topics include adviser-advisee guidance, interdisciplinary teaching, self-concept, young adolescents and their teachers, classroom management, and working with parents. NMSA conducts local, state, and national conferences.

The many professional organizations representing support services professionals make a comprehensive list unrealistic; however, organizations include American Speech and Hearing Association, American Association of School Librarians, Association for Educational Communications and Technology, National Association of School Musicians, and American Counseling Association. Again, hundreds of other organizations function to support specific professional interests and specializations. Support services professionals will need to decide on the specific organization that will most contribute to their continued professional development.

Mentoring Programs

During the 1980s, educators began to regard mentoring as a key component in teaching and developing professionals. Proponents have not offered a rigorous theoretical basis for advocating the mentor's role but, rather, have found easy acceptance on the basis of the cultural legacy of the mentoring relationship and its potential for providing support for beginning teachers and a new professional responsibility for experienced teachers. The spread of mentoring programs became a national phenomenon by the end of the decade. Interest in these programs remains strong. However, mentoring in some cases has proven to be less than ideal, especially when programs have been implemented with too little conceptual understanding of mentoring, unrealistic expectations, and poorly thought-out implementation strategies (Wildman et al., 1992).

Mentor characteristics cited as important by mentors and beginners were the mentor's position-specific responsibilities, personality characteristics, and emotional stability. Mentors often had numerous other responsibilities that took time and attention from the mentoring relationship. These other activities included serving on committees, accepting extracurricular assignments and duties, coaching, being a cooperating teacher, and evaluating other teachers – not to mention the responsibility for the management of their own classrooms.

The following characteristics were reported consistently across all data sources by both mentors and beginners:

(1) Willing to be a mentor
(2) Sensitive – that is, they know when to back off
(3) Helpful, but not authoritarian
(4) Emotionally committed to their beginners
(5) Astute – that is, they know the right thing to say at the right time
(6) Diplomatic – for example, they know how to counteract bad advice given to their beginners by others
(7) Able to anticipate problems
(8) Nurturant and encouraging
(9) Timely in keeping the beginners apprised of their successes
(10) Careful to keep the beginners' problems confidential
(11) Enthusiastic about teaching
(12) Willing to be good role models at all times

Each of the characteristics emerged as crucial at varying points in the relationship. The prime trait, however, that supported and maintained the relationship was the willingness of the experienced teacher to be a mentor. Although this list of characteristics is indicative of an ideal mentor, the success of the relationship was judged by both mentors and beginners based on the extent to which these characteristics were displayed sincerely (Wildman et al., 1992).

Support services professionals especially need mentors. Often working alone or with a limited number of other educators, these professionals sometimes do not feel a sense of collegiality found in many professional relationships. A support service professional, knowing another professional in the school cares about his or her personal and professional welfare, can be a major contributing factor to the person's success.

National Certification

A move, in full swing in the 1990s, proposes national certification standards for educators and governed by educators. The 1986 Carnegie document, *A Nation Prepared: Teachers for the 21st Century*, proposed forming a national self-governing board to establish high standards for teachers. The National Board for Professional Teaching Standards (NBPTS) proposed to develop, encourage, and provide a means for recognizing the professionalism of teachers and also to help students meet standards by increasing the quality of teachers and schools. A stated goal of the NBPTS is to maintain a majority of active classroom teachers on the board, numerous committees, and all working groups. Such a policy allows that people formulating standards and methods of evaluation will mostly be teachers ("National certification: Reflection of excellence," 1993).

Benefits of a national certification board include certification will give educators an opportunity to examine their practices; will elevate the status of educators in the eyes of the general public; and will empower educators to make significant changes in the profession ("National certification: Reflections of excellence," 1993).

Five core propositions, drawn from an early document of the NBPTS, considered educators to be committed to students and learning, knowledgeable of the subjects they teach and know how to teach the subjects to students, responsible for managing and monitoring student learning, thinking systematically about their practice and learning from experience, and members of learning communities ("National certification: Reflections of excellence," 1993).

The NBPTS presently focuses only on certifying regular classroom teachers; however, as the board gains respect among the profession, the possibility exists for a board for support services personnel. One might argue that the vast diversity among support services personnel and their specializations will make such a board an impossibility. Proponents of such a board could argue that the present national board has considerable diversity. For example, reading, science, and mathematics educators teach their respective curricular areas, yet common criteria for excellence can still be identified by boards. Support services personnel can benefit from the advantages of national boards, just as classroom educators. Increased employment, enhanced perceptions of the general public, and thoughtful examination of practice cross professional area lines.

In summary, doctors and lawyers have been board certified for decades and in the near future, the NBPTS will begin to issue national certification to classroom teachers. These board efforts and the overall increase in professionalism among educators can be the impetus to motivate support services personnel to begin their own board. Rather than a threat or another obstacle to overcome, support services personnel should view national boards as a means of furthering one's professional expertise and one's status both in the profession and in the school.

SUMMARY

Support services professionals, during the 1990s and in the future, will only be as good as their general education, professional cores, and field experiences. Several challenges face educators responsible for preparing support services personnel: accountability, increased professionalism, technological advances, and new support roles necessitated by 21st century demands. Growing professionalism among educators and the need for support services personnel to grow more proficient in their respective areas suggest the need for continuous and lifelong education. Effective support services personnel realize their professional preparation does not end at graduation. Instead, preparation to meet the responsibilities of one's profession includes learning and improvement of skills through continuing education, staff development, and taking advantage of programs offered by professional associations. Undoubtedly, the 21st century will bring improved professional preparation before graduation, as well as more opportunities to continue professional growth throughout one's life.

REFERENCES

American Association of School Librarians/American Library Association. (1989). *Curriculum Folio Guidelines for NCATE Review Process.* AASL/ALA.

Allen, H. A., Splittgerber, F. and Manning, M. L. (1993). *Teaching and Learning in the Middle Level School.* Columbus: Merrill.

Ayers, J. B. and Pratt, G. W. (1990). "Evaluating preparation programs for school library media specialists," in *Evaluating Preparation Programs for School Leaders and Teachers in Specialty Areas*, M. F. Berney and J. B. Ayers (Eds.), pp. 53–71, Boston: Kluwer Academic Publishers.

Barron, D. and Bergen, T. (1992). "Information power: The restructured school library for the nineties," *Phi Delta Kappan*, 73:521–525.

Baruth, L. G. and Robinson, M. (1987). *An Introduction to the Counseling Profession.* Englewood Cliffs: Prentice-Hall.

Burks, M. P. (1988). *Requirements for Certification.* Chicago: The University and Chicago Press.

Callister, T. A. and Dunne, R. (1992). "The computer as doorstop: Technology as disempowerment," *Phi Delta Kappan*, 74:324–326.

Council for Accreditation of Counseling and Related Educational Programs. (1988). *Accreditation Procedures Manual and Application.* Alexandria, VA: CACREP.

Cranton, P. (1989). *Planning Instruction for Adult Learners*. Toronto: Wall & Emerson.

Foucar-Szocki, D. and Mitchell, F. (1993). "A new view: Adult literacy education," *Adult Learning*, 4(6):21–22, 25.

Friedman, M. I., Brinlee, P. S. and Dennis-Hayes, P. B. (1980). *Improving Teacher Education: Resources and Recommendations*. New York: Longman.

Griffin, G. A. (1986). "Clinical teacher education," in *Reality and Reform in Clinical Teacher Education*, J. V. Hoffman and S. A. Edwards (Eds.), pp. 1–23, New York: Random House.

Henry, M. A. (1989). "Change in teacher education: Focus on field experiences," in *Reforming Teacher Education: Issues and New Directions*, J. A. Brown (Ed.), pp. 69–95, New York: Garland.

Howsam, R. B., Corrigan, D. C. and Denemark, G. W. (1985). *Educating and Profession*. Washington: AACTE.

Jarolimek, J. and Foster, C. D. (1989). *Teaching and Learning in the Elementary School*. New York: Macmillan.

Knoff, H. M. (1986). "Supervision on school psychology: The forgotten or future path to effective services?" *School Psychology Review*, 15(4):529–545.

Manning, M. L. (1993). *Developmentally Appropriate Middle Level Schools*. Wheaton, MD: ACEI.

Martin, S. K. (1986). "Library education: An administrator's view," *Library Journal*, 111:115–117.

Mead, E. J. (1991). "Reshaping the clinical phase of teacher preparation," *Phi Delta Kappan*, 72:666–669.

"National certification: Reflections of excellence." (1993). *Virginia Journal of Education*, 86(9):7–12.

National Council for Accreditation of Teacher Education. (1986). *NCATE Standards, Procedures, and Policies for the Accreditation of Professional Education Units*. Washington: NCATE.

Noll, J. W. (1993). *Taking Sides* (7 ed.). Guilford, CT: Dushkin.

Ritz, J. M. (1990). "Evaluating preparation programs for vocational education teachers," In *Evaluating Preparation Programs for School Leaders and Teachers in Specialty Areas,*, M. F. Berney and J. B. Ayers (Eds), pp. 73–89. Boston: Kluwer Academic Publishers.

Scheneman, S. (1993). "Continuing professional development: Education and learning," *Adult Learning*, 4(6):6.

Thomas, A. C. (1990). "Evaluating preparation programs for school counselors and psychologists," in *Evaluating Preparation Programs for School Leaders and Teachers in Specialty Areas*, M. F. Berney and J. B. Ayers (Eds.), pp. 33–53. Boston: Kluwer Academic Publishers.

Wentling, T. L. and Lawson, T. E. (1975). *Evaluating Occupational Education and Training Programs*. Boston: Allyn and Bacon.

Wiggins, G. (1993). "Assessment: Authenticity, context, and validity," *Phi Delta Kappan*, 75:200–214.

Wildman, T. M., Magliaro, S. G., Niles, R. A. and Niles, J. A. (1992). "Teacher mentoring: An analysis of roles, activities, and conditions," *Journal of Teacher Education*, 43:205–213.

CHAPTER 6

Consultant and Leadership Roles

OVERVIEW

SUPPORT SERVICES PERSONNEL will assume both consultant and leadership roles in the 21st century. Whether counselors, school psychologists, speech correctionists, or any of the newer support roles suggested in Chapter 5, these professionals will be expected to serve in consultant roles and to take active leadership roles. As consultants, support services professionals will offer advice, perform specialized services, and complement the efforts of administrators and classroom educators. These professionals will accept positions of leadership, which will require the professional ability, as well as personal and professional qualities, necessary to lead others toward meaningful goals. Prerequisites to consultants and leaders being successful include their response to accountability demands, their professionalism to their specialty and those they serve, and their willingness and ability to use technology to improve their effectiveness.

THE 21ST CENTURY: CONTEMPORARY ROLES

Consultant

Support services personnel can play valuable consultant roles such as identifying problems, coordinating efforts, taking advantage of others' strengths, promoting team efforts, and offering expertise and specialized advice. This section looks at support services professionals' consultant responsibilities and suggests appropriate practices.

Identifying Problems and Possible Solutions

The consultant's first step is to identify the problem, either singularly or in conjunction with other professionals working closer to the problem.

An accurate identification requires the gathering of information as an aid to understanding the problem and its various dimensions. Next, the consultant needs to utilize all available assessment information in order to determine actual goals. Third, the consultant needs to analyze and synthesize information in search of the most effective solution to the problem (Kurpius, 1978).

The steps to identifying problems and possible solutions may not always be clearcut and may require considerable critical examination to perceive possibilities for positive and significant change. The consultant should seek the opinions of others working closer to the situation, should seek the advice (when possible) of other support services professionals, and should strive for collaborative efforts. Likewise, it is probably not a wise idea for consultants to propose only one possible solution to a problem. Instead, whenever possible, educators seeking consultative advice should be given two or perhaps more possible solutions, so educators will feel empowered to make the final decision. A sense of ownership in the decision-making process will likely lead to a greater willingness to implement the solution.

Working Collegially

While closely related to the collaborative efforts suggested in identifying the problem, the consultant's ability to "work collegially" is of such importance that a separate section is warranted. Forming and maintaining collegial relationships may be the most influential factor in determining the consultant's effectiveness.

Consultants working to help people identify and solve a problem need to be considered friendly, understanding, flexible, knowledgeable of interpersonal relationships, and wanting to help. Too often, educators, as well as other professionals, have a "turf mentality" where other professionals should not tread. In fact, the support services professionals may sometimes have to convince educators of their willingness and ability to help. Working collegially is a requirement for positive and productive working relationships. Working collegially includes developing positive, interpersonal relationships; showing respect for all participants and their ideas; promoting team processes and group dynamics; working as co-professionals toward a common goal; responding to conflict in a positive manner; and making all participants feel like a part of the solution.

Consultants and others will not achieve desired goals when conflict takes precedence over harmony, competition occurs rather than cooperation, and chaos takes the place of orderly deliberation. The consultant might be considered an "outsider" (yet a much needed one) and, thus, may have to work deliberately to promote collegial relationships. While all educators should assume responsibility for collegiality, the support service professional acting in a consultant role needs to make special efforts to promote collegial relationships.

Perceiving Others' Strengths

The consultant should bring considerable knowledge and expertise to problem situations and to suggesting plausible solutions; however, this responsibility does not mean the consultant should singularly solve the problem. Perceptive consultants recognize the necessity of empowering other professionals to reach possible solutions. Professional educators formulating their own plans will feel more accountable for their efforts to make the solution work. The consultant should be viewed as one who offers advice and helps others to realize the strengths they bring to a problem-solving or task-addressing situation.

Such a philosophy of the consultant's role requires the tapping of others' strengths, resources, and expertise. Sometimes, people do not realize the "powers" they bring to problem-solving situations and, therefore, need to be encouraged to offer opinions. Several steps lead to tapping others' strengths and resources:

- Ask others to list on paper the strengths they bring to a given situation.
- Meet individually, if possible, with others to determine strengths.
- Ask administrators or other supervisors to suggest participants' strengths and expertise.
- Encourage all members of the team or group to participate.
- Show respect for all comments and suggestions, being careful not to stifle creativity or input.
- Help others to realize they have worthwhile ideas to contribute to the problem-solving process.

Encouraging others to survey their strengths and personal resources should not be a threatening process. Participants should not perceive the consultant as badgering or overly demanding. People threatened may withdraw from the process or feel resentful, contributing to a breakdown of communication and group processes required to solve problems or reach desired goals.

Relating Knowledge and Experiences to Individual Situations

Successful consultants direct their attention and experience to individual situations, rather than offering only "canned solutions" — solutions expected to solve more than one problem. Each problem to be solved or task to be addressed deserves individual attention. Therefore, the consultant needs to direct his or her knowledge and experience to the situation needing to be addressed.

First, the consultant needs the knowledge, skills, and attitudes necessary to address the problem or task. Such preparation requires professional knowledge, first-hand experiences, and, of course, willingness to work with others toward established goals. If educators ask the support service professional for consultant services and he or she does not feel competent in that area, he or she should either admit to a lack of expertise or make a deliberate effort to gain the knowledge needed to make a significant contribution. It is unreasonable to expect consultants to have expertise in all areas; however, it is equally unreasonable for consultants not to admit their areas of weaknesses.

Second, as previously suggested, consultants' knowledge and skills need to be directed toward *individual* situations. Before offering any consultative advice, efforts should be directed toward considering the dimensions of the given problem or task, possible solutions, and the strengths and talents of individual team or group members. Assuming that so-called "textbook solutions" work for all problems and tasks can lead to disenchantment with the consultant, the deliberation process, and the actual plan of action.

Promoting Team Efforts

As Chapter 3 suggested in considerable detail, team efforts greatly enhance the likelihood of successful ventures. Team efforts have the potential for engaging a number of professionals toward a given task, tapping multiple resources and strengths, contributing to feelings of collegiality, and enjoying the satisfactions of team members working toward common goals. Rather than having an exhaustive discussion of team efforts at this point, readers are reminded that Chapter 3 focuses entirely on the various aspects of teaming and the teaming process.

Support services professionals, working in consultant roles, need to explain the benefits of working in teams, encourage team efforts, and model effective teaming skills. As previously suggested, professionals need ownership of their decisions and to feel responsible for their actions. Also, teams can contribute considerably more expertise to given problems and tasks than individuals. Rather than consultants working singularly to solve problems or address tasks, they should encourage team efforts and should implement team processes that reflect the research on effective teaming. The nature of the consulting process suggests consultants should assume major responsibility for implementing the team process, rather than risking splintered and disjointed efforts.

Understanding Group Dynamics

Theories of group dynamics should not be viewed as a rigid set of structures that prescribe a step-by-step approach to a consultant's or leader's actions. Instead, theories should serve as a general framework that helps to make sense of the many facets of group process and dynamics (Corey and Corey, 1987). Consultants knowledgeable of group dynamics can consider themselves and their groups when determining directions to take to achieve desired objectives.

Questions that support services personnel, acting in consultant roles, should ask themselves as they decide on approaches and attitudes to adopt (Corey and Corey, 1987, pp. 7−8) are as follows:

- What is the basic nature of human beings?
- How can I incorporate my philosophy of human nature into the way I lead groups?
- Can people be trusted to determine their own direction in a group, or do they need strong intervention from the leader to keep them moving productively?
- Who should determine the goals of the group, the members or the group leader?
- How specific should the goals be?
- What is the group leader's role? Facilitator? Director? Expert? Consultant? Resource person?
- How much responsibility for the group's work lies with the leader? With the members? To what degree should the group be structured by the leader?
- What are your views on selecting a co-leader and working with

one? Ideally, how would you divide responsibility with a co-leader?
- Should the leader work with one person at a time or encourage maximum interaction among members?
- How much personality change is desirable? Should the focus be on attitude change or on behavior change?
- What are the functions of group members?
- What techniques are the best? Why?
- What are the criteria for measuring the success of a group?

Working on consultant roles, support services professionals should adopt a number of personal characteristics (Corey and Corey, 1987):

- courage to be vulnerable at times, to admit to mistakes and imperfections, to confront in a professional manner when necessary, to continually examine one's own role, and to be direct and honest with others working in the group or team
- willingness to model behavior and attitudes such as openness, seriousness of purpose, acceptance of others, and the benefits of taking risks
- sincere interest (e.g., goodwill and caring), which includes neither abusing their role for their own purposes nor exploiting members to enhance their ego
- belief in the group process as being a constructive means to positive outcomes
- openness to themselves, to others working toward a goal, to new experiences, and to differing values
- nondefensiveness in coping with attacks, e.g., both fair and unfair criticism, which might result from expressions of jealousy, testing of authority, power seeking, or projection onto the leader of feelings for other significant people
- personal power excluding domination of group or team members or manipulation of them toward the leader's end
- stamina (both physical, psychological, and the ability to stand pressure) to remain vitalized to meet tasks and eventually accomplish goals
- self-awareness, which includes an awareness of one's goals, identity, motivations, needs, limitations, strengths, values, feelings, and problems
- sense of humor, which allows one the ability to laugh at oneself and to see humor in one's own frailties

- inventiveness to be spontaneously creative and to approach each new problem or task with fresh ideas

Leadership

Leadership can be described in terms of its various definitions, characteristics of leaders, roles of effective leaders, and ways of becoming an educational leader. Likewise, support services professionals can examine the various issues and dimensions managing conflict; management versus leadership; forces affecting leadership; and the permeating themes of this text: accountability, professionalism, and technology.

Definitions of Leadership

Bennis and Nanus (1985), in their book *Leaders* reported approximately 350 definitions of leadership. Stogdill (1974) reported, "There are almost as many definitions of leadership as there are persons who have attempted to define the concept."

Leadership has been defined in terms of individual traits, behaviors, influence over others, interaction patterns, role relationships, and hierarchical position (Conger, 1992). Conger chose a single definition that captures many of the important manifestations of leadership in organizations and that also outlines the general behaviors leaders need to develop:

> Leaders are individuals who establish direction for a working group of individuals, who gain commitment from these group members to this direction, and who then motivate these members to achieve the direction's outcomes. (Conger, 1992, p. 18)

Three dimensions of the leadership of complex organizations naturally flow from this definition: 1) establishing direction, 2) aligning people in terms of that direction, and 3) motivating and inspiring people to move in that direction. These functions can take many forms. Setting direction can range from devising a company's strategic mission to establishing production goals for a manufacturing unit. In other words, they cover the span from grand to mundane (Kotter, 1990; Conger, 1992).

Goens and Clover (1991) offer examples of new definitions of leadership and point to a significant change in what leaders must become to influence the organizations of the 21st century.

The new leader . . . is one who commits people to action, who converts followers into leaders, and who may convert leaders into agents of change. (Bennis and Nanus, 1985, p. 3)

Leadership is the reciprocal process of mobilizing, by persons with certain motives and values, various economic, political and other resources, in a context of competition and conflict, in order to realize goals independently or mutually and held by both leaders and followers. (Burns, 1978, p. 425)

Leaders must also help people know what they can be at their best by calling for the kind of effort and restraint, drive and discipline that make for great performance. In leadership at its finest, the leader symbolizes the best in the community, the best in traditions, values, and purposes. (Gardner, 1978, p. 133)

Leadership in the self-renewing and thriving enterprise is characterized by its willingness to move beyond tidy models of what leadership is and does. Leaders establish order and discipline, and simultaneously foster skepticism, incredulity, experimentation and change. They encourage the generation of new forms and actions that may have neither precedent nor accustomed approval. They inject creative enzymes into the system, with results that can be destabilizing and disorderly and are rarely parametric. They know that to achieve more and better results, more resourcefulness is as important as more resources. (Levitt, 1988, p. 7)

The wide array of definitions of leadership and leaders suggest support services personnel should formulate their own definition, one that relates specifically to their respective specializations. Likewise, perhaps they could look to their own professional organizations for relevant definitions. The formulated definition should include the aspects of leadership they feel are important to their specialization and should reflect 21st century perspectives such as accountability, professionalism, and the role of technology in the specialization.

Characteristics of Leaders

What kind of support services professionals become leaders? What characteristics should potential leaders try to develop? In the early 20th century, leadership researchers concentrated almost solely on the personal traits of leaders. The characteristics of successful leaders were studied, and conclusions led to generalizations about all leaders. As each study about a different kind of leader uncovered new characteristics, the list of characteristics grew until it was too large to be of any use. Critics of the "trait" approach to leadership theory pointed to the unwieldy nature of the list and to the widely varied characteristics to substantiate their claim that there are no leader traits that will hold for all leaders (Mazzarella and Grundy, 1989).

After years of research and data collection, it was concluded that leaders were not born with any particular traits that determine leadership ability. In other words, trait theories took a back seat to other theories of leadership, i.e., situational theories, which suggest leaders in one situation may be followers in another. However, it may be premature to discard trait research and theories. The renewed interest in characteristics of effective leaders suggests it might be time to reexamine early trait research to determine what is worth saving and its implications for present leaders. It is important to remember that research does not reveal any single characteristic that determines leadership. Rather, research suggests groups of qualities that appear to correlate with leadership. Not all leaders have these traits and not all effective leaders have all of them (Mazzarella and Grundy, 1989).

Characteristics of leaders, just as definitions of leadership, vary according to the researchers and writers. Smith and Piele (1989) place characteristics in several broad categories:

Social participation – The ability and desire to work with different kinds of people having various needs, interests, and expectations. (Gorton and McIntyre, 1978)

Communication – A natural facility with language, e.g., well-developed interpersonal skills and able to communicate effectively in face-to-face interaction with a diverse range of individuals and groups. (Blumberg and Greenfield, 1986)

Listening – Effective leaders have an ability to listen, to be sensitive to others and to events going on around them, to absorb others' ideas, and to know when silence is the most effective means. (Blumberg and Greenfield, 1986)

Conger (1992) suggests a shorter and perhaps more specific list of characteristics that describes effective leaders:

- staying in touch
- caring
- listening
- having vision
- understanding
- feeling responsible

- taking initiative
- empowering
- having courage
- encouraging risk taking
- being unconcerned about failure

Yukl (1989) and Goens and Clover (1991) concluded that characteristics most frequently found in successful leaders showed that they are

- adaptable to situations
- alert to social environments
- ambitious and achievement-oriented
- assertive
- cooperative
- decisive
- dependable
- dominant (desire to influence others)
- energetic (high activity level)
- persistent
- self-confident
- tolerant of stress
- willing to assume responsibility

Other research (Mazzarella and Grundy, 1989) suggests that leaders need specific character qualities that distinguish between effective and ineffective leaders. This work suggests that, in addition to the positive human relations skills, leaders need to be goal-oriented, secure, proactive, and well aware of the dynamics of power (Mazzarella and Grundy, 1989).

Two reasons indicate that this research on leadership traits is even more valuable to school people than the earlier trait research. First, contemporary researchers are focusing on educational leaders only and are looking for leadership characteristics that are unique to this group. Second, the research looks at the characteristics that distinguish effective from ineffective leaders. Rather than examining the traits that identified good leaders, early researchers looked only at the traits that distinguish leaders from nonleaders. This lumping of both good and bad leaders made it unlikely that researchers would pinpoint characteristics of effective leaders. The present subjects under scrutiny have demonstrated leadership abilities, skills, and potential. Using leaders with proven leadership skills can provide a better idea of the characteristics that leaders need.

What Effective Leaders Do

After considering definitions of leadership and descriptions of characteristics of leaders, readers will not be surprised when they find that descriptions of "what effective leaders do" also vary. One characterization of leaders' work combines three skills:

- *Mental Functioning:* The leader applies complex and simple tasks to reach desired goals.
- *Technical Skills:* The leader has appropriate technical skills (in this case, the support service professional's area of specialization).
- *Social Skills:* The leader has the social power to lead others to a goal (Lombardo, 1978; Goens and Clover, 1991).

Such a view portrays leaders as having the ability to perceive in many different ways and apply all levels of thinking to their problem-solving tasks. Likewise, leaders must have sufficient technical expertise in their specialization to organize and implement plans toward an established goal (Goens and Clover, 1991).

In his discussion of leaders' roles, Cuban (1989) explained three roles: instructional, managerial, and political. The instructional role is to change beliefs and behavior, whereas the managerial role is to ensure stability. The political role involves the process of determining and transforming goals into policies and programs. It includes the authority and influence used to work with a board and to govern a district. Cuban points out that the instructional, managerial, and political roles are often at cross-purposes, creating role conflict for the leader (Goens and Clover, 1991).

Regardless of their positions or professional roles, leaders' actions and behaviors in the 21st century will need to reflect several dimensions (Goens and Clover, 1991):

- modeling values
- interpreting processes
- creating conflict
- exerting influence
- making decisions
- managing change
- creating new structure

- building teams
- communicating mission
- embracing technology
- transforming data into information

Support services professionals leading other educators and administrators have special challenges. They must understand the concept of leadership, the various characteristics of leaders, and the various leader roles. Likewise, they must be able to mesh their leadership expertise and skills with the technicalities of their professional specializations.

Management versus Leadership

Most contemporary research draws the conclusion that there are significant differences between leaders and managers, which provide dimensions for comparison and contrast (Goens and Clover, 1991). Zaleznik (1986) stated that managers and leaders are motivated by different types of situations, their historical perspectives are unlike one another's, and they think and behave in contrasting ways regardless of the type of organization. He believes that the managerial ethic is associated with a bureaucratic culture, whereas leaders create entrepreneurial cultures.

Many organizations tend to be overmanaged and underled. Managers are efficient, whereas leaders are effective; also, leaders ask different questions than managers. The focus of managers' attention is on the physical resources, such as capital and workers' skills and technology, whereas leaders concern themselves with emotional and spiritual resources, like values, commitment, and aspirations (Bennis and Nanus, 1985).

Support services professionals can take deliberate steps to become effective leaders, rather than only managers. The following suggests the task the leader will face and possible leadership activities to address the task:

Creating an agenda	Establishing direction – developing a vision of the future, often the distant future, along with strategies for producing the changes needed to achieve that vision

Developing a human network for achieving the agenda	Aligning people—communicating the direction by words and deeds to all those whose cooperation may be needed so as to influence the creation of teams and coalitions that understand the vision and strategies and accept their validity
Execution	Motivating and inspiring—energizing people to overcome major political, bureaucratic, and resource barriers to change by satisfying very basic, but often unfulfilled, human needs
Outcomes	Produces change, often to a dramatic degree, and has the potential of producing extremely useful change (e.g., new products that customers want, new approaches to labor relations that help make a firm more competitive (Kotter, 1990; Conger, 1992)

As Chapter 3 emphasized, the leader should take advantage of the combined expertise and many talents of teams. Effective leaders continually encourage team approaches to addressing tasks and solving problems. As a team builder, the leader attempts to reduce the dysfunctional friction, while recognizing that in a complementary team, strength lies in differences; hence he or she need not attempt to clone people or make everyone else over in his own image. As long as people have the same goals, it is not important that they have the same roles. When team members regard each other with mutual respect, differences are utilized and are considered strengths rather than weaknesses.

The basic role of the leader is to foster mutual respect and build a complementary team where each strength is made productive and each weakness made irrelevant. The essential role of a manager is to use leverage to multiply the work and role of the producer. A producer rolls up his or her sleeves and does what is necessary to solve problems and get results (Corey, 1991).

Managing Conflict

The nature of leadership and leading other people often leads to conflict. A number of factors and situations may lead to conflict: educators hanging on to the mind-set that support services personnel should perform services only when called upon, participants feeling threatened by change on the team process, lack of trust of leaders and their ability, and a desire to maintain the status quo. Regardless of the reason, the support services professionals acting in leadership roles will face conflict and will be expected to manage the conflict with the least amount of "fallout" possible.

First, it is important to state that, while conflict has its negative consequences, conflict can also lead to positive occurrences. The negative aspects of consequences include

- diverting energy from the task at hand
- destroying morale
- polarizing individuals and groups
- deepening differences
- obstructing cooperative action
- producing irresponsible behavior
- creating suspicion and distrust
- decreasing productivity

On the positive side, conflict

- opens up an issue in a confronting manner
- develops clarification of an issue
- increases involvement
- improves problem-solving quality
- provides more spontaneity in communication
- is needed for growth
- strengthens a relationship when creatively resolved (Lindelow and Scott, 1989)

Perceptive support services personnel will readily recognize constructive and destructive conflict. Constructive conflict supports the goals of the team or group and eventually improves performance. Destructive conflicts, just the opposite, hinder team or group progress and eventually its ability to reach desired goals. Support services professionals, working in leadership roles, need to determine the constructive or destructive nature of conflict and plan an agenda accordingly. Appropriate strategies include either taking advantage of constructive conflict or reducing the negative consequences of destructive conflict.

Support services personnel can take several steps to manage conflicts among educators being led and members of teams and groups. It is important to note that conflicts should be considered individually so the correct management technique will be selected. While support services personnel have a number of management theories at their disposal, this section examines only representative examples: avoiding conflict, setting goals requiring cooperative participation, mutual problem solving, compromise and the use of third parties, and the use of authority to arbitrate conflicts. These examples should provide a beginning point for support services personnel as they continue to build a repertoire of conflict management strategies.

1) *Avoiding Conflict*—This conflict management technique involves simply trying to avoid situations with the potential for conflict and avoiding situations in which conflict already exists. Avoidance techniques include "ignoring and procrastinating" or ignoring that the conflict exists or simply putting off action to deal with it; "isolating conflicting parties" is placing team or group members in situations or positions where they seldom interact; "withholding feeling" includes individuals who cannot avoid each other withholding feelings or conflicting beliefs in the presence of the other; "seeking like-minded people" involves staffing the team or group with like-minded people; and "smoothing" is the process of playing down differences between conflicting parties while emphasizing their common interests.

2) *Setting Cooperative Goals*—This management technique requires the creation of a super ordinate goal, a highly valued goal that two conflicting groups or team members can reach only by cooperating with each other.

3) *Mutual Problem Solving*—Perhaps the most effective means of conflict management, mutual problem solving often addresses situations resulting from a lack of or problems in communication. Bringing conflicting parties together to discuss differences can lead to increased understanding, clarification of differences, and constructive collaboration. Guidelines for this technique include the following:

- Welcome the existence of differences within the organization as a valuable resource.
- Listen with understanding, rather than evaluation.
- Recognize and accept the feelings of the individuals involved.

- Clarify the nature of the conflict.
- Indicate who will make the decision being discussed.
- Suggest procedures and ground rules for resolving the differences.
- Create appropriate vehicles for communication among the disputing parties.
- Encourage the separation of ideas from the people who propose them.

4) *Compromise and the Use of Third Parties* — Compromise is probably the most widely used technique for resolving conflict; compromise does not result in clear winners and losers, and the process requires each conflicting party to make concessions. Sometimes this process requires a third-party arbitrator or mediator — the mediator can either convince the conflicting parties to settle a dispute or assume responsibility for making a decision. Perhaps easier said than done, using a moderator to settle a dispute requires that he or she develop a compromise both sides consider fair and equitable.

5) *Use of Authority* — This technique uses the traditional power of position to overrule a subordinate. While this technique solves conflicts quickly and neatly, the overuse or misuse of authority, without meaningful input from subordinates, can lead to other serious forms of conflict (Lindelow and Scott, 1989).

Conflict can pose a serious threat to support services professionals' leadership efforts: goals may not be met, potential for change may be lost, and general feelings of dissatisfaction can lead to low morale and forms of resistance. The skilled leader will understand individual situations and be able to select a management plan with the most potential for resolving a particular conflict.

Forces Fostering Leadership

While the debate over leaders being born or made has made interesting reading (Conger, 1992), support services personnel need to have a firm understanding of the forces fostering leadership. For example, how can support services personnel who do not consider themselves "born leaders" develop leadership abilities? What forces or actions contribute to their leadership effectiveness? This section acknowledges the support for a genetic predisposition for leadership and then examines other forces influencing one's ability to lead others.

Conger (1992) suggests there is some support for the belief that genetics may be an important role in determining leadership traits and abilities. For example, two qualities often described in leadership studies—intelligence and physical energy—appear to be rooted in genetics (Conger, 1992). Assuming that the support for leaders having genetic traits is valid, other factors enter the picture. People often have to be taught early in life the value of independence, of making decisions, of taking responsibility, and of learning the importance of ethical behavior accompanying leadership. Children born with intelligence and physical energy may not see their leadership abilities blossom when parents do not value independence and risk taking. In other words, a person's childhood experiences must complement his or her intelligence and physical energy.

The majority of writers on leadership abilities and effective leaders believe the origins of leadership are more complex than genes and family. Other factors also affect whether a person becomes an effective leader: work experiences, hardship, opportunity, education, role models, and mentors. These factors or adult experiences that catalyze leadership include (Kotter, 1990; Conger, 1992):

- challenging assignments early in a career
- visible leadership role models who were either very good or very bad
- assignments that broaden knowledge and experience
- task force or committee assignments
- mentoring or coaching from others
- attendance at meetings outside a person's core responsibility
- special development opportunities
- special projects
- formal training programs

Other factors contributing to peoples' ability to lead and, generally speaking, influence others toward a set goal, include personal desire and willingness to lead. Some people simply do not want to lead—the responsibilities and hardships of leadership, a need to conform to others' expectations, the risk of being considered unconventional, and a need for social acceptance might lead to a person not wanting to lead. The personal and professional satisfactions do not equal the sacrifice a person must make.

Support services professionals who feel they were not born with leadership ability should not be disheartened to a point they do not attempt to lead. While a ''born leader'' may have a head start, support services personnel can learn many leadership traits. Attending leadership workshops, working with mentors with proven leadership abilities, and even reading books and manuals can contribute to an improvement of leadership abilities.

Motivating Others

In nearly all cases, leaders will be challenged to motivate others to act toward established goals. Kotter (1990) thought dimensions of all leadership efforts included 1) establishing direction, 2) aligning people in terms of that direction, and 3) motivating and inspiring people to move in that direction.

In school situations, it would appear that professionals would be motivated; however, sometimes, several factors may result in a lack of motivation: an already full schedule, feeling overwhelmed by another committee or task, feeling unconfident or threatened by the newly assigned task, and perhaps uncomfortableness over support services personnel assuming active leadership roles. In these situations, support services professionals assuming leadership roles will need to work toward motivating groups or team members to work toward established goals. Directions for the support services professionals include

- allowing those being led to have active decision-making roles in establishing goals
- encouraging intrinsic, rather than extrinsic, motivation
- showing the benefits and advantages of groups working toward common goals
- working with individual members to show how their efforts can contribute to the achievement of goals
- understanding (and letting people being led realize this understanding) school professionals have many other responsibilities in the school and profession
- establishing firm deadlines (with the collaboration of others) for completing tasks
- encouraging collaboration, group decision making, and cooperation in all deliberation and goal-setting efforts
- encouraging efforts of all people rather than only a select few
- clarifying the responsibilities of professionalism and the demands of accountability

A leader's expertise and efforts to motivate others might be the single most important role she or he might play. A leader usually cannot accomplish goals alone; those being led need a voice in the process and need to feel they contributed to the goals and, eventually, the final product. This sense of involvement leads to ownership, which leads to commitment. Leaders, lacking confidence in their motivational abilities or feeling they can carry the total responsibility themselves, need to study theories of motivation, learn techniques of motivating others, take small steps at a time (if necessary), and eventually become masters of motivation. It is important to note that motivating others should be for the overall welfare of the team, group, or school rather than the leader's personal or self-serving gain. People being led, who feel they are being exploited, may be even more difficult to lead in future ventures.

Promoting Collegiality

The support service professional acting in a leadership capacity has a responsibility to instill and promote a sense of collegiality, both with other support services personnel and other educators and administrators. A sense of collegiality, positive in and of itself, can have a number of benefits and can contribute to the meeting of goals and the addressing of tasks. In fact, establishing and promoting collegiality needs to be among the leader's prime responsibilities.

First, collegiality can lead to increased motivation to work cooperatively and collaboratively toward accepted and established goals. Professionals enjoying collegial relationships feel their efforts are appreciated and are more likely to work diligently toward a goal being met or a task being addressed. Working together toward a common goal usually has a more powerful effect than individuals working alone.

Second, collegiality and interpersonal relationships go hand-in-hand; working in an atmosphere of collegiality, without doubt, is more pleasant than working in situations characterized by conflict, competition, and agitation.

The support service professional's role includes making efforts to instill feelings of collegiality. Sometimes, the nature of leading individuals, teams, or groups results in uncomfortableness or threatening feelings. In these cases, support services personnel need to make special efforts to ease feelings of uncomfortableness and to work toward more positive feelings of collegiality.

Several ways of promoting collegiality include

- making all participants feel like an important and contributing member of the team, group, or school
- addressing situations that might result in conflict
- learning about individual educators and their strengths and weaknesses
- arranging for occasions (perhaps a recognition dinner) that promote collegiality
- making people feel like both an individual and a functioning member of a team, group, or school
- demonstrating and modeling behavior conducive to collegiality

Leaders who realize the importance of collegiality will probably be more successful than the leader who allows conflict and ill feelings. However, collegiality does not come automatically; it must be initiated and nurtured and at the forefront of the leaders' agenda.

Collegial Leadership

Collegiality can be taken one step further where leaders or authority figures actually share leadership positions. Traditionally, principals occupied "authority and leadership positions" in schools; however, as support services personnel take more active roles, positions of leadership may change. The increasing trend toward site-based management (allowing individual school principals and educators to make decisions concerning the school's destiny) may change the traditional perception of the principal and may eventually lead to a sense of collegial leadership.

Collegial leadership should not do away with the lines of authority and accountability in a school. For instance, unless the boundaries of teachers' duties as leaders are spelled out clearly, some may assume they have the authority to make decisions the principal would prefer to make. However, some believe total-group decision making tends to be overused in schools. In the early stages of a change process, wide participation is appropriate, but during the time new programs are implemented, the lines of authority should be clearly defined (Weber, 1989).

The authors recognize the need for an authority figure in the schools and do not recommend support services professionals usurping administrator power or causing any disruption in the chain of command. However, ideas toward leadership could evolve to include collegial leadership—a process where support services personnel and administrators (and, in fact, other professionals in the school) could share leadership roles and decisions. Obstacles could include handling professional disagreements, accountability expectations, personality conflicts, and visions for the future. As with any professional endeavor, barriers have to be confronted and, if possible, settled to a point where they will have a minimal impact on meeting goals and addressing tasks. Positives of collegial leadership include the magnified benefits of shared leadership, more professionals working toward a given goal, and another step toward making site-based management a reality.

Administrators and support services personnel participating in collegial leadership activities can set an example for other educators in the school to work together as a team. Distractors or critics of collegial leadership often base leadership expectations on past perceptions and fail to recognize increased demands on schools and changing perceptions of how schools should be run. Twentieth century mind-sets toward leadership, especially collegial leadership, will not suffice in the 21st century.

Leadership for the Next Age

Adrian and Apps (1993) believe leaders should prepare for the next age, rather than holding onto perspectives of the past. Their theory suggests leader development should include a working philosophy of leadership, creating organizational change or renewal, living diversity, and gaining an international perspective. This process of leadership development involves a four-stage process: recognizing a task or a problem, investigating alternatives, making decisions about how to change, and acting in ways consistent with the decisions. Within this process, ''developing'' leaders are doing the following (Adrian and Apps, 1993):

- Reflect on beliefs and values within the contexts of life experiences, culture, and society.
- Examine long-accepted truths, which are actually social constructions like time is linear, progress is beneficial, and nature is controllable.
- Write personal credo statements.
- Create a shared organizational vision.
- Learn to communicate both the credo and the vision in ways that build bridges between people and ideas while challenging

assumptions, structures, and beliefs held by individuals and organizations.
- Take risks and redefine failure as growth.
- Solicit/hear diverse perspectives, whether they are expressed in academic jargon or in improving English.
- Learn to tolerate and, sometimes, encourage discomfort.
- Embrace ambiguity.
- Encourage artistry in leadership and as an approach to communicating with others (through metaphor, for example).
- Appreciate humor.
- Experience emotion.
- Become socially aware and act on that sensitivity.
- Seek an integration of mind-body-spirit.

Adrian and Apps (1993) hope that professionals undergoing leadership training will

- Value lifelong learning.
- Have new esteem for the power of diversity.
- Act on heightened social awareness.
- Use ethical perspectives and a long term, wide-angle view to decision making.
- Have the capacity to assess novel problems and create the tools needed to resolve them.
- Implement collectively developed shared visions.

Undoubtedly, Adrian and Apps have a valid point about leaders preparing for a future we might know little about today. While we need to look toward the past for perspectives and insights, leaders do need to prepare for the future—a changing world of professional expectations (i.e., changing perspectives toward support services professionals and their roles in educational ventures), increasing demands for accountability at all levels, technological breakthroughs unheard of today, rapidly changing demographics of our nation, and a host of other unforeseen events. Leaders and professionals that prepare leaders need to utilize techniques such as those that Adrian and Apps recommend in order to be prepared for the demands and challenges of the 21st century.

CONSULTANTS AND LEADERS: PREREQUISITES TO SUCCESS

Consultants and leaders, regardless of support service position, face several prerequisites to their personal and professional successes: their attitudes toward and commitment to accountability, degree of professionalism toward their colleagues and their profession, and their willingness to use technology as a means of attaining or reaching goals. This section examines these three themes—accountability, professionalism, and technology—which will either determine or significantly influence consultants' and leaders' success.

Accountability

Just as educators in all positions and professional areas, support services personnel serving in consultant and leadership roles will be held accountable. The national mood or perception that schools can and should be more productive will likely continue (and perhaps grow more intense) during the late 1990s and early 21st century. This insistence on effectiveness and proven results will undoubtedly affect support services personnel. Likewise, consultants and leaders will not be immune to scrutiny and demands for increased effectiveness. Accountability, however, should not be perceived as an obstacle or nuisance. Instead, professionals should view accountability as a means of documenting effectiveness, a mechanism to build upon strengths and to remedy weaknesses, and as a means of reviewing personal and professional goals. Support services professionals, acting as consultants and leaders, have a responsibility toward the general public, to the professionals requesting services, and to the profession itself.

School districts and other educational agencies hold consultants and leaders accountable for achievement, productivity, and mission implementation. The accountability process must satisfy district or agency requirements and expectations (Goens and Clover, 1991) and must provide concrete and measurable results that document effectiveness.

While the individual situation dictates accountability measures to be considered, several determinants seem to cross situational lines. The following list is by no means exhaustive; however, it does suffice to show factors to be considered. The organization, whether a school district or other educational agency, should expect support services professionals working in consultant and leadership roles to demonstrate

- knowledge, skills, and attitudes necessary for the particular situation
- consultant or leadership abilities to assist others in the meeting of goals

- knowledge and ability to work through an established and methodical process to set clear goals having consensus among team or group members
- ability and motivation to implement a plan of action designed to accomplish goals or to address tasks
- ability to manage conflicts with the least degree of confusion and interruption of group plans
- ability and determination to "lead" rather than "manage"
- ability and desire to model and instill interpersonal relationships necessary to accomplish collegiality among all team members
- motivational techniques to encourage others to work toward established goals
- ability to create a shared organizational vision in which all team members feel a sense of ownership
- willingness to take risks to accomplish tasks and meet goals
- ability and willingness to listen to diverse opinions and thoughtfully scrutinize one's own position
- willingness to accept and abide by a code of professional (and personal) ethics
- ability and desire to create a culture of excellence
- ability and willingness to accept the demands of accountability and to encourage others to perceive accountability as a positive means of personal and professional growth
- ability and motivation to empower individuals, teams, and organizations to work as a group toward established goals
- ability to use (and encourage others to use) technological advances to assist in meeting team goals
- knowledge of teams and the team process (as discussed in Chapter 3), as well as the skills to tackle problems and tasks through teams

Consultants and leaders are also accountable to the profession, both the overall profession and their area of specialization. Similarities in responsibilities, obligations, and benefits undoubtedly exist in leaders' and consultants' professional organizations and their specialty organization. Support services professionals might question belonging to two organizations—how can I commit time, effort, and financial resources to two organizations? What is the rationale for being accountable to two organizations? Such questions warrant explanation and deserve careful consideration, yet the authors feel several reasons suggest the need for such professional involvement and for professionals committing to support the organization and the profession.

First, support services personnel considering themselves accountable to a professional association representing a diverse group of educators has several benefits: consultants and leaders learn professional dimensions other than their own; learn the challenges facing education as a profession; develop contacts and collegiality with other educators; and, generally speaking, develop a group of the overall accountability demands of a profession. A number of professional organizations exist (for a sampling, see the list in Chapter 5) — National Education Association, Association for Childhood Education International, Association for Supervision and Curriculum Development, National Middle School Association, National Association for the Education of Young Children, National Association of Secondary School Principals, to name a few — which can offer support services consultants and leaders valuable advice, publications, and various learning opportunities. Accountability expectations include adherence to the association's professional ethics; obligations to consider candidates and vote; and learning the roles, behaviors, and attitudes associated with being a member of a profession and a professional organization. Through newsletters, journals, and conferences, consultants and leaders can become acquainted with the overall profession and take an active role at the local, state, and national levels.

Second, support services personnel should consider themselves accountable to the organization representing their specialty. Such specialty associations may include American Library Association, American Association of School Librarians, Association for Educational Communications and Technology, American Speech and Hearing Association, American Association for Counseling and Development, National Association of School Musicians, and National Association of Elementary School Principals. These associations represent the concerns and challenges of particular support areas. Consultants and leaders can gain valuable knowledge and information concerning their respective specialties and should consider themselves accountable to the expectations of the professional specialty association.

In summary, support services professionals face a number of accountability measures and demands—to their school district or education agency, colleagues and professional organizations, and ultimately, to themselves, knowing that they have contributed their maximum effort to consulting and leading endeavors. Accountability, however, should be viewed as a "positive," a means of measuring and enhancing one's personal and professional contributions to colleagues and the profession as a whole.

Professionalism

Professionalism, a second prerequisite to consultants' and leaders' success, has many benefits for both individuals demonstrating professionalism and colleagues. Participation in professional organizations and demonstrating professional behaviors has the potential for enhancing interpersonal relationships, the motivation to achieve goals, and the effectiveness of the decision-making process. This section looks briefly at how consultants and leaders need to demonstrate professional behaviors in all endeavors with colleagues and professional organizations.

Support services consultants and leaders committing to the expectations and ideals of the profession can gain a sense of professional empowerment and the ability and confidence to meet goals and lead others to move collegially toward goals. The roots of professional empowerment lie in knowledge and competence. Without mastery of skills, knowledge, and strategies (Goens and Clover, 1991), consultants and leaders cannot demonstrate the competence needed to garner respect and commitment to a task. While professionalism may take many forms, three aspects seem to hold potential for support services personnel working as consultants and leaders:

(*1*) Aspect 1 – Consultants and leaders meet professional responsibilities. Support services professionals know their professional responsibilities and strive to meet expectations of the district or agency, as well as colleagues and members of teams. Those dealings should be conducted in an ethical manner and should demonstrate knowledge, abilities, and attitudes necessary for goal setting and attainment. Other aspects include fair treatment of colleagues and team members, fostering positive interpersonal relationships rather than conflict, and recognizing the need for confidentiality when discussion of issues should be kept silent.

(*2*) Aspect 2 – Consultants and leaders continue to learn and to grow professionally. Support services professionals need to continue their professional education – to learn changing theories of leadership, to learn recent advances in specialty areas, to learn issues and challenges facing educators outside their support area, and to develop enhanced means of maintaining collegial relationships. Professionals cannot grow stagnant and continue to maintain consulting and leading effectiveness. Continuing to learn and to grow professionally can occur through professional seminars, reading journals, and books; attending courses and workshops; and working collegially with others. Being a professional and working in professional roles and relationships, one cannot maintain professional energy and expertise without deliberate and planned effort.

(*3*) Aspect 3 – Consultants and leaders commit to helping others and the profession. Effective support services personnel have a sincere desire to help others and to contribute to the profession. Helping others includes having concern for their personal and professional welfare, working to involve them in team endeavors, recognizing and encouraging other people to utilize strengths toward common goals, and modeling behaviors necessary for positive and collegial relationships. Similarly, helping the profession includes belonging to and participating in professional organizations; continuing to learn and grow as a professional; and, generally speaking, doing whatever possible to promote the education profession and one's specialty.

Technology

Technology, another strand permeating this text, will continue to enhance consultants' and leaders' effectiveness and overall chances of success. To make the most of technological advances, support services professionals will need to 1) understand how technological advances can contribute to consultant and leadership effectiveness and 2) encourage others to use and promote the use of technological advances. Recently, increasing evidence (Kemp and Smellie, 1994) has documented the effectiveness of carefully designed, high-quality media. Consultants and leaders can make work more interesting and enjoyable, as well as more goal-directed (Kemp and Smellie, 1994):

- Support services professionals, knowledgeable of technological advances, realize how technology enhances consultant and leadership efforts. Many support services professionals are not fully acquainted with technological advances and how technology contributes to consulting and leadership functions. Others have made considerable progress learning how to use technology to enhance presentations. What contributions can technology offer to consulting and leadership efforts?

- The content of a topic can be more carefully sequenced and organized.
- The delivery of efforts, i.e., presentations, can be more standardized.
- Efforts, whether presentations or written documents, can be more interesting.
- The length of time for efforts and teamwork can often be reduced.
- The quality of efforts can be enhanced.
- The needs of individual team members can be addressed.
- The role of the consultant or leader can be appreciably changed in positive directions.

As with any presentation to a group, careful thought should be devoted to preplanning the consulting or leadership effort. For example, consultants and leaders might ask themselves (Kemp and Smellie, 1994).

(1) What preparation should the audience have before experiencing the materials? (reading, activity, etc.)
(2) How will you introduce the materials to a group or individuals so they are properly alerted as to what is coming? (outline, questions, problem situation, etc.)
(3) What will you be required to do during use of the material? (show items, stop/start VCR, raise questions, etc.)
(4) What will be required of the group or individuals of the materials? (take notes, answer questions, practice a skill, etc.)
(5) What should be done after use of materials? (answer questions, encourage discussion, complete follow-up activities, etc.)

Similarly, after the presentations, whether a consultant or leadership effort, reflection is necessary: What needs to be changed the next time? What points were overemphasized? What points needed more elaboration? Was there sufficient time for group participation? Did materials meet the objectives? Should the consultant or leader become more skillful in using technology? After a consultant or leader completes a presentation or other effort, he or she will be able to devise his or her own list, which addresses specific points and individual situations. Such reflection in an age of accountability has the potential for serving both the consultant and leader, as well as the audience being served.

- Support services professionals encourage and model to other professionals how to use technological advances. This entire book calls on support services professionals to take active leadership roles to address problems, tasks, and challenges of the late 1990s and early 21st century. Rather than waiting to be called upon, support services professionals, especially those assuming consultant and leadership roles, need to be powerful advocates for positive change and an empowered profession. Such leadership includes consultants and leaders modeling and encouraging other professionals to recognize the benefits of technology and to use these advances on a daily basis. This encouragement should be nonthreatening and constructive; i.e., consultants and leaders should 1) inform other professionals of roles technology can play, 2) provide instruction in specific methods, and 3) suggest other sources of information, i.e., books, magazines, workshops, and courses.

SUMMARY

Support services professionals' changing roles will include consultant and leadership dimensions. In consultant positions, support services professionals will assist in identifying areas to address, working collegially with other professionals, encouraging team efforts, and promoting group dynamics. Similarly, their leadership roles will include all the customary expectations of professional leaders, as well as newer challenges resulting from a rapidly changing world. Two points surface when considering professionals' changing roles: perceptive support services professionals will view consultant and leadership roles 1) using 21st century perspectives—looking toward the present and future will be more productive than planning an agenda using perceptions of the past—and 2) successful consultants and leaders will consider accountability, professionalism, and technology essential to their success. Events such as team processes, empowerment, and site-based management indicate the coming century will place new demands on support services personnel. These new demands will be even greater for consultants and leaders; however, the rewards can be equally great, especially for support services personnel prepared to meet the professional challenges.

REFERENCES

Adrian, J. G. and Apps, J. W. (1993). "Leadership development in the next age," *Adult Learning*, 4(6):9–10, 25.

Bennis, W. and Nanus, B. (1985). *Leaders: The Strategies for Taking Charge*. New York: Harper and Row.

Blumberg, A. and Greenfield, W. (1986). *The Effective Principal: Perspectives on School Leadership* (2nd ed.). Boston: Allyn and Bacon.

Burns, J. M. (1978). *Leadership*. New York: Harper and Row.

Conger, J. (1992). *Learning to Lead: The Art of Transforming Managers into Leaders*. San Francisco: Jossey-Bass.

Corey, M. and Corey, G. (1987). *Groups: Process and Practice* (3rd ed.). Monterey: Brooks/Cole.

Corey, S. R. (1991). *Principle-Centered Leadership*. New York: Summit.

Cuban, L. (1989). "The district superintendent and the restructuring of schools: A realistic appraisal," in *Schooling for Tomorrow*, T. Sergiovanni and J. H. Moore (Eds.), pp. 251–271, Boston: Allyn and Bacon.

Garner, J. W. (1978). *Morale*. New York: Norton.

Goens, G. A. and Clover, S. (1991). *Mastering School Reform*. Boston: Allyn and Bacon.

Gorton, R. A. and McIntyre, K. E. (1978). *The Senior High School Principalship. Volume II: The Effective Principal*. Reston, VA: National Association of Secondary School Principals.

Kemp, J. E. and Smellie, D. C. (1994). *Planning, Producing, and Using Instructional Technologies* (7th ed.). New York: HarperCollins.

Kotter, J. P. (1990). *A Force for Change: How Leadership Differs from Management*. New York: Free Press.

Kurpius, D. (1978). "Consultation theory and process: An integrated model," *Personnel and Guidance Journal*, 56:335–338.

Levitt, T. (1988) "The innovating organization," *Harvard Business Review*, 1:7.

Lindelow, J. and Scott, J. J. (1989). "Managing conflict," in *School Leadership – Handbook for Excellence* (2nd ed.), S. C. Smith and P. K. Piele (Eds.), pp. 338–355, Eugene, OR: University of Oregon, ERIC Clearinghouse on Educational Management.

Lombardo, M. (1978 January). "Looking at leadership: Some neglected issues," *Center for Creative Leadership*, p. 3.

Mazzarella, J. A. and Grundy, T. (1989). "Leadership styles," in *School Leadership – Handbook for Excellence* (2nd ed.), S. C. Smith and P. K. Piele (Eds.), pp. 9–27, Eugene, OR: University of Oregon, ERIC Clearinghouse on Educational Management.

Smith, S. C. and Piele, P. K. (1989). *School Leadership – Handbook for Excellence* (2nd ed.). Eugene, OR: University of Oregon, ERIC Clearinghouse on Educational Management.

Stogdill, R. M. (1974). *Handbook of Leadership: A Survey of the Literature*. New York: Free Press.

Weber, J. R. (1989). "Leading the instructional program," in *School Leadership – Handbook for Excellence* (2nd ed.), S. C. Smith and P. K. Piele (Eds.), pp. 191–224. Eugene, OR: University of Oregon, ERIC Clearinghouse on Educational Management.

Yukl, G. A. (1989). *Leadership in Organizations*. Englewood Cliffs: Prentice-Hall.

Zaleznik, A. (1986). "Managers and leaders: Are they different?" *Harvard Business Review*, 64:67–78.

PART III

Challenges and Prospects for the 21st Century

CHAPTER 7

Support Services in a Culturally Diverse Society

OVERVIEW

SUPPORT SERVICES PERSONNEL in the 21st century will live and work in a rapidly changing world—increasing culturally diverse populations, increasing numbers of limited-English proficiency learners, and a growing recognition of how culture influences motivation and perceptions of educational success. Undoubtedly, our nation's increasing cultural diversity requires rethinking and restructuring of professional roles. Major attention must be directed toward equal opportunity, addressing the educational and overall needs of culturally diverse learners, and involving all school professionals in multicultural efforts. This chapter examines our nation's increasingly culturally diverse population, looks at several problems and challenges, and suggests how support services personnel's roles will change and how they can contribute to a more equitable and democratic society.

THE MELTING POT IDEOLOGY—PERSPECTIVES FROM THE PAST

Historically, culturally diverse populations were expected to assimilate toward majority culture perspectives, values, and customs. Culturally diverse groups, as the perspective proposed, came to America with their cultural heritages, values, and customs and ''melted'' or assimilated into majority culture Americans. Glazer and Moynihan (1970), in their book *Beyond the Melting Pot*, proposed that the melting pot did not, in reality, work or provide an accurate description of our nation's changing cultural diversity. Glazer and Moynihan, explaining their point, told how Jews, Italians, and the Irish of New York City chose to retain their old-world heritages. Similarly, other cultural groups also failed (or did not try) to forsake long-held cultural heritages in order to become "Americanized." Giving up characteristics that have been a part of one's cultural heritages for generations is not an easy task. Asians and Hispanics are often reluctant to give up ethnic customs and traditions in favor of middle-class American habits that might appear contrary to beliefs instilled as a young child. Likewise, African-Americans have fought to overcome cultural dominance and discrimination and, through efforts such as the Civil Rights Movement, have sought to understand and maintain their rich cultural heritages. Historical perspectives also considered culturally diverse groups to be basically alike and failed to consider geographical, generational, and social class differences among the various cultural groups.

THE SALAD BOWL IDEOLOGY—A MORE ENLIGHTENED AND CONTEMPORARY PERSPECTIVE

Undoubtedly, some cultural assimilation occurred as culturally diverse populations adopted Anglo-American customs and standards. This assimilation may have been a result of pressure, financial hardship, or intimidation, rather than a conscious decision to become more like mainstream America. This assimilation, however, was not as widespread as some historians believed. In fact, the melting pot ideology began to adjust to a perspective of the United States society as a "salad bowl," wherein each group reflects its unique identity (McCormick, 1984). Allowing people to hold onto cultural heritages, yet live together as a nation, is a more humane and realistic expectation for the United States to adopt. Whether arriving from Southeast Asia, from one of the many Spanish-speaking countries, or from other foreign lands, it is unrealistic to expect people to forsake values, customs, and heritages they have had for years. Such a position in favor of the salad bowl ideology does not overlook the possibility that some assimilation might be necessary for survival or successful participation in the United States, e.g., sufficient English proficiency to survive economically and to participate successfully in everyday life. Some assimilation may be necessary for survival; however, culturally diverse people can be allowed and, in fact, encouraged to hold on to cherished cultural backgrounds. An important point remains—the melting pot ideology held that cultural differences be eliminated, while the salad bowl ideology takes a more enlightened approach by viewing cultural characteristics as enriching to the United States society.

Support Services Personnel's Roles in a Changing Society

How will changing demographics, specifically rapidly increasing culturally diverse populations, affect support services personnel's roles? While specific roles vary within geographical locations and extent of diversity, one basic role is prerequisite to all roles. It is imperative that support services personnel view our increasing culturally diverse population as positive and enriching to our nation. Support services personnel harboring any other perceptions or attitudes will not give their best effort to helping all learners and to making schools a more harmonious and democratic place to learn and teach. Once support services personnel bring the proper mind-set to the task, specific roles include modeling respect for all learners, leading other educators to view differences as enriching and positive, leading team efforts to devise culturally appropriate curricula, working within one's professional specialty (e.g., speech specialists may work with limited-English proficiency learners and testing specialists may work to address cultural influences on testing), and working for equity and equality for all learners.

As the authors have previously espoused, support services personnel addressing our increasing cultural diversity cannot wait for other professionals to take action. One cannot assume other educators will plan and implement an agenda for cultural diversity. Support services personnel must take the lead in guiding all professionals to work effectively with culturally diverse learners and to provide curricular experiences that reflect the diversity of our nation.

THE CULTURALLY DIFFERENT

This section looks at current and projected population numbers of selected culturally diverse groups and provides geographical information when available. The U.S. Census Bureau does not report the same information on all cultural groups, so population projections available for one cultural group may not be available for another group.

Native Americans

Of the four cultural groups addressed in this book, Native Americans have the smallest population numbers and the smallest increases in recent decades. Native Americans, however, still warrant consideration because they represent significant numbers in several states and because Native American children have many problems that schools need to address (Sanders, 1987). The total Native American population is approximately 1.5 million or one-half percent of the total United States population. Approximately one-half of Native Americans live on Native American lands, while the other half lives outside reservations in urban or other predominantly Anglo-American geographical areas (Axelson, 1985). In 1990, 437,000 Native Americans lived on reservations and associated trust lands. Of the Native Americans living on the 314 reservations, 388,000 lived on the seventy-eight reservations with 1,000 or more Native Americans. The Navajo Reservation and Trust Lands in Arizona, New Mexico, and Utah comprise the largest of the reservations (U.S. Bureau of the Census, 1991). States with the greatest population of Native Americans include California, Oklahoma, Arizona, New Mexico, and Washington ("America's first . . ., 1989).

African-Americans

The African-American population increased to nearly 30 million in 1990. A 13.2% increase since 1980, their growth rate was one-third higher than the national growth rate (U.S. Bureau of the Census, 1991). In fact, the African-American population has been growing faster than the total population for a number of years; i.e., their population increased from 11.8% in 1980 to 12.2% in 1987 ("Black population is growing . . .," 1988). Likewise, the African-American population during the next few decades will probably outpace the Anglo population because of the relatively young age of the African-American population (U.S. Bureau of the Census, 1986). The African-American population in 1990 exceeded one million in sixteen states and exceeded two million in three states—New York, California, and Texas. Other states with significant African-American populations include Florida, Georgia, Illinois, North Carolina, Louisiana, Michigan, and Maryland. Projected population data include 7.9 million of five to seventeen year olds by the year 2000 (U.S. Bureau of the Census, 1991).

Asian-Americans

While there is danger in categorizing all Asian-Americans into one group, it is also unrealistic to present all the diverse Asian groups currently living in the United States. Refugees just from Southeast Asia often include Blue, White, and Striped Hmong; Chinese, Krom, and Mi Khmer Cambodians; Chinese Mien, Thai Dam, and Khmer Laotians; and Lowlander and Highlander Vietnamese. Each Asian group has their own history and culture, as well as many stratifications within each group (Kitano, 1989).

Boosted by high levels of immigration, the Asian population more than doubled from 3.5 million in 1980 to 7.3 million in 1990 (U.S. Bureau of the Census, 1991). The ten states with the largest Asian-American population in 1990 included California, New York, Hawaii, Texas, Illinois, New Jersey, Washington, Virginia, Florida, and Massachusetts (U.S. Bureau of the Census, 1992).

Hispanic-Americans

Describing Hispanic-Americans becomes virtually impossible due to the tremendous range of Spanish-speaking countries. The Hispanic population from 1980 to 1990 increased from 14.6 million to 22.4 million. This 53% increase resulted from a high birth rate, as well as high levels of immigration (U.S. Bureau of the Census, 1991).

In 1990, California had the largest Hispanic population, a total of 7.7 million, which represented a 69% increase over the 1980 numbers. Three other states, Texas, New York, and Florida, had Hispanic populations of one million or more. Other states with large Hispanic populations include Illinois, New Jersey, Arizona, New Mexico, Colorado, and Massachusetts (U.S. Bureau of the Census, 1991). Ten to fourteen year olds in 1990 totaled 2,002,000 (U.S. Bureau of the Census, 1992); however, projections suggest Hispanic five to seventeen year olds will reach 6,207,000 by the year 2000, a 28.6% increase (U.S. Bureau of the Census, 1991). If predictions become reality, Hispanics will outnumber African-Americans and people of any other single minority background. In fact, Hispanics currently outnumber African-Americans in cities such as New York, Los Angeles, San Diego, Phoenix, San Francisco, and Denver (U.S. Bureau of the Census, 1988).

European, African, Australia, and Other Cultural Groups

Other cultural groups also inhabit the United States, adding to its diversity. Population numbers of European, African, Australian, and other cultural groups include (U.S. Bureau of the Census, 1992)

Country of Birth	Population Numbers: 1990 (in thousands)
Europe	112.4
Africa	35.9
Australia	1.8
Other countries (New Zealand and other unknown countries)	4.5

LINGERING PROBLEMS CHALLENGING THE UNITED STATES SOCIETY

Stereotyping

Stereotyping can be described as the prejudicial attitude of a person or group that superimposes a generalization about behavioral characteristics on a total race, sex, or religion (Lum, 1986). Stereotypes produce an overly general mental picture that usually results in a judgmental, negative, or positive image of a person or an entire culture. Educators can readily understand the dangers associated with stereotyping, especially when these mental images become the basis for educational decisions and also contribute to people being victims of racism.

Stereotypes that school educators need to address include negative images of young people themselves. All too often, educators and the general public stereotype young people as being difficult to teach and preoccupied with the opposite sex when, in actuality, many young people completely defy this stereotype. Other stereotypes include Asian-Americans being bright, hard-working, and a model minority or, perhaps, describing Native Americans as lazy and unmotivated. Stereotyping can be devastating to learners. Educational experiences may reflect erroneous beliefs and, thus, be too easy or too difficult, may be based upon expectations that certain culturally diverse groups will misbehave, and may predetermine learners' behavior and success in school.

Racism

Signs of racist behavior and racial unrest indicate that "racism is alive and well in the public school" (Stover, 1990, p. 14). Indicators of continuing racism include three students bringing a white doll to school wearing a Ku Klux Klan robe and a black doll with a noose around its neck; racial tensions sparked when several white students displayed Confederate flags during a black history program, and fights erupted between whites and Asian immigrants in a mostly white, affluent neighborhood (Stover, 1990).

Racism can have serious effects on culturally diverse young adolescents. First, culturally diverse learners interpret the actions of others as discriminatory and racist. Second, victims of racism attribute the cause to the person behind the action, to themselves, to social circumstances, or to some combination of the three. Third, they form conclusions about themselves and their self-worth and make decisions about how they will react to future racist acts. An overall effect of racism is that learners suffer lower academic achievement and self-esteem, apathy, and poor perception of the future (Murray and Clark, 1990).

Institutional racism, another insidious plague on United States society, occurs when schools (or any other organization serving the public) has rules, expectations, and policies that exclude certain populations. One outstanding example, homogeneous ability grouping, all too often results in segregation of learners. Other examples include any organizational type that excludes learners, separates learners by culture or social class, and, as previously mentioned, bases performance expectations on cultural stereotypes.

Prejudice

Allport (1954, 1979) in his *The Nature of Prejudice* defined prejudice as a feeling, favorable or unfavorable, toward a person or thing, which is not based on actual experience. Prejudice can hold a negative or positive tone or a racial and ethnic connotation. Key components of prejudice include a negative nature that can be individually or group focussed, a feeling that can be only an attitude or belief or can be overtly expressed, a belief based on faulty or unsubstantiated data, and an attitude rooted in generalizations. In light of new evidence, the person harboring prejudicial attitudes would be resistant to evidence that would contradict the negative belief (Ponterotto, 1991). As with racism, prejudice can interfere with learner development, school expectations for achievement and behavior, and a host of other negative behaviors. Educators have a responsibility to treat all learners in an objective fashion, to provide equal educational experiences for all learners, and to have objective perceptions and expectations for all learners, regardless of cultural, gender, and social class backgrounds.

Responsibilities of Support Services Personnel

Support services personnel undoubtedly have a moral and professional responsibility to address the dangers associated with stereotyping, racism, and prejudice. Too often, these three evils are ignored in the hope that they will go away or that the damage will not be too severe. Other times, they are not recognized. Considerable evidence just presented suggests that stereotyping, racism, and prejudice continue to exist and continue to limit learners' potential. It is also important to note the effect of these three on self-esteem, cultural identities, social development, and overall school achievement.

Support services personnel, working as neither classroom educators nor administrators, might be in the best position to view the whole picture and, thereby, identify stereotyping, racism, and prejudice that others might miss. One might say, "Stereotyping, racism, and prejudice have been with us for centuries—what can we do?" Without doubt, this question has been asked by some caring and conscientious professionals. While these three evils need to be the focus of natural attention, support services personnel can be the guiding force in initiating an attack. Specific roles to combat stereotyping, racism, and prejudice may include

(1) Recognizing that the three evils exist and limit learners' potential
(2) Ridding oneself of all vestiges of these plagues on society
(3) Taking a public stand in school meetings (perhaps team meetings) for a just and equitable society where people are objectively perceived and treated equally
(4) Addressing, in a positive manner, individual's statements that convey myth, hatred, or misperception
(5) Modeling personal characteristics that complement a humane and democratic society
(6) Identifying school situations that, intentionally or unintentionally, might result in discriminatory or prejudicial acts, e.g., separating learners by ability, which results in separation of cultures and genders
(7) Conducting or arranging for workshops on racism, discrimination, and prejudice; identifying and helping others to change; helping

learners who feel victimized; and working daily toward a more humane and caring society

Progress may appear slow, people may appear unwilling to change, and incidents of racism and stereotyping may even increase as our nation grows more culturally diverse. Obstacles and frustrations do not provide support services personnel just cause to stop their efforts. Becoming active leaders in the push for accurate perceptions and just treatment can result in both learners and educators changing their attitudes toward people who are different and altering perceptions of how a democratic society should operate.

ROLES OF SUPPORT SERVICES PERSONNEL IN OUR CULTURALLY DIVERSE SOCIETY

Support services personnel can play vital roles in our culturally diverse society—recognizing and appreciating cultural diversity; leading others to work toward a more accepting and humane society; and understanding how culture affects motivation, school achievement, language decisions (e.g., whether to learn English or maintain one's native tongue), self-esteem, and cultural identities. Without doubt, all professional educators need to assume active roles toward making our culturally diverse society more accepting and harmonious; however, support services personnel's changing roles can include leadership roles and being a catalyst toward positive change.

Recognizing, Accepting, and Appreciating Cultural Diversity

Our society, for many years, placed major concern (e.g., legal rights and genuine concern for welfare) on its Anglo-American citizens. For many years, the rights and overall welfare of culturally diverse groups, primarily African-Americans, took second-class status. African-Americans were denied opportunities readily available to the Anglo population. Likewise, Asian-Americans, primarily of Chinese ancestry, performed back-breaking work building the railroad linking the Missouri River to the Pacific Coast (Banks, 1987). Fortunately, through the efforts of Civil Rights leaders and Supreme Court decisions, culturally diverse groups increasingly were accorded long-denied rights. With these legal rights, however, did not come genuine acceptance and respect.

Support services personnel need to work toward more positive attitudes toward culturally diverse groups. Rather than subscribing to the outdated melting pot mind-set, support services personnel need to perceive culturally diverse learners' differences as positive and enriching to the United States society. Only then will support services personnel genuinely work toward culturally diverse learners' overall welfare and also lead other professionals to work toward humane and equitable treatment.

Specifically, support services personnel can

- recognize cultural, gender, social class, generational, and individual differences among people
- accept culturally diverse learners' characteristics as differences on which to build learning experiences, rather than negatives to be eradicated
- appreciate differences as positive and enriching to our nation

One point deserves to be highlighted as a prerequisite to any efforts that support services personnel may initiate. Efforts to promote cultural diversity should be genuine and sincere; any other attitudes will result in support services personnel giving a half-hearted effort and providing only "lip service" to multicultural efforts (Manning, 1991).

Understanding How Culture Affects Perceptions toward Motivation and Achievement

Support services personnel need to convey to educators, teams, and professionals working with children and adolescents that perspectives of motivation and success are often based upon middle class Anglo-American perspectives. These perceptions hold that one has excelled or "done something" with their abilities or talents. Such achievement usually captures the attention and respect of educators. It is important, however, that support services personnel convey to other educators that learners in other cultures might not share these perceptions of motivation, success, and school achievement. Some cultures might prefer noncompetitive and harmonious learning situations over competitive situations where learners are expected to excel at peers' expense. For example, Native Americans might appear to be unmotivated or disinterested to educators when, in fact, this cultural group is more concerned with harmonious situations, rather than any kind of competition. Maintaining harmony with one's friends and families might be considered a greater priority than excelling in academic endeavors or accumulating great wealth. Similarly, Asian-Americans' quiet demeanors may prevent them from choosing to participate in class discussions or raise their hands during questioning sessions. Last, Hispanic-American learners may not demonstrate the motivational characteristics many educators expect, because this culture might not want to excel or stand out from their peers.

While support services professionals working in specific areas, e.g., counselors, librarian/media specialists, and speech correctionists, should encourage all learners to perform at their maximum potential, it is important to realize that not all cultures demonstrate the same motivational characteristics. Educators' perception of behaviors indicating motivation and desire to achieve might differ significantly from the culturally diverse learner. Serious harm could be inflicted upon a learner when educators insist upon specific behaviors that may be totally out of character or contradict long-accepted cultural characteristics.

Understanding the Importance of One's Language and One's Ability to Communicate in Mainstream Society

Most educators are native-English speakers and probably do not understand the value culturally diverse learners place on their language. Similarly, most educators have not been in situations where their language was not the language of the majority; therefore, they do not understand the difficulties and frustrations language minority speakers experience. In some aspects, one's language is a defining characteristic of one's cultural heritage. A significant personal trait, language and one's ability to communicate, affects many aspects of a person's life — cultural identity, self-esteem, socialization, and the ability to cope with everyday demands. Not being able to speak and understand the language spoken in school can pose a serious problem. The student may not be able to understand the language of instruction and, perhaps equally severe, may begin to consider his or her language inferior. Being asked to forsake one's language in favor of the language of the teacher or school can be traumatic, especially when parents and family members continue to speak the native language at home.

How can support services personnel help other educators to react to speakers of other languages and to help culturally diverse learners speaking native languages to deal with school and overall life expectations? First, support services personnel must understand the importance of helping both educators and students, especially when educators fail to understand the importance of one's language or feel frustrated with teaching these youngsters. In addition, the support service professional may be the most appropriate person to help the educator and the learner since they serve in the most appropriate position to understand both perspectives. The support service professional can

- serve as a liaison between classroom educators and culturally diverse learners, parents, and families
- provide assistance (actually complementing classroom educator's efforts) and suggest other sources of help, e.g., appropriate social services agencies
- work with culturally diverse learners, helping them to learn English and to cope with everyday demands of living without forsaking their native language or conveying that their language is inferior or wrong
- help classroom educators and administrators to understand the personal cultural significance of language

Support services personnel addressing language needs offer a significant contribution to culturally diverse learners, as well as their educators. As our society grows more culturally diverse and, subsequently, as educators encounter more learners speaking languages other than English, support services personnel's challenges will increase. Rather than language diversity being a challenge that will resolve itself or diminish over the years, classroom educators will increasingly be faced with learners speaking native languages. Educators will need specialized assistance for years to come—perceptive support services personnel will be prepared to meet language challenges.

Understanding Self-Concept and Cultural Identity Development

The work of Purkey and Novak (1984) in *Inviting School Success* documented the need to address learners' self-esteem. To a significant extent, one's perception of oneself determines behavior, school achievement, and overall social development. Perceptive educators realize the importance of learners' self-esteems and plan teaching-learning experiences and educational environments that enhance feelings of self-worth. While all learners sometimes experience obstacles to positive self-esteem, even greater obstacles face culturally diverse learners – often speaking a language other than the majority, attending a school and living in a community with different customs and expectations, facing confusing school expectations, and learning that teachers and peers have differing traditions and value systems. Without doubt, educators need to make special attempts to help culturally diverse learners to have positive feelings about themselves and to consider their school experience worthwhile.

The cultural identity, or the degree of worth learners attach to their cultural heritage, also deserves serious consideration. Identity has been defined as answers to questions such as "Who am I?" and "Who am I to be?" Identity is a person's sense of place within the world or the meaning that one attaches to oneself in the broader context of life (Vander Zanden, 1989). It is important that educators show children and adolescents that people may have several identities at once, i.e., one might be Hispanic-American, a member of any of the Spanish-speaking cultures, one's brother, a Catholic, an inhabitant of a specific geographic region in the United States, or any number of identities (Baruth and Manning, 1992).

The challenge for support services personnel becomes clear as one considers learners from culturally diverse backgrounds. Culturally diverse individuals need to be able to clarify personal attitudes toward their cultural and ethnic backgrounds. The educator's goal is to teach individuals to learn self-acceptance, thus developing the characteristics needed to accept and respond more positively to other ethnic groups. Similarly, educators should strive to instill in learners an acceptance and understanding of both the positive and negative attributes of their cultural or ethnic groups and to teach learners the importance of acquiring genuine ethnic pride, rather than hate or fear (Banks, 1988; Baruth and Manning, 1992).

Individuals who have positive ethnic, national, and global identifications value their ethnic, national, and global communities highly, and are proud of these identifications. They both desire and have the competencies to take actions that will support and reinforce the values and norms of their ethnic, national, and global communities (Banks, 1988; Baruth and Manning, 1992).

TRADITIONAL PERSONNEL: ROLES IN AN INCREASINGLY MULTICULTURAL SOCIETY

Traditionally, support services personnel have included counselors, speech correctionists, and librarians/media specialists. These professionals specialized in their respective areas and performed valuable services to both learners and teachers. Many of these professionals attended excellent training institutions and, thus, are experts in their areas. However, more than likely, these specialists received training prior to the emphasis on addressing the needs of culturally diverse groups. The roles of these traditional support services personnel will be affected by our nation's increasing culturally diverse society and the push for appropriate multicultural experiences. In the 21st century, many of these professionals will continue performing similar tasks as previously; however, they will also take on some new roles and change other roles to reflect the cultural diversity of the nation.

Counselors

Counselors' roles include understanding culturally different children and adolescents, counseling culturally different learners, understanding testing and assessment issues, and working with classroom teachers for the welfare of the learners. Cultural, intracultural, ethnic, and racial differences deserve understanding and consideration when counseling children and adolescents in multicultural situations. Rather than being a homogeneous population, learners have many differences that vary according to individuals, individual cultures, gender, generation, and socioeconomic status.

Counselors may work with individuals, small groups, and large classes. The first contact between a school counselor and a troubled student may be initiated by the classroom educator, who has daily contact with learners and who may be the first professional to detect a potential problem. Individual teachers, then, are in a prime position to either ask the counselor for direct assistance or to refer students with problems to the counselor. It is wise for both the teacher and the counselor to determine the best means of referring students, of coordinating and scheduling large-group counseling, and of determining the correct needs of the culturally diverse learners.

Counselors may provide several forms of assistance to classroom teachers and their students. Considering the many demands on the counselor's time and expertise, however, the teacher might have to initiate contact or inform the counselor of special areas of concern. Generally speaking, the counselor can assist with the following (Baruth and Manning, 1992):

(*1*) Determining and providing joint efforts of administrators and other educators to improve learners' self-concepts and cultural identities
(*2*) Providing assistance in suggesting culturally appropriate instruments and in interpreting test scores of culturally diverse learners
(*3*) Working with culturally diverse families (both immediate and extended) in parent education endeavors
(*4*) Offering parents meaningful roles in school governance and offering families opportunities to support the teaching and learning process at home and at school
(*5*) Providing individual and small-group counseling in areas of concern to culturally diverse learners, i.e., peer acceptance and approval
(*6*) Providing large-group counseling sessions in areas such as involvement meetings, rules meetings, thinking meetings, values clarification meetings, and group councils (Thompson and Rudolph, 1988)
(*7*) Suggesting culturally relevant materials for helping all children and adolescents to better understand one another's culture
(*8*) Working with older students in career planning and suggesting appropriate subjects needed to pursue career plans
(*9*) Helping learners deal with concern over body development, the desire for social acceptance, and the conflicts between adult expectations and peer expectations of culturally appropriate behaviors
(*10*) Designing special programs for at-risk, culturally diverse learners

Support services professionals should view their roles and the counselor's roles as complementary, rather than as two professionals working alone. Since classroom educators have the most daily contact with culturally diverse learners, they are usually in the best position to detect learners with problems, make referrals, and to follow up on the counselor's efforts. Likewise, the classroom teacher and the counselor should always know each other's purposes and strategies and, whenever possible, should provide joint efforts for the benefit of the learners (Baruth and Manning, 1992).

Speech Correctionists

The speech correctionist who works in multicultural settings has a broad knowledge of communication and understands the unique communication situations of culturally diverse learners: dialects, bilingualism, and TOESL, as well as the differences between home and school language and the various assessment challenges.

Since communication is such a vital human aspect to learners of all cultural and ethnic backgrounds, speech correctionists play an important role in helping educators distinguish between disorders and variations. They can also help learners who are experiencing differences with communication, regardless of the reason. There is a need for all speech correctionists to become sensitive to cultural diversity and to develop cross-cultural communication competencies as they work with children classified as non-English proficiency (NEP) and limited-English proficiency (LEP) (Cheng, 1987).

The primary role of the speech correctionist is to distinguish between communicative disorders and communicative variations and to convey to classroom educators the differences between the two. Communication disorders include speech disorders (an impairment of voice, articulation of speech sounds, and/or fluency) and language disorders (the impairment, or deviant development, of comprehension and/or a spoken or written symbol system). Communicative variations include communicative differences or dialects (a variation of a symbol system used by a group of individuals that reflects and is determined by shared regional, social, or cultural/ethnic factors) and argumentative communication (systems used to supplement communication skills, such as prosthetic devices) (McCormick, 1990). It is imperative that communications disorder specialists in multicultural situations distinguish between disorders and variations. Culturally different learners who use a particular dialect or regional accent should not be labeled as having a "disorder" in need of elimination (Baruth and Manning, 1992).

A second, closely related role of the speech correctionist is to understand and to help classroom educators to understand the difference between school language and home language. A learner may appear so "quiet" and "withdrawn" that the educator wonders if the child or adolescent has physical or emotional problems. However, the child or adolescent at home and in the community shows considerable verbal proficiency. When there are substantial differences between language use and conversational use in the home and in the classroom, children and adolescents often appear to have low verbal ability. Despite being verbal in nonschool settings, these learners may talk very little in the classroom and, even then, using only simple words and sentences (McCormick, 1990). In such a situation, the speech correctionist might have to convince the classroom educator that the child or adolescent is not speech-handicapped and is not in need of remediation or therapy.

The classroom educator should view the speech correctionist as a valuable resource person, especially since this professional has such a wide range of expertise and abilities in dealing with communicative disorders. Working in a complementary fashion for the welfare of learners, the speech correctionist can assist the classroom educator in determining whether communication problems are to be remediated or whether variations are to be accepted and appreciated.

Considerable interaction should occur between classroom educators and the speech correctionist. First, the speech correctionist and the teacher need to consult with each other about their goals for a learner, how they expect to accomplish these goals, and what success has been achieved. Such interaction can be formal or informal or by the speech correctionist providing the teacher with copies of written therapy progress reports sent home to parents. Second, the teacher in the classroom has more contact with parents and spends more school hours with learners, who may talk about their feelings, wants, and life at home. Some information that a teacher receives from learners or their parents may be important to the speech correctionist. Third, the teacher is also in an ideal position to provide the speech correctionist with information regarding a learner's speech and language functioning within the classroom and in informal situations, such as in the hallway, the lunchroom, or on the playground. The teacher may also be able to provide reminders to the child during the habit-forming stages of therapy, when the child can best produce the targeted speech behaviors but still must make them a habit in all communicative situations. Fourth, the speech correctionist will need the teacher's input with regard to referrals and in establishing whether or not there is an adverse effect on education due to communicative problem (Oyer et al., 1987; Baruth and Manning, 1992).

The speech correctionist's responsibilities include appropriate assessment, therapy, scheduling, and consultation with teachers and parents (Oyer et al., 1987). Other responsibilities in multicultural situations include understanding the communication problems of culturally different children and adolescents, being able to convey to teachers an assessment of disorders and variations, and providing a climate of understanding and acceptance for all learners.

Librarians/Media Specialists

The librarian, or media specialist, in multicultural settings has the usual responsibilities of any professional serving in this capacity. However, working with culturally diverse children and adolescents requires an understanding of cultural diversity and also includes building a library and media collection that shows positive portrayals of culturally diverse groups. Another role of library or media specialists is to work with classroom educators in positive, constructive ways that demonstrate a respect and commitment for providing appropriate multicultural experiences (Baruth and Manning, 1992).

School librarians/media specialists today have discovered that there have been radical changes in the cultural and ethnic backgrounds of the children and adolescents attending their schools (Nauman, 1987). Libraries/media centers are responsible for ensuring that books, magazines, audiovisual materials, computer software, and all library and media materials have positive and realistic culturally diverse characters with whom learners can relate. For example, culturally diverse children and adolescents should be shown in accurate and objective terms, not in stereotypical images. One of the better and more pragmatic solutions has been offered by the Council on Interracial Books for Children, which regularly evaluates children's materials, trade books, textbooks, and other educational resources (Nauman, 1987).

In a world of children's and adolescents' books and textbooks that continues to grow daily, librarians/media specialists can refer to the following guidelines suggested for professionals (Nauman, 1987):

(*1*) Books and other library materials should reflect authentic cultural and ethnic perspectives.

(*2*) Books and other library materials should reflect differences in lifestyles, socioeconomic levels, interests, and abilities.

(*3*) Books and other library materials should portray characters who represent positions in society apart from, and uninfluenced by, their ethnic heritage.

(*4*) Books and other library materials should reflect a variety of geographic locations of culturally diverse groups.

(*5*) Books and other library materials should use language that shows the richness of the culture portrayed, with dialect used only as a positive, differentiating mechanism.

(*6*) Books and other library materials should accurately depict history and include opportunities to see differing viewpoints.

Like other professionals working in elementary and secondary schools, it is important that librarians/media specialists and classroom educators work together for the welfare of children and adolescents. Librarians/media specialists can be valuable resources for regular classroom teachers and can supplement learning experiences or use a literature-based approach that bases instruction entirely on children's literature. Since the possibility exists that some classroom teachers received training in teacher education before experiences in multiculturalism were required by accrediting associations, library and media specialists can be especially valuable in pointing out the problem of the many children's books that portray characteristics from middle class Anglo perspectives and can be helpful in suggesting culturally appropriate books for all children.

The librarians/media specialists' roles in an increasingly multicultural society include stocking the library and media center with books, magazines, and other materials that accurately portray culturally diverse children and adolescents; assisting classroom educators to choose and use these books; ensuring that library collections have works by non-Anglo authors and illustrators; ensuring that library holdings and materials are accessible to all students, regardless of social class and cultural backgrounds; and assisting students as they search for reading materials (Baruth and Manning, 1992).

Summary of Traditional Personnel

In summary, these three support services personnel have addressed the needs of literally thousands of students and have worked effectively to complement regular classroom educators' efforts. Similarly, their efforts during the last decade to address their particular specialties and to address our nation's changing demographics have been both commendable and successful. These support services personnel will need to continue to recognize cultural differences as positive and enriching and also to provide culturally appropriate teaching-learning experiences. This next section proposes an entire array of possible support services roles the future might bring, especially as our nation, schools, and individual educators work to restructure schools to meet the needs and challenges of the 21st century. However, proposing support services roles in no way negates the significant contributions that support services personnel in the past have offered to schools, teachers, and learners. New support services personnel positions are proposed because our pressure to reform schools in changing demographic times suggests that

United States schools will need more specialized assistance or professionals who can complement classroom teachers' daily efforts.

FUTURE SUPPORT PERSONNEL AND THEIR ROLES IN A MULTICULTURAL SOCIETY

Future support services professionals will reflect the needs of a culturally diverse society and the expectations for accountability and professionalism.

Learning Diagnostician

Support services personnel in the 21st century can play valuable roles in diagnosing learning problems. Rather than assuming a student cannot or will not learn, the learning diagnostician will determine the actual reason for a child or adolescent not learning. The significant populations of culturally diverse learners in today's schools require that support services personnel consider cultural backgrounds and the influence of culture on learning and achievement.

Determining specific cultural influences include, first, considering the previously mentioned effects of culture on perceptions of motivation and academic success. Once the learning diagnostician understands the learner, efforts can then be directed to diagnosing actual learning needs.

While the relationship between culture and learning still needs study, several authors have pointed out how culture affects learning styles and overall cognition. Support services personnel, working in this diagnostic role, can help classroom educators plan teaching-learning experiences that reflect culturally diverse students' learning styles and cognitive characteristics. In their focus of Native Americans and Alaskan Native youth, Swisher and Deyhle (1989) based their study on the premise that "people perceive the world in different ways, learn about the world in different ways, and demonstrate what they have learned in different ways" (p. 2). Their findings included differences in learning to learn, visual approaches to learning, influences of culture, and attitudes toward cooperating and competing. Another study reported that many Native Americans showed strengths in visual/spatial/perceptual information; used mental associations to remember concepts and words; demonstrated tendencies toward being reflective rather than impulsive and watching-then-do rather than engaging in trial and error; and exhibited tendencies toward participating in global processing on both verbal and nonverbal tasks, for example, students might process using the whole and the relationships between the parts, rather than emphasizing the parts to build the whole (More, 1987).

African-Americans view things in their environment in entirety, rather than in isolated parts; prefer intuitive rather than deductive or inductive reasoning; approximate concepts of space, number, and time, rather than aiming at exactness or accuracy; and rely on nonverbal, as well as verbal, communication (Shade, 1982). Differences have also been found in learning styles between African-American students of varying academic levels. High achievers tended to be teacher-motivated, while average achievers preferred to learn in the late mornings. Also, the low achievers preferred nonparental authority figures present while learning (Jacobs, 1990; Manning, 1993).

Dunn et al. (1990) examined the learning styles of African-, Chinese-, Mexican-, and Greek-American fourth, fifth, and sixth graders and described cultural differences in learning styles. Their suggestions included providing all four cultures with both quiet areas and student interaction areas, providing both conventional and informal seating arrangements, and allowing learners to work alone, in pairs, in small groups, or with teachers. Some students, such as Chinese-Americans, preferred a variety of instructional approaches, while others (i.e., African-Americans) felt more comfortable with established patterns and routines (Manning, 1993).

Software Specialists and Writers

As technological advances become commonplace events in our daily lives, support services personnel can direct efforts in several directions. This software specialist will need to have the technological skills to

- design culturally appropriate software
- communicate effectively with classroom educators about the possibilities technology offers
- help classroom educators in the design of software that meets the learning needs of culturally diverse learners

Software specialists will need to know the various modes and then recognize the need for diversity in all education endeavors:

- Drill and practice, as the name implies, allows learners to practice learning by completing drills.

- Programs can tell learners whether an answer is correct, offer a short remedial lesson, and provide a management section to indicate to the teacher how the student is progressing.
- Tutorial lessons, providing opportunities for enrichment or remediation, can introduce new concepts or reinforce previously learned concepts.
- Simulations provide learners with learning experiences that approximate real-world situations.
- Problem-solving programs take a set of data, teach the learner how to organize the information, come up with a scientific role, and solve the problem.
- Videodisks present visual and sound images, which can be recorded and played back later (Blough and Schwartz, 1990; Allen et al., 1993).

The support service specialist will need to locate or write software programs that reflect the cultural diversity of our nation. Such an effort will include software that reflects culturally diverse learners' interests; that makes use of positive, nonstereotypical references to culturally diverse people; and that recognizes our increasingly culturally diverse society, as well as our genuine respect for diversity.

Curriculum Designers

Curriculum design reflects decisions reached about what actually must be planned and delivered as a final result of the curriculum design effort. The actual design will reflect curriculum sources, external influences, general orientations, and, of course, local and state requirements. Curriculum designers need to answer questions such as the selecting, organizing, and sequencing of content. Once these questions have been answered, then curriculum designers need to decide how the curriculum can be most effectively transmitted and eventually evaluated (Armstrong, 1989).

Support services professionals designing or supporting other educators in the curriculum design effort will need to include content and teaching-learning experiences reflective of the cultural diversity of our nation.

Support services personnel designing culturally appropriate curricula can rely on several guidelines as a starting point. The curriculum should (Sleeter and Grant, 1988)

(1) Present and teach concepts representing diverse cultural groups and both sexes
(2) Include materials and visual displays that are free of race, gender, and handicap stereotypes and that include members of all cultural groups in a positive manner
(3) Include concepts related to diverse groups, rather than teaching fragments of information
(4) Provide as much emphasis on contemporary culture as on historical culture, and groups should be represented as active and dynamic, e.g., while the women's suffrage movement should be addressed, more contemporary problems confronting women also should be addressed
(5) Be viewed as a "total effort," with multicultural aspects permeating all subject areas and all phases of the school day
(6) Ensure the use of nonsexist language
(7) Endorse bilingual education and the vision of a multilingual society
(8) Draw on children's experiential background, and the community and curricular concepts should be based on children's daily life and experiences
(9) Allow equal access for all students, i.e., all students should be allowed to enroll in college preparatory courses or other special curricular areas

Banks (1988) contended that ethnic pluralism should permeate the total school curriculum and environment. Similarly, school policies and procedures should foster positive cross-cultural interactions and understandings among students, teachers, and staff members. The entire curriculum and school environment should reflect the learning styles of all learners, and should provide students with continuous opportunities to develop a more positive self-concept and cultural identity. Other guidelines include the multicultural curriculum (Banks, 1988):

(1) Addressing students' needs to understand the totality of the experiences of ethnic groups
(2) Addressing students' needs to understand conflicts between ideals and realities in human societies
(3) Exploring and clarifying ethnic alternatives and options within society
(4) Promoting values, attitudes, and behaviors that support ethnic pluralism

(5) Helping students develop the skills necessary for effective interpersonal and interethnic group interactions
(6) Being comprehensive in scope and sequence, presenting holistic views of ethnic groups, and being an integral part of the total school curriculum
(7) Including interdisciplinary and multidisciplinary approaches
(8) Using comparative approaches in the study of ethnic groups and ethnicity
(9) Maximizing use of local community resources
(10) Including assessment procedures that reflect individual ethnic cultures

Support services personnel, helping in the design of such a curriculum, will have both short- and long-term effects. In the short-term, learners will see their culture reflected in the school curriculum, and in the long-term, learners and educators will benefit from multiculturalism permeating the curriculum and overall school environment.

Mental Health Diagnostician

As schools increasingly accept greater responsibility and attempt to serve all learners, it is likely that more attention will be directed toward mental health concerns. For example, in an effort to understand how personal problems affect academic and social growth, support services professionals will seek to diagnose mental health problems and plan appropriate intervention. Such an effort will require a consideration of culture and cultural backgrounds on mental health intervention.

Draguns (1989) suggested several resources for addressing mental health concerns: (a) research-based findings on the cross-cultural process; (b) published accounts of personal experiences; (c) personally transmitted accounts; (d) one's own experiences with culturally different people; and (e) one's professional, cultural, and personal sensitivity.

Axelson (1985) compiled a list of fundamentals for working in multicultural settings. Understanding of these guidelines contributes to more accurate perceptions, more cooperative working environments, and increased effectiveness. Mental health diagnosticians (and their students) will benefit from having

(1) Self-awareness and comprehension of one's own cultural group history and experiences

(2) Self-awareness and comprehension of one's own environmental experiences in mainstream culture
(3) Perceptual sensitivity toward one's own personal beliefs and values
(4) Awareness and comprehension of the history and experiences of the cultural group with which the person might identify or encounter
(5) Awareness and comprehension of the environmental experiences in mainstream culture with which the person might identify or encounter
(6) Sensitivity toward the person's personal beliefs and values
(7) Commitment to careful and active listening, not casual attention and a broad repertoire of genuine verbal and nonverbal responses
(8) Concern about the person and his or her situation in the same way that you would care about yourself if you were in that situation
(9) Commitment to avoid misunderstandings and being patient, optimistic, and mentally alert

Evaluation and Testing Specialists

A professional's goal in assessment is to minimize ethnocentrism and maximize culturally appropriate information. Assessment includes interviewing, observing, testing, and analyzing documents. Basic questions revolve around the issue of the extent to which cultural diversity affects assessment. Will a characteristic indigenous to a specific culture be mistakenly perceived and assessed using Anglo-American middle class standards? Two important issues in multicultural assessment include 1) whether psychological constructs or concepts are universally valid and 2) the effects of diagnosing and placing false labels. Other questions related to multicultural assessment include (Lonner and Sundberg, 1985):

(1) What level and type of assessment is indicated?
(2) Which tests are most useful and why?
(3) What are the ethical and legal responsibilities associated with multicultural assessment?

Support services personnel, accepting the role of evaluation and testing specialists, will need to administer culturally appropriate assessment strategies in order to diagnose problems and concerns, develop appropriate goals, and assess the outcomes of intervention (Lonner and Ibrahim, 1989). Other issues for evaluation and testing specialists to consider include determining feasibility of standardized testing, the effects of testing on culturally diverse learners, and how to most effectively help classroom educators design culturally appropriate tests.

THE NEED FOR CULTURALLY DIVERSE SUPPORT SERVICES PERSONNEL

The number of culturally diverse support services personnel should reflect the cultural diversity of our nation. Even the loftiest goals and philosophical commitments toward diversity become superficial when learners see support services personnel, all or mostly from one culture. Schools, now and in the future, need support services professionals from culturally diverse populations. Reaching the goal of a culturally diverse faculty and staff can be achieved by deliberate recruitment programs aimed at employing culturally diverse professionals.

Rationale

Defending the goal of employing culturally diverse support personnel is not difficult. First, having diverse support personnel shows students a commitment to include all people, regardless of cultural, ethnic, and racial backgrounds; second, such a policy shows a respect for the legal mandates that ensure equal opportunity for all people, regardless of cultural diversity. Third, culturally diverse support services professionals can add a much-needed cultural perspective to all professional deliberations and team decisions. Having the staff reflect the diversity of the student body is undoubtedly a fundamental goal and a prerequisite to showing respect for cultural diversity and for equal opportunity under the law (Baruth and Manning, 1992).

Efforts to Recruit and Retain Culturally Diverse Support Services Personnel

Efforts to recruit and retain culturally diverse support services personnel will grow increasingly important as our schools continue to reflect the diversity of our nation. Recruitment efforts may include school representatives

(*1*) Attending job fairs and college interview sessions to employ culturally diverse professionals
(*2*) Writing letters to prospective graduates inviting them to visit schools and interview for positions
(*3*) Contacting organizations working for the welfare of culturally diverse groups to request names of potential employees
(*4*) Contacting Deans of Colleges of Education to request names and majors of potential graduates
(*5*) Offering incentives, e.g., specialized equipment, which contribute to support services professionals' effectiveness

Culturally diverse support services personnel undoubtedly enrich school environments: showing learners the school's commitment to diversity, adding culturally diverse perspectives, and contributing to the school population being more representative of the society. Recruitment efforts offer the potential for employing culturally diverse professions; however, efforts cannot stop at the hiring stage — efforts must be made to retain these professionals. Many professionals, unhappy or feeling unfulfilled in their jobs, seek employment in other school systems or, unfortunately, leave the education profession altogether.

Efforts to retain culturally diverse support services personnel include

(*1*) Creating supportive working environments that demonstrate acceptance and appreciation of cultural differences
(*2*) Offering first-year support or assistance programs to help in the transition from college or university life or from another employment position to the professional life or the new position
(*3*) Providing staff development opportunities to help newly employed professionals in their daily activities
(*4*) Emphasizing the team concept, whereby newly employed professionals can benefit from other educators' experiences and also whereby teams can benefit from new perspectives

Special meetings of support services professionals should be conducted periodically to determine problems that need to be addressed. Culturally diverse professionals may experience problems and frustrations that others do not experience. Changing perspectives of support services personnel must be considered and appropriate assistance offered to professionals feeling frustrated, either by the changing roles or the stress of the position.

ACCOUNTABILITY AND PROFESSIONALISM

As in all school endeavors, it is imperative that accountability and professionalism permeate all areas of the school. The 21st century will require increased accountability, especially as school budgets fall due to lowered tax revenues and as educators are held more accountable, both by their own professional agencies and by outside agencies. Accountability and professionalism, however, should be perceived as positives or as challenges with the potential for making the teaching professional stronger and better able to meet the needs of learners.

All professionals in our increasingly culturally diverse society will be held accountable for their actions – their efforts to work toward equality for all learners, to work toward acceptance and appreciation of all learners, and to provide culturally appropriate teaching and learning experiences for all learners. Support services personnel will be held accountable for those efforts and for their reactions to culturally diverse populations in their own specialized areas.

While the following list applies to all educators, culturally diverse support services personnel (as well as all support personnel) will need to pinpoint how their particular expertise can particularly address each accountability measure. Professionals responding to our school's cultural diversity will

(1) Address culturally diverse (as well as all) learners' learning and developmental needs
(2) Recruit and retain facilities representative of our nation's diversity
(3) Provide teaching and learning environments that are conducive to harmony and acceptance of cultural diversity

While culturally diverse support services personnel should be held accountable for their actions, the school administration and other educators should also be held accountable for addressing the needs of support professionals. These professionals should consider themselves an integral part of the school and realize that their efforts are appreciated. Likewise, the overall school district should be held accountable for attracting and retaining culturally diverse support services personnel and for providing professionally satisfying working conditions.

Accountability and professionalism are closely intertwined — one complements the other and, in fact, makes the other necessary. Both require educators to work toward the educational and overall welfare of all learners, toward the teaching profession reflecting our nation's cultural diversity, and toward all professionals modeling acceptance and appreciation of all learners.

Again, accountability and professionalism should be perceived as challenges having the potential for enriching schools and the nation as a whole. Responsibilities to these two have grown more demanding over the years and will grow even more demanding as educators work to meet the needs of increasingly diverse school populations.

SUMMARY

Changes in our society are being reflected in our schools and vice versa: changing United States demographics and an increased recognition of the need for more humane perspectives toward culturally diverse populations. These changes are occurring at a time when perspectives toward support services personnel's roles are also evolving and schools are being called upon to meet the needs of all learners, regardless of cultural, ethnic, gender, and socioeconomic backgrounds. Support services personnel can play significant roles in this change process, both the changes that affect their professional roles personally and also the demographic changes that affect all professional educators. Perceptive support services professionals will view these changes necessary for a more effective school and a more humane nation. Some holdover lingers from the melting pot mind-set; however, perceptive educators see the need for culturally diverse learners retaining cherished cultural characteristics. The challenges will grow for support services personnel in the 21st century; the personal and professional satisfactions from meeting these challenges will be rewarding in and of themselves.

REFERENCES

Allen, H. A., Splittgerber, F. L. and Manning, M. L. (1993). *Teaching and Learning in the Middle Level School.* Columbus, OH: Merrill.

Allport, G. W. (1979). *The Nature of Prejudice* (25th anniversary edition). Reading, MA: Addison-Wesley.

Allport, G. W. (1954). *The Nature of Prejudice*. Reading, MA: Addison-Wesley.

"America's first . . ., (1989). *Census and You*, 24(3):1.

Armstrong, D. G. (1989). *Developing and Documenting the Curriculum*. Boston: Allyn and Bacon.

Axelson, J. A. (1985). *Counseling and Development in a Multicultural Society*. Monterey, CA: Brooks/Cole.

Banks, J. A. (1988). *Multiethnic Education: Theory and Practice* (2nd ed.). Boston: Allyn and Bacon.

Banks, J. A. (1987). *Teaching Strategies for Ethnic Studies* (4th ed.). Boston: Allyn and Bacon.

Baruth, L. G. and Manning, M. L. (1992). *Multicultural Education of Children and Adolescents*. Boston: Allyn and Bacon.

"Black population is growing . . ." (1988) *Census and You*, 23(6):3−4.

Blough, G. O. and Schwartz, J. (1990). *Elementary School Science and How to Teach It* (8th ed.). Fort Worth: Holt, Rinehart, & Winston.

Cheng, L. L. (1987). "Cross-cultural and linguistic considerations in working with Asian populations," *American Speech and Hearing Association*, 29(6):33−36.

Draguns, J. G. (1989). "Dilemmas and choices in cross-cultural counseling: The universal versus the culturally distinctive," in *Counseling across Cultures* (3rd ed.), P. D. Pedersen, J. G. Draguns, J. Lonner and J. E. Trimble (Eds.), pp. 1−21, Honolulu: University of Hawaii Press.

Dunn, R., Gemake, J., Jalali, F., Zenhausern, R., Quinn, P. and Spiridakis, J. (1990). "Cross-cultural difference in learning styles of elementary-age students from four ethnic backgrounds," *Journal of Multicultural Counseling and Development*, 18:68−93.

Glazer, N. and Moynihan, D. P. (1970). *Beyond the Melting Pot: The Negroes, Puerto Ricans, Jews, Italians, and Irish of New York City* (2nd ed.). Cambridge, MA: The M.I.T. Press.

Jacobs, R. L. (1990). "Learning styles of Black high, average, and low achievers," *The Clearing House*, 63:253−254.

Kitano, H. H. L. (1989). "A model for counseling Asian-Americans," in *Counseling across Cultures*, P. B. Pedersen, J. G. Draguns, W. J. Lonner and J. E. Trimble (Eds.), pp. 139−151, Honolulu: University of Hawaii Press.

Lonner, W. J. and Ibrahim, F. A. (1989). "Assessment in cross-cultural counseling," in *Counseling across Cultures* (3rd ed.), P. B. Pedersen, J. G. Draguns, J. Lonner and J. E. Trimble (Eds.), pp. 299−333, Honolulu: University of Hawaii Press.

Lonner, W. J. and Sundberg, N. D. (1985). "Assessment in cross-cultural counseling and psychotherapy," in *Handbook of Cross-Cultural Counseling and Therapy*, P. D. Pedersen (Ed.) *pp. 173*−179, Westport, CT: Greenwood.

Lum, D. (1986). *Social Work Practice and People of Color: A Process-Stage Approach*. Monterey, CA: Brooks/Cole.

Manning, M. L. (1993). "Cultural and gender differences in young adolescents," *Middle School Journal*, 25(1):13−17.

Manning, M. L. (1991). "More than lipservice to multicultural education," *The Clearing House*, 64:218.

McCormick, L. (1990). "Communication disorders," in *Exceptional Children and Youth*, N. G. Haring and L. McCormick (Eds.), pp. 327−363. Columbus, OH: Merrill.

McCormick, T. (1984). "Multiculturalism: Some principles and issues," *Theory into Practice*, 23:93–97.

More, A. J. (1987). "Native-American learning styles: A review for researchers and teachers," *Journal of American Indian Education*, 27(1):17–29.

Murray, C. B. and Clark, R. M. (1990). "Targets of racism," *The American School Board Journal*, 177(6):22–24.

Nauman, A. K. (1987). "School librarians and cultural pluralism," *The Reading Teacher*, 41(2):201–205.

Oyer, H. J., Crowe, B. and Hass, W. H. (1987). *Speech, Language and Learning Disorders*. Boston: Little, Brown, and Company.

Ponterotto, J. G. (1991). "The nature of prejudice revisited: Implications for counseling intervention," *Journal of Counseling and Development*, 70:216–224.

Purkey, W. W. and Novak, J. M. (1984). *Inviting School Success* (2nd ed.). Belmont, CA: Wadsworth.

Sanders, D. (1987). "Cultural conflicts: An important factor in the academic failures of American Indian students," *Journal of Multicultural Counseling and Development*, 15:81–90.

Shade, B. (1982). "Afro-American cognitive styles: A variable in school success?" *Review of Educational Research*, 52:219–244.

Sleeter, C. E. and Grant, C. A. (1988). Making Choices for *Multicultural Education: Five Approaches to Race, Class, and Gender*. Columbus: Merrill.

Stover, D. (1990). "The new racism," *The American School Journal*, 177(6):14–18.

Swisher, K. and Deyhle, D. (1989). "The styles of learning are different, but the teaching is just the same: Suggestions for teachers of American Indian youth," *Journal of American Indian Education* (Special Issue August):1–11.

U.S. Bureau of the Census. (1992). *Statistical Abstracts of the United States: 1992* (112 ed.). Washington, DC: U.S. Government Printing Office.

U.S. Bureau of the Census. (1991). *1990 Census Profile, Race and Hispanic Origin* (no. 2 June): 1–8.

U.S. Bureau of the Census. (1988). *Current Population Reports, Series P-20, No. 431*. Washington, DC: U.S. Government Printing Office.

U.S. Bureau of the Census. (1986). *Current Population Reports, Series P-25, No. 985. Estimates of the Population of the United States, by Age, Sex, and Race*. 1980–1985. Washington, DC: U.S. Government Printing Office.

Vander Zanden, E. (1989). *Human development* (4th ed.). New York: A. A. Knopf.

CHAPTER 8

Issues and Challenges

OVERVIEW

TWO POINTS REGARDING support services professionals become clear as the 21st century nears. First, support services personnel have made significant strides within the profession and specialty areas, as well as have gained increased professional status among peers and school teams. Second, several issues continue to thread themselves through various support professions, and, similarly, a number of challenges continue to test support services professionals' determination to become integral members of school teams. Why focus on issues and challenges? How do issues and challenges affect support services personnel? Why consider their effects on support services personnel? How will support services professionals and the profession as a whole benefit from working to address issues and challenges? This chapter examines these and other questions and shows how consideration of issues and challenges can lead to a more effective and responsive profession.

ISSUES AND CHALLENGES

It is important to mention at the outset that issues and challenges should not be viewed as obstacles or hurdles causing frustration or dismay. Rather, issues such as rapidly advancing technology and challenges such as defining boundaries of authority can lead to richer professional lives, whereby professionals grow more productive and effective, as well as more confident in their abilities to meet everyday demands and expectations.

Effects on Support Services Professionals

Developing positive perspectives toward issues and challenges, however, should not deny the fact that they continue to have effects on support services professions; stress levels, morale, and determination levels can be affected positively or adversely. A challenge for supports services professionals is to use their empowered status to deal with issues and challenges and to encourage others to seek greater power and control of decisions that directly affect them and their personal and professional lives.

What are the possible effects of the many issues and challenges affecting support services professionals today? Positive effects may include

- feelings of increased empowerment – the power to make professional decisions affecting one's professional life
- beliefs that one has made significant contributions to colleagues and learners in the school
- increased feelings of job security, knowing that their professional roles contribute to overall school efforts
- satisfactions resulting from increased levels of responsibility
- satisfactions resulting from successfully meeting accountability expectations and taking advantage of technological innovations
- enhanced respect of colleagues, administrators, and parents
- positive feelings resulting from increased professionalism and being an active member of a profession helping people

On the other side of the coin, negative effects may include

- feelings of being overwhelmed with changing demands, e.g., technological advances and professional expectations
- increased stress
- lowered morale
- feeling unable to cope with increased accountability demands
- fear of lawsuits resulting from malpractice

While the authors believe the positive effects outweigh the negative, both deserve to be considered. For support professionals to be confident of their roles and expertise, they must work toward collegial relationships, whereby all educators (including administrators and regular classroom teachers) can work for the benefit of other professionals, which will eventually benefit the children and adolescents in the schools.

Using Empowerment to Address Issues and Challenges

Using empowerment to address the issues and challenges includes identifying sources of empowerment and encouraging others to feel empowered. Only when these two points are addressed will support services personnel be able to grow professionally and be able to develop positive perceptions of issues and challenges. This section examines a definition, looks at sources of empowerment, and explains the need to empower others.

The dictionary defines empowerment as giving authority or power to others. How effectively this power is used to produce results determines the efficacy of those empowered. Bennis (1989) indicates that empowerment is the collective effect of leadership, which has four strands. First, empowered people feel like they can make a critical difference, are significant, and have meaning. Second, learning and competence do matter. Leaders value mastery, and mistakes are allowable because they provide knowledge and feedback. Third, empowered people feel a sense of community. Unity, team, and family are evident. Finally, in an empowered environment, work is exciting and challenging. Empowerment by leadership is magnetic, in that it pulls people to a sense of mission and energizes them to act individually in the pursuit of collective goals (Goens and Clover, 1991).

Sources of empowerment include 1) structure, practices, and policies and 2) personal choices that professionals make in their own actions. In essence, empowerment is just as much state of mind as it is authority for decision making. Empowered people feel that (Block, 1988; Goens and Clover, 1991)

- Their survival is in their hands because they take responsibility for their situation and do not blame others.
- They have a sense of purpose, and work means more than making money. They work for things that have meaning for them.
- They are committing themselves to achieving that purpose; they know what they want to do and get it done

Knowing one has increased empowerment should result in feelings of influence over one's personal and professional life. Support services personnel can make decisions or be involved in the decision-making process that affects their daily roles and actions. Likewise, people's belief in themselves and their power to influence professional decisions can add new dimensions: renewed commitments to support services positions, a new sense of professionalism, and a new sense of confidence to meet challenges. Empowerment, however, should not be perceived as "control" over others or a license to impose personal decisions on other professionals in the school; empowerment should be shared with other professionals, both team members and others, and, in fact, others should be helped toward empowerment and toward feelings of being able to influence personal and professional decisions.

Support services personnel can take several steps to empower others:

(*1*) Emphasize site-based management (professional decisions being made at the individual school, rather than the district level) and team processes, whereby professionals play integral roles in making decisions that affect them and their learners.
(*2*) Emphasize a sense of community characterized by collegiality and professionalism.
(*3*) Encourage colleagues to take active roles and actually provide worthwhile and meaningful roles.
(*4*) Promote others' self-concepts and their beliefs in their abilities to make decisions toward significant change.
(*5*) Encourage competence to deal with situations, skills to work toward specific goals, and attitudes appropriate to making positive changes.
(*6*) Encourage other professionals to accept responsibility for their work, to realize the need for self-accountability, and to develop favorable opinions toward external accountability measures.

In summary, empowerment means having the knowledge, skills, and attitudes to meet professional challenges and to influence the conditions under which one works. Empowerment, however, should not result in the control of others, the abuse of power, the running roughshod over colleagues, and treating others unfairly. Professionals feeling empowerment that includes these dimensions will likely have little long-term successes in meeting goals, establishing professionalism, and promoting collegiality. Quite the contrary, encouraging others to feel empowered means helping them to feel a sense of power and ability to make (or significantly influence) decisions affecting their daily lives.

ISSUES

Three issues serving as a thread throughout this text, professionalism, accountability, and technology, will continue and in all likelihood increase in importance as support services personnel move into the 21st century. Indeed, issues result from support services personnel taking more active roles in the profession; from advocates for accountability growing more vocal and gaining power, political and otherwise; and from technology, which continues to expand professionals' horizons by leaps and bounds. This section examines professionalism, accountability, and technology; deliberates on the sometimes uncomfortable nature of change; and also insists that these three phenomena can result in a more effective profession, one that provides support services personnel with increased satisfaction in their work and their interaction with others.

Professionalism

The professionalization movement touched almost all facets of education—curriculum, teaching methodology, training of school service personnel (administrators, counselors, librarians/media specialists, and other specialists), in-service teacher training, teacher organizations, and even school building construction. To understand this professionalization movement, one need only compare pictures of an old one-room country school with a modern school building or contrast a mid-20th century high school curriculum with one from today or compile a list of the teaching materials found in a 1940 school and a similar list for a typical contemporary school (Johnson et al., 1994).

Developing 21st century perspectives toward an increasing complex society and educational enterprise will require support services professionals to commit to professionalism, which includes working collegially with others, acquiring a belief system or code of ethics, committing to help all learners, continuing one's education in an attempt to increase effectiveness, and, generally speaking, modeling professional behavior in all interactions. Undoubtedly, support services professionals have felt a professional obligation to their specialty area; however, no longer working in isolation or waiting to be called upon, support professionals in the 21st century will need to broaden their perspectives by assuming active leadership roles in the schools.

Support services professionals, regardless of specialty areas, have always been bound by a code of ethics. Ethics can be defined as rules of conduct or moral principles.

> When a person becomes a member of a profession, he or she joins a historical community of practice with a telos, a general purpose, that one must be committed to in order to be a professional. In medicine the general purpose is to promote health, and in education it is to promote learning. The clients, in these cases patients or pupils, put their trust in

the professional's honest commitment to the purpose. There is thus built into the form of the practice itself a moral obligation on the part of the practitioners. To breach that obligation is to act unprofessionally. Likewise, in the tradition of a practice like teaching, certain standards of conduct and of manner develop in support of the telos and become recognized as a desirable part of the moral climate of the practice. In the treatment of students, of subject matter, and of colleagues, honesty, truth, and justice become central virtues of the practice. (Soltis, 1986, p. 2)

All professions have a code of ethics, requirements for behavior, and daily practice. Law, medicine, and education, to name a few selected professions, have ethical obligations to the profession, to professional associations, to the people they serve and work with, and to themselves to engage in ethical and moral behavior. It is important to note support services professionals also have obligations to codes of behavior for two professions—their specialty area and the education profession as a whole.

To ensure all ethical guidelines are met, support services personnel need to look to their own professional specialty, i.e., school psychologists and guidance counselors should consult the ethical standards subscribed to by the AACD (American Association for Counseling and Development) and the APA (American Psychological Association).

While many ethical codes are lofty (yet vitally important), more specific guidelines can be suggested for support services professionals' daily work. For example, support services professionals should (Calabrese and Nunn, 1993):

- Prepare thoroughly to meet responsibilities to both other educators and administrators and to learners.
- Treat other professionals and all students fairly, equally, and with dignity.
- Work with parents so students can learn under the most optimal circumstances.
- Seek continuous professional growth.
- Encourage participation of students, other professionals, and parents.
- Accept responsibility for all endeavors being successful to the maximum extent possible.
- Affirm and nurture all learners, as well as professional relationships and interactions.

There are a number of ways to think about professional ethics, depending upon one's position within the profession, individual situations, and areas of specialty. Each way has its merits and its shortcomings (Soltis, 1986). However, one important element stands above all ways of thinking about professional ethics: professionals have an ethical and moral obligation to consider their attitudes and behaviors and to decide whether their ways of thinking and behaving reflect professional organizations' guidelines and proper treatment of learners and other professionals.

Accountability

Accountability, another issue facing support services professionals, will grow more demanding as people and political factions increasingly expect schools to prove their effectiveness. Programs, old and new, must be assessed to determine their educational effectiveness with the results reported to parents, school boards, and the general public.

Accountability has its roots in two fundamental modern problems. One is the continuous escalation of educational costs, and closely related is the loss of faith in educational results. The failure of the American educational system, particularly in the cities and in some remote rural areas, has been accurately documented. The expectations of citizens for their children have not been met. Although American public schools historically have done the best job of any nation in the world in providing education for all the children of all the people, they still have failed for some of their constituents (Johnson et al., 1994).

Just as with all educators, support services professionals will face increasing scrutiny and accountability demands in coming years. The crucial issue is for support services professionals to reconcile themselves to more than one type of accountability. Accountability is also an issue of concern with regular classroom educators; however, some support services personnel experience several sources of accountability. Am I accountable to the principal or to the supervisor representing the specialty area? Where are the boundaries of authority? If the principal and supervisor agree on expectations, accountability responsibilities are made a little easier. Is one accountable to the regular classroom teacher? To other school professionals? To the learners and their parents? Undoubtedly, the list could continue.

Admittedly, the issue of feeling accountable to both school administrators and supervisors or directors of support areas might depend upon the individual school or school system. However, generally speaking, support services professionals are accountable to people they serve, whether learners or teachers. Since schools are a collaborative effort, it is difficult to say a support service professional would be accountable to one individual or group yet not be accountable to another. In reality, all education professionals (as well as professionals in other areas) have multiple accountability expectations.

Rank ordering is difficult and risks negating individual situations; therefore, this discussion of where responsibility lies takes a more random approach, especially since the nature of school efforts involves collaborative efforts focused toward a common goal—helping learners to develop and learn at their maximum potential. The next section proposes that support services personnel are accountable to learners; to classroom educators, administrators, and other support services professionals; and to the profession. While separated for ease and clarity, the need to consider all three as essential to educative attempts should not be forgotten.

Public schools have been created primarily to meet the state's need for an educated citizenry. Indeed, public education is not so much a right accorded to students as an obligation to which they are compelled by law. State goals include 1) socialization to a common culture (education to meet social needs); 2) inculcation of basic democratic values and preparation of students to responsibly exercise their democratic rights and responsibilities (education to meet political needs); and 3) preparation of students for further education, training, and occupational life (education to meet economic needs). To meet these goals, the state further defines what types of socialization are desired, what manner of democratic preparation is to be given, and what forms of preparation — forms useful to the state's economic goals—are to be offered (Darling-Hammond, 1989).

Such a position suggests that support services personnel's bottom-line accountability is to the students they serve. Learners attend school to learn (albeit they are required by state law); the state sets forth goals to be met; and educators are responsible or accountable for making sure students learn and state goals are met. Support services professionals assist in these roles, adding the specialized services that classroom teachers need or that are mandated by law. In any case, the eventual beneficiary of the specialized service is the learner.

Support services professionals' accountability expectations do not stop with learners, although addressing their individual and collective needs is a significant responsibility. Support services professionals are also considered accountable for their actions toward classroom educators, administrators, and service specialists in other areas. Given a particular education situation, an accountability issue is the degree to which a support service professional is accountable, i.e., who is ultimately responsible for students' learning – the classroom educator or the support professional? Where do boundaries of accountability begin and end for each professional?

First, one accountability measure should be the support service professional's effectiveness in assisting in providing complementary, specialized services to classroom educators – for example, the counselor who intervenes to improve a low-achieving youngster's self-concept, the speech correctionist who works with a learner's articulation and fluency disorders, and the hearing specialist who complements instruction through sign language or provides specialized hearing equipment. Assistance should be evaluated on the support professional's knowledge of the respective specialty areas, attitudes toward helping the teacher and the learner, and actual procedural skill in meeting objectives. Another accountability factor should be the support professional's leadership ability – the ability to suggest appropriate directions, to arrange for the help of social service agencies, and the ability to lead others toward collaborative goals.

A second somewhat related goal is to work (perhaps even initiate and establish) effectively in teams. As Chapter 3 explained in considerable detail, perceptive support services professionals can take advantage of teachers, administrators, and other support services professionals' various types and levels of expertise. Likewise, the support professional can offer specialized services to assist in the meeting of team objectives. Either leading the team or working as a team member, effective teamwork requires collegiality; the knowledge, abilities, and skills to decide upon and reach objectives; and the ability to resolve conflicts and disputes. Accountability as related to teams can take two forms. Support leaders can be held accountable for actions and behaviors, and the overall team can be held accountable for its work. The emphasis on collegiality, collaboration, and effective teaming, major thrusts of this book, are all aspects for which support services professionals should be held accountable. As with other abilities demonstrated with individual teachers and teams, support services personnel can also be held accountable for their leadership ability, as well as their ability to teach leadership skills to others.

Staff development represents a third accountability area for support services professionals. Most districts have a staff development specialist who accepts primary responsibility for staff development activities. A support service professional might be the staff development specialist. As restructuring occurs and professional roles evolve to meet 21st century expectations, the staff development specialist might be at the actual school site, rather than the district office. Such an arrangement might result in the staff development professional actually being a support service professional of the school.

Staff development professionals cannot be expected (and their interests and qualifications might not allow) to provide all staff development activities; therefore, support services professionals may be expected to supplement professional development. Several examples come to mind: the speech correctionist may need to share specialized knowledge with teachers whose knowledge is limited to information gained in a survey course; counselors and school psychologists may need to assist teachers and administrators to understand and work with culturally diverse learners; and testing and assessment specialists may need to provide staff development activities in proper test construction. One cannot assume staff development specialists have the time and expertise to meet all educators' expectations. Perceptive support services professionals can supplement and complement staff development efforts, especially in esoteric areas.

Last, as discussed in Chapter 6, support services professionals are accountable to the profession. Such professional accountability includes adhering to ethical and moral codes, treating all learners with respect, maintaining one's effectiveness by additional education and training, treating colleagues in a collegial manner, and having commitment to promote the profession. While these provide only representative examples, they serve to illustrate the point that accountability includes one's allegiance and commitment to the profession as a whole.

Technology

As technological development continues to accelerate, it can either become increasingly difficult for people to understand and use, or it can become "user friendly." It is necessary for all people to understand technology to function effectively in today's society; therefore, technology education needs to be responsive to the demands of society. To accomplish this, the study of technology should be a part of the learning experiences of all students. The mission of technology education is to prepare individuals to comprehend and contribute to a technologically based society (Savage, 1993).

Undoubtedly, technology and technological innovations will continue into the 21st century and well beyond. Support services professionals knowledgeable of recent advances can testify to how technology has contributed to the education of children and adolescents and also to the tremendous possibilities for the future.

As with other educators, support services professionals face a number of technology-related issues such as whether: technology will become more difficult or easier to use, learners' needs for human interaction will take a backseat to technology, technology will be affordable for schools, and technology specialists can convince other school educators to tap into this vast resource.

Admittedly, support services personnel have little control over school districts' financial ability to purchase computers and other technological equipment. A school system either has the financial means and propensity to invest in technology or it does not. Support services professionals, however, can offer significant contributions by building a solid case for what technology can do for educators and learners. Often, administrators must be shown how technology can contribute to the overall school program and, in particular, to learners' academic achievement.

Support services professionals have greater control over other issues. In these situations, support services professionals' success and effectiveness will depend upon their commitment to address issues and to take leadership roles toward making the school day reflect 21st century technology.

First, technology will probably become easier to use as hardware and software developers design products with consumers in mind. However, for educators and students still not understanding how to use technology, the support service professional, perhaps a person especially trained in technology, can provide either one-on-one instruction or staff development programs for groups.

Second, support services professionals can take a major role in recognizing that some learners need individual attention and human interaction. Even with technology's tremendous strides, some learners need a teacher, someone capable of helping, caring, explaining, and encouraging. Support services personnel can help in the identification of these learners, as well as in helping classroom teachers to provide this human interaction.

Third, support services professionals might have to work at the forefront of helping other professionals to understand the "positives" that technology offers. Either slow to change or failing to understand what computers and technology can offer, teachers might not take advantage of technological advances. These teachers need to be identified and trained in how computers and technology can benefit their learners.

What if support services personnel do not understand technology's potential contributions to educators and their learners? In these cases, professionalism and accountability should be a rallying cry for support specialists to educate themselves on technological advances and how these breakthroughs can contribute to the meeting of goals. Being a professional means one keeps up with the latest innovations in his or her profession. Whether knowledge, skills, or attitudes, maintaining one's professionalism requires being prepared to meet changing demands. Likewise, accountability measures could consider professionals' ability and motivation to use technology in their daily schedules. Neither professionalism or accountability in this situation should be considered from a negative perspective. Instead, these two entities should be viewed as a mechanism of growth, a means of becoming more effective and more responsive to the expectations of the profession.

Support services professionals can also promote and use technology as a means of motivating learners and expanding educational opportunities. A powerful motivational tool, technology can capture learners' attention, involve the inattentive, and challenge learners who feel that doing the minimum suffices.

What steps can support services professionals take to help classroom educators use technology most effectively?

(*1*) Provide workshops and seminars addressing specific information (such as word processing, database, spreadsheet, computer art, and Hypercard) that classroom educators have indicated a need for.
(*2*) Emphasize that technology should not replace human interaction.
(*3*) Help design lesson and unit plans using technological advances.
(*4*) Show teachers how technology can reduce clerical time, such as maintenance of student records.
(*5*) Show teachers how technology can provide both remediative and enrichment experiences.
(*6*) Show teachers how visual aids can be motivational and also address specific learning styles.
(*7*) Help teachers learn specific terminology so communication can be clear and effective.

Innovations in previous decades that received considerable publicity has a means to change or improve educational efforts. For example, filmstrip projectors and overhead projectors were touted as innovations with tremendous potential. While these innovations undoubtedly enhanced instruction, they did not radically change educational procedures and did not live up to the expectations of proponents. Technology and technological advances will have a far more dramatic impact on education and the lives of learners. The difference lies in the extent to which computers and technology have engulfed the United States society. Learners see in their daily lives how computers can be used—in supermarkets, department stores, and in many homes. Also, as technology becomes more available, the possibility of declining costs becomes an increasing possibility. Perceptive support services personnel, realizing technology is not a passing fad, work toward the integration of technology in everyday school practice. The degree to which they provide direct services to classroom educators will determine the success of technology in schools, and subsequently, their own effectiveness and contributions to schools.

Issues: Summary

In summary, these three issues—professionalism, accountability, and technology—cannot be neglected or underestimated. The three will continue to influence the personal and professional lives of educators in the 21st century. Change is inevitable and should be met with preparation and a positive attitude. Professionalism among teachers, administrators, and support services personnel will grow stronger; demand for the public getting its money's worth will continue to challenge all educators; and technology will affect both the ''what and why'' of educational efforts. Support services professionals will not be immune from issues and challenges facing other educators, and they can, in fact, be a major force in helping others to develop positive perspectives toward the challenges facing the educational profession.

CHALLENGES

Reform movements and restructuring efforts have resulted in the education profession receiving considerable attention and, in fact, being changed in significant ways—the beginning of professional development schools, site-based management, new levels of professionalism, and proposed national certification, to name a few examples. The one-room schoolhouse has been replaced by a massive education system, whereby support services professionals enjoy heightened professional status and work collaboratively for the education and overall welfare of students. Even with improvements in the education profession and heightened levels of respect for support services personnel, readers should not assume that all challenges have been met. Quite the contrary, support services professionals during the 21st century will have a full agenda — changing mind-sets toward special area personnel, further defining roles in the profession, working toward teams and teaming becoming a reality, and a host of other challenges. Support services professionals' emphasis should focus on continuing the momentum that began in the 1990s and on working toward acceptance as fully participating members of the education team.

Lingering Mind-sets toward Support Services Professionals

While evidence reveals that restructuring and reform efforts are having positive effects, there are undoubtedly educators who hold onto mind-sets of the past: support services personnel should wait for educators to request help; should avoid leadership roles; should take passive roles rather than advocacy; should work alone or with others sharing their specialty rather than working on teams; should "do their own things" instead of collaborating; and, generally speaking, should intervene only when called upon. Such perspectives among educators are a holdover from previous decades of classroom teachers, administrators, and support personnel working in isolation. For example, the speech correctionist might work with a speech-handicapped child several times per week, yet he or she and the language arts teacher do not know what the other's efforts are. Likewise, the guidance counselor might work with a young boy with low self-esteem and at risk of experimenting with drugs, yet the health and physical education specialist might not be aware of the counseling intervention. Such isolated efforts have been the norm in previous years, rather than the exception. Unfortunately, these practices continue in some schools in the 1990s and, unless support services professionals take deliberate steps, might continue into the 21st century.

Realistically speaking, it is unlikely (albeit possible) that perceptions toward specialty areas will change dramatically unless support services professionals take bold and determined moves to make change a reality. Two moves are in order: 1) to prevent regression of thought—in other words, avoid educators regressing to more traditional expectations toward support services professionals—and 2) to continue the impetus toward changing mind-sets toward roles that support services professionals can play in schools. To foster changed perspectives and to avoid mind-sets regressing to more traditional perspectives of support services professionals and their roles, these professionals should do the following:

- Work collaboratively and professionally with individual educators to demonstrate how expertise in specialty areas can contribute to the meeting of goals.
- Work through professional associations to achieve increased status and recognition as integral and functioning team members.
- Keep up with trends, innovations, and research findings in one's professional area.
- Give presentations at professional conferences in one's professional area, as well as for a professional association representing education and educators.
- Support efforts of professional associations, individuals, and political groups to elevate professional status.
- Support the highest moral and ethical standards and codes of behavior.
- Recognize one's expertise, ability, and potential to lead and take an active role in the effort to be recognized by other educators and the general public.
- Insist on representation on school and district committees and task forces to demonstrate willingness to participate in a collegial manner.

Defining Roles—Collaborators, Consultants, and Leaders

Fully functioning support services personnel work in three main roles: collaborators, consultants, and leaders. This separation does not imply that the roles are mutually exclusive nor does the separation suggest that support services professionals cannot work in all three roles at once. Likewise, in team situations, a support service professional might work in all three roles during various stages of the team effort. Last, support services professionals should perceive their roles as being in all three areas and, in fact, as being able to "switch gears" from one role to another, i.e., from a collaborator to an actual leader.

As collaborators, support services personnel will work with other educators to design and implement appropriate educational experiences (e.g., curriculum development, instructional methodology, and education environments), rather than waiting for policy decisions to come from upper echelons of administration.

As the chapter on consultants and leaders indicated, support services professionals will work as consultants, sharing expertise and knowledge in areas of specialty and, generally speaking, working collegially and collaboratively with teams to meet agreed-upon goals. As leaders, support services personnel will actually serve as a team leader or leader in another capacity to lead others toward goals.

The challenge will lie in knowing when to assume each role and the responsibilities associated with each role. Likewise, effective performance of responsibilities in the three areas requires appropriate attitudes, motivation, and commitment to use one's roles to instigate change or to work toward common goals. Support services personnel that feel uncomfortable with consultant, collaborator, and leadership roles can take deliberate steps—workshops, seminars, classes, books, and journals—to gain feelings of competence.

Reaching Maximum Potential—Personal and Professional

Realistically speaking, some educators, support services professionals, and others do not reach their maximum potential. A number of reasons can account for this loss of potential: lack of confidence, other personal and professional interests, work with administrators who expect decisions regarding education policy to be made from the top downward, lack of professional preparation or knowledge of working collaboratively, and a host of other factors. Nearly all educators know other educators who only "do enough to get by," who are burned out, or who, for one reason or another, fail to contribute their maximum to their school or district.

Several factors suggest that support services personnel can reach higher levels of effectiveness. First, they selected the professional specialty, and, therefore, they are stakeholders in the professional area. Second, they had the determination to attain professional preparation in their specialty area, and third, they successfully secured the professional position.

How can support services professionals realize their maximum potential? Such a question is, indeed, difficult, especially since achieving maximum personal and professional potential is an individual entity—one professional may be just more motivated than another, one professional may respond more to intrinsic motivation while another might expect extrinsic rewards, and many other individual situations. With these limitations firmly in mind, several things that contribute to support services personnel reaching their maximum personal and professional potential can be suggested:

- working collaboratively where other team members encourage and challenge other educators to think and achieve maximum potential
- having high expectations of oneself (as well as others), rather than accepting mediocrity or lackadaisical performance
- avoiding burnout and boredom through varied activities and assignments
- having collaborative meetings and social get-togethers where collegiality is encouraged
- taking "refresher" courses, seminars, and workshops to increase interest in one's professional area
- having an administrative structure that rewards and encourages, rather than punishes and chastises

As previously stated, reaching maximum personal and professional potential is an individual situation, one which depends upon many factors. Many factors and conditions can be changed; those that cannot be changed need to be "worked around" or addressed in the most effective manner. To be candid, while education can be rewarded, it can also be frustrating—bureaucratic administrative structures, uncooperative team members, and children and adolescents who do not respond to educational experiences and efforts. The effects of these frustrations, while undoubtedly taking a toll, should be minimized whenever possible. It is hoped that the 21st century will bring new theories of motivation, as well as professionally designed workshops, seminars, and other means of helping support services professionals to reach their maximum personal and professional potential.

Making the Team Concept a Reality

Chapter 3 explained teams and the teaming concept in considerable detail. Therefore, this section will look only at the challenge of making the team concept a reality.

Sustaining (and in some cases, actually beginning the teaming process) can present support services professionals with a challenging endeavor. Change often comes slowly, and some professionals, like all people, have a tendency to regress to previous ways and habits. Professional educators have worked in isolation for many decades, others may feel uncomfortable working in teams or feel more effective working alone. Such conditions challenge support services professionals to work toward an effective teaming process.

Perceptive support services professionals realize that effective implementation of the team concept will take continuous efforts. One cannot assume that a successful team effort in one situation will result in success in another situation (or even be tried in another situation). Support services professionals can take several steps to increase the chances of teaming becoming a reality:

- Promote the team concept as a viable means of reaching collaboratively agreed goals.
- Demonstrate effective teaming behaviors in all committee meetings and other deliberations.
- Work to eliminate or reduce the effects of conditions creating obstacles to effective teaming.
- Watch for tendencies toward regression, whereby educators work effectively in teams on one occasion yet return to isolationist or singular efforts in others.

Several advantages suggest support services professionals should promote team efforts whenever possible: enhanced collegiality, increased collaboration, renewed benefits from capitalizing on a number of expertises, and a number of other positives. As educational decisions grow more complex in the 21st century, the need for a team effort will grow more important. Making these potential advantages a reality, however, will require deliberate effort. Support services professionals can play valuable roles in the effort to making teaming a reality.

Responding to Societal Conditions and Changes

Few would doubt that our society is experiencing a number of changes, all of which have the potential for affecting educational practices. Undoubtedly, societal changes have always affected education and have resulted in educators changing both the curricular emphases and instructional practices. Because of their specialized training, support services professionals might particularly help classroom educators and administrators design and implement educational responses to societal changes.

Several societal conditions and changes affect education and challenge educators to provide appropriate responses: increased accountability from the general public (and from within the profession), increased expectations for schools to address more than educational needs, problems associated with urban living, changing familial structures, increasing multiculturalism, more violence, increased substance use and abuse, and increasing poverty. While support services professionals cannot be expected to solve all problems or to provide educational practices to reflect all societal changes, support services professionals do work in a prime position to initiate efforts, to complement others' efforts, and to encourage team efforts toward addressing changes.

Realistically speaking, some readers may feel that the magnitude of societal problems prevent support services professionals from having a dramatic impact. Increasing violence, widescale poverty, and substance abuse—what can support services professionals do to curb violence, help the poor, or lessen the drug problem? Admittedly, these are severe problems—out of the control of one person or group. However, these problems will continue to affect the nation and its schools in the 21st century. Support services professionals can take action at least in their own schools and neighborhoods. Working with other educators in the school, support services professionals can take several general directions:

(*1*) Bring societal conditions and their efforts, e.g., the consequences of poverty on learners, to the attention of others.

(*2*) Organize groups within the school designed to address problems, e.g., support groups for learners with changing family structures.

(*3*) Organize efforts against violence in the schools, e.g., efforts to end gang violence.

(*4*) Work with local and regional groups to offer a response to societal changes, e.g., Children's Defense Fund and the National Urban League.

(*5*) Work with individuals experiencing poverty and engaging in dangerous behaviors, e.g., drugs.

(*6*) Commit to be an advocate for learners affected by societal changes and act to lessen the negative effects of changes on learners' learning and overall welfare.

How can support services professionals specifically change schools and educational practices to assist other educators to formulate responses to societal conditions and changes?

- Provide curricular experiences and materials that help learners deal with a changing society, e.g., technological changes,

enhanced and accepting perspectives of cultural diversity, and general education experiences that prepare learners for lifelong learning and employment.
- Provide instructional groups representative of our changing population demographics, e.g., using cooperative learning groups, rather than homogeneous ability groups.
- Provide discussion groups and counseling sessions (individual, small-group, and large-group), which deal with issues of concerns such as drug addiction and changing family structures.
- Work with linguistically different learners to improve their English proficiency while maintaining respect for their native language; likewise, help other educators in efforts to teach learners whose native language is other than English.
- Provide curricular experiences and instructional methods that reflect respect and understanding of cultural and gender differences.

While these suggestions provide only representative examples, perceptive support services professionals can think of other ways to assist both learners and other educators. In summary, efforts must include recognizing how societal changes affect learners and planning appropriate responses (and help others to plan responses in team situations). A commitment to lead a school response to address societal changes can reap such dividends, especially when efforts are carefully planned to address specific changes.

Responding to Reforms and the Reform Movement

Educators during the last decade of the 21st century experienced substantial pressure to restructure an education system, thought by many to be outdated and inefficient. Proposed changes include decisions regarding educational practice being made at the school level rather than the district level; the implementation of Professional Development Schools so that, among other things, prospective teachers could be trained with the assistance of practicing educators; increased accountability measures or, in this case, the profession holding itself accountable; changing the way schools are financed; and the implementation of a national certification system to enhance the status of the teaching profession. While criticizing and proposing drastic changes to the education profession is nothing new, the impetus to reform and restructure schools took hold during the late 1980s and early 1990s and did, indeed, result in a call for change.

Support services personnel have been affected in at least two ways: first, their roles evolved and became more clearly defined as administrators and classroom educators changed perceptions of support area specialists, and second, many support services professionals joined the reform and restructuring effort. The challenge, however, will continue into the future, especially if the quick results expected by reformers do not materialize as soon as expected. As stated before, educational systems are slow to change, and changing centuries of tradition will be a difficult task. This is not to imply that education reform should not be tackled; however, it does mean educators of all levels and specialties must work collegially and collaboratively to bring about needed changes.

The efforts of support services personnel in these reform efforts will be much needed. Support services personnel have several strengths that can prove valuable to sustaining the movement to change educational practices and, more specifically, the education profession. These strengths include: the ability to see the reform movement and educational efforts as a whole; special leadership skills and knowledge of teaming processes; opportunities to work with and between administrators and classroom educators; and the training and expertise to address important concerns such as accountability, technology, and professionalism. Likewise, support services professionals can play active roles in decision-making processes at the school level, can offer significant expertise and experience in the professional training of other support specialists, can work toward a system of national certification for support services professionals, and can offer help in designing and implementing accountability measures. In other words, perceptive support services professionals will not wait for outside agencies to impose changes. These professionals will be challenged to play major roles in the changes affecting them and the profession as a whole and will, in fact, be part of the change process.

Making Potential Support Roles a Reality

Many possibilities exist for new support services roles, depending upon a school district's commitment, visions of how learners' needs can be met, and financial resources. This text has suggested continuing traditional support areas such as school psychologists, guidance counselors, speech correctionists, media specialists, and specialists for the hearing impaired. However, this text has also proposed other possibilities such as home-schooling specialists, testing and assessment specialists, curriculum designers, media producers, technology specialists, and specialists trained to address cultural and gender differences. These possibilities provide only representative examples. Types of specialists trained and employed to address the individual needs of learners are limited only by the district's imagination and the mind-sets toward roles of schools.

These proposed specialist roles, however, will not become reality without deliberate work, conscientious planning, careful attention being given to financial concerns, and determination to change outdated mind-sets toward education and educators' roles. Support services professionals can play instrumental roles in this effort—proposing new specialist roles to classroom educators, school administrators, and district-level administrators. Simply proposing new professional roles, while exciting and promising, will not suffice. Professionals making decisions and financial planners must be shown how these new support roles will contribute to educational efforts—how learners will be helped, how achievement scores will rise, how the positions will be cost-effective, how services will not be duplicated, how the roles will complement others' efforts, how the professionals will fare within the state's certification system, how positions can be financed, and how these professionals will be held accountable. In other words, even the most farsighted and wealthy districts will not buy into the concept of additional support services professionals unless they can see a need, can understand the person's role, and see the financial advantage and educational worth of employing such professionals.

The challenge will be for support services professionals to be able to provide a sound rationale based upon student need and public expectation. While this challenge will be difficult, especially if economic forecasts are less than bright, one hope remains: educators and the education process must change with society and public expectations. An educational system effective in the 21st century cannot be representative of 19th century rural America or the post-industrial state of the 20th century. In other words, the education system needs to take a stand toward positive and planned change and must be at the forefront of change, rather than reacting to change.

Support services professionals' efforts in making potential support roles a reality need to be soundly based in several tenets:

- sound rationales for the proposed roles
- specific role descriptions and responsibilities
- accountability measures
- cost-effectiveness

The challenge of new support roles will not be easy; however, the benefits will be worth the effort. The profession will be better meeting its responsibilities; more learners will be served; more specialized services will become the norm, rather than the exception; and, at least the authors hope, public opinions of the nation's school systems will improve. It goes without saying that these are lofty and perhaps idealistic goals, but the changes and demands of the 21st century will take a significant toll on school systems that do not offer an adequate response. Schools' tasks might be less difficult and the rewards greater if educators make the choice to lead rather than follow — this is an ideal time for support services professionals to lead administrators and classroom educators into the 21st century.

SUMMARY

As with all educators and administrators, support services professionals will face a number of issues and challenges during the 21st century. Enhanced professionalism, increased accountability, and rapid technological innovations will both challenge support services professionals and assist them in changing roles. These professionals will be in a prime position to meet these and the various other issues and challenges: they are better educated, the reform movement has empowered them to make decisions affecting their professional lives, many have leadership ability and an understanding of team processes, and the time is ripe for significant and positive changes. However, it is important that these changes not be met with 19th or 20th century perspectives. Support services professionals cannot make decisions based upon "what was" or, in some cases, "what is" — considerable foresight will be needed to perceive future learner needs, possible school roles, and "what can be." It will also be important for support services professionals to be visionary to a degree that they can envision future demands and possibilities. Most issues and challenges can be addressed by support services professionals with professional preparation and commitment. Tackling issues and challenges will not be an easy task, yet significant benefits can accrue: learner needs being better met and professionals experiencing higher degrees of satisfaction in their efforts.

REFERENCES

Axelson, J. A. (1985). *Counseling and Development in a Multicultural Society*. Monterey, CA: Brooks/Cole.

Bennis, P. (1989). *Why Leaders Can't Lead*. San Francisco: Jossey-Bass.

Block, P. (1988). *The Empowered Manager*. San Francisco: Jossey-Bass.

Calabrese, R. L. and Dunn, G. (1993). "A teacher code of ethics: Defining what students can expect," *NASSP Bulletin*, 77(551):50–56.

Darling-Hammond, L. (1989). "Accountability for professional practice," *Teachers College Record*, 91:59–80.

Goens, G. A. and Clover, S. I. R. (1991). *Mastering School Reform*. Boston: Allyn and Bacon.

Johnson, J. A., Dupuis, V. L., Musial, D. and Hall, G. E. (1994). *Introduction to the Foundations of American Education* (9th ed.). Boston: Allyn and Bacon.

Savage, R. (1993). "Technology education: Meeting the needs of a complex society," *NASSP Bulletin*, 77(554):41–53.

Soltis, J. F. (1986). "Teaching professional ethics," *Journal of Teacher Education*, 37:1–5.

CHAPTER 9

The Future of Support Services Personnel

OVERVIEW

SEVERAL EVENTS INDICATE a promising future for support services professionals: the reform and restructuring effort currently embracing all levels of education; a sense of renewal resulting from professionals feeling empowered to determine professional agendas; and other indicators such as increased collegiality, collaboration, and professionalism. For this promising future to become a reality, support services professionals will need to take proactive efforts to promote their specialty areas, as well as the education profession as a whole. This final chapter looks at how the reform and restructuring movements might affect support services professionals and also examines several indicators suggesting a bright future.

THE REFORM/RESTRUCTURING MOVEMENT—
IMPETUS AND OPPORTUNITIES FOR SUPPORT
SERVICES PROFESSIONALS

The reform and restructuring movements have different meanings for different people and range from selecting curricular materials to educating teachers and support services professionals in school settings (i.e., Professional Development Schools), rather than the traditional teacher education institution. The many articles appearing in the 1990s document this belief: Goodlad (1990) suggests changing teacher education; Watts and Castle (1993) feel solving school's time dilemmas is necessary for school restructuring; Donahoe (1993) adds changing the school culture to the list; Canady and Rettig (1993) suggest unlocking school schedules; and Tye (1992) argues that educators must move beyond restructuring rhetoric to more substantial changes.

Emphasis on Changing Schools and the Status Quo

Regardless of the advocate for educational reform, change is a key ingredient. Schools' roles accepted for centuries must change; mind-sets toward learners must change; and decision-making processes must change. In other words, the status quo (which admittedly has worked for many students) has not worked for many low achievers, dropouts, learners with their self-esteems destroyed, and many others. While some question (Tye, 1992) whether restructuring efforts will have a dramatic impact, it does appear that the scrutiny being focused on schools and educators will have a positive effect. Questioning long-held assumptions and traditions can have positive effects — both the consideration process and the actual change (if, indeed, change actually occurs).

Examining Expectations and Assumptions of Schools and Professionals

As previously suggested, long-held expectations and assumptions about schools and professionals need to be examined. Why does our nation have so many low achievers? Why do dropout rates remain too high? Why are many teachers less able academically and unable to teach? Why are educational decisions affecting the future of learners and professionals' everyday actions made at higher levels of administration? Why do we have school from September to June rather than all year? Why do learners attend school only five days a week and then do not stay all day? This list of questions is endless. Some questions may have sound and logical answers; however, some may not have even undergone intense consideration.

The reform and restructuring movement, while varying significantly in emphases, calls for a consideration of these questions and almost everything educators do. What benefits or changes can support services professionals (as well as other educators and the general public) expect as a result of these movements? Again, the list could be endless, depending on schools' and educators' efforts at genuine reform; however, some benefits might include

- professionals making decisions affecting their lives and daily school routines
- support services personnel experiencing enhanced professional status

- curricula aligned throughout a state for increased consistency
- parents and educators jointly and collaboratively selecting curricular materials and instructional methods
- educators trained (at least to some extent) by practicing educators
- closer contact and collaboration between communities and schools
- less bureaucracy in individual schools and school systems
- increased collaboration between and among classroom educators, administrators, and support services professionals

While other changes or benefits could undoubtedly be predicted, it is safe to suggest that support services professionals will experience increased respect as they assume more integral roles. Likewise, as will be addressed in more detail in a later section, the increased collegiality, collaboration, and professionalism resulting from working together will also lead to more productive personal and professional lives.

Renewal—Toward New Roles and Goals

The benefits or changes mentioned in the previous section will, in all likelihood, lead to a sense of renewal—a sense of increased enthusiasm and of being a renewed professional ready and capable of meeting new roles, goals, and challenges. This sense of renewal could take various forms: a willingness to accept new levels of responsibility; a desire to further one's graduate work to be better prepared for professional roles; a new sense of confidence allowing an ambitious agenda to make significant changes; an increased willingness to work collaboratively with other team members; and a tendency to "try new things"—innovations once thought too difficult, too time-consuming, or unworthy of trying.

Empowerment—Making Professional Decisions

One of the major benefits of the reform and restructuring movement will be teacher and support services professional participation in educational operations, commonly called teacher empowerment. There is a growing belief that educators conducting the day-to-day operation of schools should assume greater responsibility for school programs.

Educators, both classroom teachers and support services professionals, should be expected to prepare educational environments that are consistent with the community's educational goals. Likewise, this empowerment should not be restricted or bound by state regulations that prohibit flexibility and one's ability to make professional decisions (Johnson et al., 1994).

Empowerment might lead teachers and support services professionals to make specific educational decisions such as

- helping to design curricular experiences
- designing in-service and staff development programs
- influencing school budgets
- selecting new team members
- selecting materials, other resources, and equipment
- making plans for community involvement activities
- setting goals (both short-term and long-term) for school practices

One might question how an emphasis on change, examining long-held expectations, gaining a sense of renewal, and feeling empowered can contribute to effectiveness, positive feelings about one's specialization area, and, generally speaking, new feelings of wanting to be a fully capable professional. The answer is severalfold: First, support services professionals will feel their opinions and professional expertise are considered and respected. Rather than professionals receiving "orders" from administrators who perhaps have not taught for years, these professionals now have the ability and opportunity to assume active decision-making roles. Second, a look at educational history suggests that education has always been examined, and, often a hotly debated subject, the reform and restructuring movement is a genuine and comprehensive effort to study education and probably the first movement to allow frontline educators to take genuine participatory roles. Third, people who feel they are active stakeholders are more willing to "go the extra mile" and to work for the benefit of learners, as well as other members of the education team and school.

INDICATORS OF A BRIGHT FUTURE

Several indicators suggest support services professionals face a bright future – a future providing job security, job satisfaction, intrinsic and extrinsic rewards, and the self-satisfaction usually associated with a profession. In all fairness, however, support services professionals' future will depend upon several factors, some of which they can influence and others they cannot. Influencing factors include the economy, the success or continuance of the reform and restructuring movements, their determination to become integral members of team efforts, administrators' willingness to share power and decision-making opportunities, and all educators' mind-sets toward roles that support services personnel can play.

Indicators suggesting a bright or promising future for support services professionals include:

- improved/more relevant professional preparation
- career incentives — promotions and reward systems
- recognition as team members
- increased collegiality and collaboration
- consultant and leadership roles
- site-based management
- business/foundation involvement
- increased professionalism
- accountability opening new opportunities
- technological advances adding to productivity

Thoughtful readers can undoubtedly think of other indicators — those signs suggesting that support services professionals will enjoy productive careers where professionalism, respect, collegiality, and collaboration are considered essential to schools and the people giving their best to learners and colleagues.

Professional Preparation Reflecting 21st Century Expectations

Recent changes in the education and training of support services personnel, as well as other educators, suggest that these personnel (whether counselors, school psychologists, speech correctionists, vocational specialists, or one of the other specializations) can take considerable pride in their professional preparation. Several impetuses have focused toward improving support services personnel's professional preparation: the reform and restructuring movements, recent redesigns of NCATE, stricter NASDTEC standards, and guidelines established by professional specialty organizations such as ASHA and CACREP. This professional preparation includes general education courses, professional education courses, and field experiences; these carefully planned and coordinated components can provide support services professionals with the knowledge, skills, and attitudes to tackle the challenges of the 21st century.

Contemporary trends provide for support services professionals using the three previously mentioned components. These trends indicate general education providing a strong liberal arts foundation; professional education including courses collaboratively agreed-upon with practicing educators in the school systems; and field experiences that are earlier, longer, and more directed and supervised than in early decades.

Professional preparation programs also include efforts to focus on 21st century problems and challenges commonly associated with

- urban and rural schools
- increasingly multicultural populations
- poverty
- drug use and abuse
- violence
- changing family structures

To address these problems and concerns with which support services professionals must deal, professional preparation programs emphasize knowledge of problems, appropriate attitudes, and skills to provide appropriate action. While means of preparing support services professionals and other educators vary, common threads emphasize teamwork, collaboration, and collegiality as essentials.

Support Services Professionals Being Considered Team Members

The benefits of working in teams have been discussed elsewhere in this text; therefore, this section will emphasize only how support services professionals working with team members is an "indicator" of a bright future. In a profession where working in isolation has all too often been the rule rather than the exception, the prospect of support services professionals engaging in team efforts with other support professionals and educators offers exciting possibilities: the personal and professional satisfaction of working collegially with others, the increased "brainpower" of a number of professionals working collaboratively, the benefits of professionals bringing areas of expertise to problem-solving situations, and professionals feeling empowered by their ability and opportunity to participate in joint decision making. Even considering the problems commonly associated with teams such as interpersonal conflicts and scheduling difficulties, effective teamwork at the school level has proven to be beneficial for both professionals and learners. Likewise, professionals working in teams is compatible with the reform and restructuring movements and the research focusing on components of effective schools.

Recognition of the Value of Collegiality

Sometimes educators, especially those accustomed to working alone, contemplate privateness in their efforts. "I would rather do it alone," or "The regular classroom educator does not understand the support service area and the many obstacles we face," one may hear support services professionals say. While one's defense of working alone may sound reasonable, there is much to be gained from collegiality, both for educators and their students. Even the most energetic and dedicated work by individual educators will not be sufficient to meet the many goals the educational system faces. Only cohesive teams of teachers, working efficiently on well-organized projects will get the job done (Clark and Cutler, 1990).

Collegiality among educators actually has the potential for changing a school's culture. Faculty members talk about practice; observe one another's work; plan, design, research, and evaluate efforts cooperatively; and instruct one another in what they know about teaching, learning, and leading (Barth, 1990; Krovetz and Cohick, 1993).

Schools benefit in at least three ways when collegial ties are maintained among educators. First, collegiality greatly facilitates the daily work of teaching and providing services. Teachers, support services professionals, and administrators function smoothly and effectively conducting the daily business of education. Second, schools that foster professional collegiality can attempt educational innovations that would exhaust a single teacher. Third, new teachers coming into a cohesive organization are given systematic assistance and are acculturated with ease and minimal shock (Clark and Cutler, 1990).

Consultant and Leadership Roles

Another bright indication is the consultant and leadership roles that support services professionals are increasingly asked to play. Once called upon only when needed, which was, in some cases, rarely or never, support services personnel now play more integral and vital roles. Educators, especially those taking advantage of team efforts, increasingly recognize support services professionals' consultant and leadership roles.

Serving in consultant roles, support services professionals can offer advice and share expertise in specialized areas, but as consistently emphasized, these professionals need to take proactive stances. Regular classroom teachers and administrators might not know the various services that support professionals can provide or might think the support professional has a "full agenda" and, thus, be reluctant to ask. Therefore, effective support services professionals take active roles to provide services to classroom educators and administrators, as well as other support services professionals.

Support services professionals are increasingly being called upon to assume leadership roles—to lead others toward school goals. While leadership opportunities vary from school to school, support services professionals may assume leadership positions in three broad areas (Leithwood, 1992):

(*1*) Helping staff members develop and maintain a collaborative, professional school culture
(*2*) Fostering teacher development
(*3*) Helping teachers solve problems more effectively

For leadership to continue to be an indicator of a bright future, effective leaders demonstrate specific behaviors such as (Leithwood, 1992)

- assisting group discussions of alternative solutions
- ensuring open communication
- avoiding commitment to preconceived solutions
- listening to different views and clarifying information at key points during meetings
- keeping groups on task
- avoiding narrowly biased perspectives
- changing own views when warranted
- sharing genuine beliefs that other groups or team members could develop better solutions than one working alone

To be effective consultants and leaders, support service professionals need to take on proactive stances to serve and lead other educators.

Twenty-first century perspectives will see support services personnel as active and vibrant professionals with the leadership and consultant ability to instigate significant and positive change.

Career Paths

In the past, educators, including support services professionals, worked in the same position for many years, perhaps for all their professional careers. A classroom teacher or a speech correctionist might serve in the same capacity for twenty or more years. The only way to improve one's salary or professional status was to move into administration or seek an advanced degree. Other professions offer a more defined and professional (and financial) career path, whereby people could move from an entry-level position through a series of stages to a higher-level position requiring more competency and responsibility.

There are some indications that the profession is recognizing the dilemma faced by educators. Often termed career paths or ladders, this concept provides educators with a number of rungs, or job roles, that carry increasing responsibility and performance of more complex tasks (Johnson et al., 1994).

Career plan models for teachers have been proposed in a number of states. In these models, there are more steps and levels of advancement for educators. With each level comes increased salary, increased roles and responsibilities, and more complex tasks (Johnson et al., 1994).

It is feasible to suggest that the restructuring and reform movements will cause educators to consider traditional and futuristic perspectives of career paths for support services professionals. A support professional, perhaps a specialist for gifted education, bilingual education, or compensatory education, may be classified at a certain level such as assistant or beginning professional and then progress to a master support professional. The ranks or levels might be determined by years in service, certifications, or competencies. The career path concept is an area where support services professionals can offer significant leadership in the development of a plan for providing career options or goals. Many options exist for career paths, and many vary with specialization area and even from state to state; however, one point is fairly clear — since the restructuring and reform movements are focusing on educational practices, this is an ideal time to consider ways to make the support services areas more exciting, rewarding, and professionally attractive.

Decisions Regarding Learners and Professionals Being Reached at School—School-Based Management

School-based management or site-based decision making permits individual schools within a school district to be involved in decision making that deals with educational operations, for example, budgeting, personnel, and instruction. The decision-making authority is granted to the schools by local boards of education. The concept came about, in part, through educational reform recommendations for greater participation of teachers in governance at the local school levels. Parents' demands to have more say in the education of their children were also a factor in promoting school-based management. Two objectives of school-based management are to reduce school district regulatory control of individual schools and to empower teachers with the opportunity to participate in making decisions for their schools.

School-based management is based on two fundamental beliefs: Those who are most affected by decisions ought to play a significant role in making those decisions, and educational reform efforts will be most effective and long-lasting when carried out by people who feel a sense of ownership and responsibility for the process (Johnson et al., 1994).

Advantages of school-based management include (Johnson et al., 1994)

- formally recognizing the expertise and competence of those who work in individual schools to make decisions and to improve learning
- giving teachers, other staff members, and the community increased input into decisions
- improving morale of teachers, because staff members see they can have an immediate impact on their environment
- shifting the emphasis in staff development—teachers are more directly involved in determining what they need
- focusing accountability for decisions
- bringing both financial and instructional resources in line with the instructional goals developed in each school
- helping to provide better services and programs to students
- nurturing and stimulating new leaders at all levels
- increasing both the quantity and the quality of communication, which is more likely to be informal—in face-to-face meetings, for example

School- or site-based management has the potential for helping all educators, including support services professionals. For many years, professional decisions were reached at the district or state level without the input of those professionals affected by the decisions. The situation for support services professionals was sometimes worse. Because they were not always considered a part of the school, decisions actually reached at schools often did not reflect their concerns or needs. This effort to involve all professionals at the individual schools can include the support services, as well as other educators. Support services professionals, regardless of specialty area, are urged to understand the concept of school-based management and take a powerful advocacy role to promote all school professionals being involved in the decision-making process.

Business Involvement in Schools

Another increasingly important set of school partnerships are those developing between businesses and schools. In the past, more of a one-way perspective existed in the relationships between businesses and schools. There were various types of "adopt-a-school" programs, where business would send often obsolete equipment and other types of resources to the schools. In many ways these programs treated schools as some sort of underprivileged client that businesses could assist; however, that simplistic one-way perspective has changed dramatically in the 1990s. Now, there truly are reciprocal partnerships between businesses and schools. It is being recognized increasingly by the business community that not only do they have things to offer schools, but also schools have many types of resources to offer to the business community in return. One of the expanding steps in the ongoing dialogue between businesses and schools has been the number of chief executive officers who have continued to express their interest in and support for schools, and they have invested in changing schools (Johnson et al., 1994).

How might business involvement affect the personal and professional lives of support services professionals? First, it is reasonable to suggest a support specialist who will solicit involvement and financial commitments from businesses and communities. Similar to a grants specialist at many colleges and universities, this support professional would seek business, community, and foundation support. Expertises would include grant writing and identifying sources for the various learning areas and specialization areas. One's knowledge might include sources of financial aid for at-risk learners, handicapped children and adolescents, and multicultural education programs. Actual work may also include helping counselors obtain funds to support sessions and experiences for learners from one-parent homes or to help learning specialists to purchase equipment. Second, support services professionals can benefit from financial contributions (monetary or equipment) or from employees donating their time and effort. Third, businesses might be able to fund sessions or workshops providing individuals or groups with specialized training. Last, all educators benefit when businesses take an interest in schools and have confidence in what educators do. Positive relationships can accrue when businesses and educators work toward common goals. Both see the benefits brought to communities by effective schools. Likewise, schools need financial (and other) assistance from businesses, and vice versa; businesses see the advantage of an educated populace. Even if the school as a whole does not solicit business support, perceptive support services personnel see the benefits of seeking their commitment to help the support area.

Professionalism Contributing to Learners and Professionals

Professionalism, another indicator of a bright future for support services professionals, has been addressed in this text. This brief look at professionalism will look only at how professionalism can contribute to a brighter future for educators and, especially, professionals in the support areas.

This assertion that positive benefits accrue from increased professionalism results from several beliefs. First, professionalism includes a number of aspects—a respect for one's role (and others' roles), increased status, enjoyment of collegiality and collaboration, and the satisfaction of working toward goals being met—that will probably play more significant roles in the 21st century. Second, professionalism is growing in the 1990s and will likely continue into the 21st century. The restructuring and reform movements, specialists with better professional preparation, educators realizing the value of working together toward goals—all these indicate that educators are seeing the value of engaging in professional behavior. Third, professionalism can be evidenced in relationships between regular classroom educators and support services professionals. Fourth, law and medicine have been considered professions for many years—high levels of training, proven competence, and commitments to high ideals have contributed to the professionalism of both. Educators, increasingly better educated and committed to collaboration among professionals, can enjoy similar levels of professionalism and the accompanying benefits.

Accountability Opening New Opportunities

For many decades, accountability had a negative connotation. A professional being held accountable often meant they were subject to dismissal or legal action. While it is true that all professionals are subject to the consequences of not performing a role at a specified level of competence, accountability does have a positive side and, in fact, can be considered an indication for a bright future.

Accountability has several positive aspects, which actually contribute to the professional and personal lives of support services specialists. Through accountability, professionals can 1) show their accomplishments toward specific goals, 2) justify their "worth" and the need for additional specialists, 3) feel a sense of accomplishment, and 4) provide a rationale for expenditures such as programs or materials.

Technological Advances Adding to Effectiveness

Considering the extraordinary technological advances already contributing to educators' effectiveness, one could reasonably predict tremendous breakthroughs in the 21st century. These advances contribute to the bright future for support services professionals. First, technology can contribute to support services professionals' daily routines such as recordkeeping, scheduling, and communicating with other educators. Time can be saved and practices made more efficient. Second, technology can contribute to learners' academic progress and overall development. A more accurate diagnosis can be made; programs can be individualized according to a learner's individual needs; and resources can be retrieved that otherwise would not have been available.

Support services professionals perceive technology as an aid, contributing to their efficiency. Technological aids may include hardware and software, instructional television, microteaching, dial-access systems, videodisks, computers, simulation, and mainframes, to name a few examples.

A prerequisite for effective use of technology is support services professionals having positive attitudes toward technological advances and the potential they bring to schools and learning situations. For technology to contribute to a bright future, professionals must perceive technological advances as a beneficial tool, rather than as a threat. Professionals feeling uncomfortable with the technological advances should take deliberate steps to learn more about these innovative tools and how technology contributes to both learners and educators.

SUMMARY

Support services professionals will undoubtedly face challenges in the 21st century: continuing to etch out their place in the educational team, changes resulting from the restructuring and reform movements, difficulties associated with assuming advocacy roles, trials resulting from taking leadership roles, and efforts to maintain professionalism in all behaviors and attitudes. While these challenges may sound like warnings or hurdles for the next century, they can actually be personally and professionally rewarding. Also, the restructuring and reform movements currently focus on positive change, renewal of professional commitments, and gaining a sense of empowerment. These impetuses and opportunities, along with other indicators, suggest a promising future for support services professionals, as well as other educators. Of course, actual futures will depend, to some extent, on the attitudes, professional preparation, and commitments that support services professionals bring to situations. However, as we enter the late 1990s and early 21st century, indications suggest support professionals are professionally prepared, committed, and empowered to act as advocates for improved support specializations, as well as the education profession as a whole.

REFERENCES

Barth, R. S. (1990). "A personal vision of a good school," *Phi Delta Kappan*, 71:512–516.

Canady, R. L. and Rettig, M. D. (1993). "Unlocking the lockstep high school schedule," *Phi Delta Kappan*, 75:310–314.

Clark, D. C. and Cutler, B. R. (1990). *Teaching: An introduction*. New York: Harcourt Brace Jovanovich.

Donahoe, T. (1993). "Finding the way: Structure, time, and culture in school improvement," *Phi Delta Kappan*, 75:298–305.

Goodlad, J. I. (1990). *Teachers for Our Nation's Schools.* San Francisco, CA: Jossey-Bass.
Johnson, J. A., Dupuis, V. L., Musial, D. and Hall, G. E. (1994). *Introduction to the Foundation of American Education* (9th ed.). Boston: Allyn and Bacon.
Krovetz, M. and Cohick, D. (1993). "Professional collegiality can lead to school change," *Phi Delta Kappan,* 75:331–333.
Leithwood, K.A. (1992). "Transformational leadership: Where does it stand? Educational Leadership", 49:8–12.
Tye, K.A. (1992). "Restructuring our schools: Beyond the rhetoric," *Phi Delta Kappan,* 74:8–14.
Watts, G. D. and Castle, S. (1993). "The time dilemma in school restructuring," *Phi Delta Kappan,* 75:306–310.

INDEX

Accountability, 24, 27–29, 51–53, 80, 88, 89, 113, 131–142, 173–176, 210–211, 221–224, 251
  evaluation, 82–85, 132
  methods of assessment, 52
  staff development, 223–224
Accountability specialist, 14–15
  accreditation reports, 15
  documentation, 15
  goals, 15
  summaries of data, 15
Accreditation/certification specialist, 60–61
Administrative support, 80, 95
Adult education specialist, 20–21, 141–142
  competencies, 141
  evaluation, 21
  legal aspects, 21
Advocacy agents, 93–114
Advocacy roles, 93–114
  assurer of legal rights, 97–98
  cultural and gender differences, 108
  equal access advocate, 100–102
  future, 108–114
  leaders, 103–104
  learner differences, 105–108
  learning styles, 107–108
  outreach coordinator, 102–103
  past and present, 93–94
  professionalism, 95
  significant adult, 96–97
  specialist, 94–95
  technology advocate, 104–105
African-Americans, 186

Agenda planning, 67–69
Asian-Americans, 186–187
Assessment, 95–96
Assessment specialist, 16–18, 96, 136–139
  learner progress, 16, 136–137
  misuse of tests, 137
  in a multicultural society, 207–208
  teacher competency, 16–17, 137–139
  tools to assess, 17, 137

Barriers, 78–79
  inappropriate task strategies, 79
  insufficient effort, 78
  lack of cohesiveness, 78
  lack of leadership, 79
  lack of understanding, 79
  reluctance to participate, 78
Building teams, 75–76
Business as a model, 73–74

Challenges, 5–6, 215–237
Change agents, 24–25, 30, 66–67
Changing roles, 29–32, 39
Community involvement, 102–103
Conflict avoidance, 80
Conflict resolution, 80–82
Consultant roles, 151–157, 172–179
  accountability, 173–176
  characteristics, 156–157
  identifying problems/solutions, 151–152
  perceiving others' strengths, 153–154
  professionalism, 176–177

Consultant roles (continued)
  promoting team efforts, 154–155
  relating knowledge/experience, 154
  technology, 177–179
  understanding group dynamics, 155–157
  working collegially, 152–153
Continuing education, 143
Council for Accreditation of Counseling and Related Educational Programs (CACREP), 121, 130
Counselors, 5–6
  as change agents, 5
  in a culturally diverse society, 196–197
  field experience, 126–127
Coursework, 118–130
  business education, 123–124
  field/clinical experience, 124–130
  general education, 118–120
  home economics education, 123
  marketing education, 124
  professional education, 120–124
  technology education, 124
  trade/industrial education, 124
  vocational education, 122–123
Culture and gender specialist, 60
Curricular experiences, 109–110
Curricular specialist, 59
Curriculum designer, 14, 59
  accountability, 134–136
  competencies, 136
  contemporary concerns, 135
  interdisciplinary courses, 135
  multicultural aspects, 135, 204–206

Delegation of tasks, 39
Developing programs, 121
Developmental needs, 98–99
Diagnosing learning and social problems, 109–114
  accountability, 113
  curricular experiences, 109–110
  evaluation and testing, 110–111
  home-based instruction, 112
  media, 111–112
  mental health intervention, 110
  team approaches, 113–114

Dialectical differences, 6–7
District office staff
  recognition of support services, 41

Educational achievements, 28
Educating support services professionals, 142–148
  continuing education, 143
  mentoring, 145–146
  national certification, 146–148
  professional associations, 144–145
Effective teams, 74–75, 79–80, 231–232
Empowerment, 23–24, 65–90, 216–218, 241–242
English as a second language, 193–194, 197–199
Equal access advocate, 100–102
Evaluation
  performance, 83, 110
  self-, 82–83
  of team effectiveness, 82–85, 110

Faculty development specialist, 18–19
  responsibilities, 19
Family structures, 26
Field/clinical experience, 124–130
  competencies, 127
  definition, 124–125
  effectiveness, 129–130
  guidelines, 125–126
Financing, 49–51, 58
  as a dilemma, 50–51
  salaries, 49–50
  school choice, 50
  taxes, 50
Future changes
  accountability, 51–53
  financing, 49–51
  length of school year, 47–49
  partnerships, 54–55
  senior volunteers, 55–56
  teachers, 46–47
  technology, 53–54
Future roles of teachers, 46–47

Goals, 87–88
Group dynamics, 155–157

Health coordinator, 8–10
    as liaison, 9
    in-service instruction, 9
Hispanic-Americans, 187
Home-schooling designers and monitors, 21–22, 112, 140–141

In-school suspension worker, 10–12
Industry as a model, 73–74
Initiatives, 65–69
    advocating teams, 65–66
    change agents, 66–67
    team agenda, 67–69
Instructional specialist, 59
Issues and challenges, 215–237
    accountability, 221–224
    defining roles, 229–230
    effects on support services, 215–216
    establishing new support services, 235–237
    maximum potential, 230–231
    overcoming past prejudices, 228–229
    professionalism, 219–221
    reform movement, 234–235
    society, 232–234
    team concept, 231–232
    technology, 224–227
    using empowerment, 216–218

Language diversity, 7
Leadership, 76–77, 86–87, 103–104
    accountability, 173–176
    behaviors, 161–162
    characteristics, 158–160
    collegial, 170–171
    definitions, 157–158
    determining traits, 166–168
    future, 171–172
    managing conflict, 164–166
    motivating others, 168–169
    professionalism, 176–177
    promoting collegiality, 169–170
    roles, 157–179
    skills, 161
    in society, 191–195
    technology, 177–179
    versus management, 162–163

Learner development, 99
Learner progress tools to assess, 17
Learning diagnostician, 12–13, 132–133
    competencies, 133
    in a multicultural society, 202–203
Learning and social problems, 109–114
Learning styles, 107–108, 192–195
Legal specialist, 19, 97–98
Library specialist, 121–122
    in a culturally diverse society, 199–201
    field experience, 127–128
Lifelong learners, 20

Management vs. leadership, 86–87, 162–163
Managing conflict, 164–166
Media instruction, 111–112, 121–122
    competencies, 127
    in a culturally diverse society, 199–201
Media producer, 139–140
Mental health diagnostician, 15–16
    intervention, 110
    in a multicultural society, 206–207
    referrals, 16
Mentoring, 145–146
Multiple intelligences, 106–107
Multiple qualifications, 58–59

National Association of State Directors of Teacher Education and Certification (NASDTEC), 119, 130
National certification, 146–148
National Council for Accreditation of Teacher Education (NCATE), 120, 121, 130
Native Americans, 185–186

Outreach coordinator, 102–103

Partnerships
    school-business/school-university, 54–55

Perceptions
  changing, 37–39
  past, 36–37
  resentment, 36–37
Professional associations, 144–145
Professional development, 39–44
  setting goals, 43–44
Professional organizations
  opportunities, 42–43
Professional preparation, 117–130
  coursework, 118–130
  field/clinical experience, 124–130
Professionalism, 27, 88–89, 94, 95–96, 130–131, 176–177, 210–211, 219–221, 250–251
  characteristics, 130–131
Programs
  developing, 121

Renewal, 39–44
  mechanisms to change, 39–40
Reform/restructuring movement, 239–252
  accountability, 251
  business involvement, 249–250
  career paths, 247
  changing schools, 240
  collegiality, 245
  empowerment, 241–242
  expectations/assumptions, 240–241
  leadership roles, 245–247
  new roles and goals, 241
  preparation, 243–244
  professionalism, 250–251
  school-based management, 248–249
  technology, 251–252

School administrators
  promoting support services, 40
School nurse, 8–10
  responsibilities, 8, 9–10
School psychologists, 6–7
  developing role, 6–7
  traditional role, 6
School year length, 47–49
  year-round education, 47–48
Self-evaluation, 82–83

Senior volunteers, 55–56
Site-based management, 23–24, 31, 50, 248–249
  win-win agreements, 24
Society
  African-Americans, 186
  Asian-Americans, 186–187
  as culturally diverse, 183–211
  Hispanic-Americans, 187
  as melting pot, 183–184
  Native Americans, 185–186
  prejudice, 189–190
  racism, 188–189
  responding to changes, 232–234
  as salad bowl, 184–185
  stereotyping, 188
  support services' role, 185, 190–195, 197–210
    accepting cultural diversity, 191–192
    accountability, 210–211
    counselor, 196–197
    culturally diverse makeup, 208–210
    curriculum designers, 204–206
    education/testing specialist, 207–208
    learning diagnostician, 202–203
    librarian/media specialist, 199–201
    mental health diagnostician, 206–207
    perceptions of motivation and success, 192–193
    professionalism, 210–211
    software specialist, 203–204
    speech correctionist, 197–199
    student self-concept, 194–195
    understanding language value, 193–194
Software specialists, 13–14, 104–105
  accountability, 133–134
  competencies, 134
  in a multicultural society, 203–204
Speech correctionist, 7–8
  in a culturally diverse society, 197–199

Staff development, 85–86
  effective programs, 86
  workshops, 85
Staff development specialist, 18–19
  responsibilities, 19
Support services personnel, 3–32
  accountability specialist, 14–15
  adult education specialist, 20–21, 141–142
  assessment specialist, 16–18, 136–139
  as consultant, 151–157, 172–179
  counselor, 5–6, 196–197
  curriculum designer, 14, 134–135, 204–206
  developing roles, 3–4, 235–237, 239–252
  the future, 239–252
  health coordinator, 8–10
  home-schooling designer/monitor, 21–22, 140–141
  as leader, 77, 157–179
  learning diagnostician, 12–13, 132–133, 202–203
  legal specialist, 19–20, 97–98
  mental health diagnostician, 15–16, 206–207
  as motivator, 87
  roles, 70
  school nurse, 8–10
  school psychologist, 6–7
  as significant adult, 96–97
  software specialist, 13–14, 133–134, 203–204
  speech correctionist, 7–8, 193–194, 197–199
  staff development specialist, 18–19, 142
  as team agents, 86–90
  training and educating, 117–148
Support services renewal, 35–61, 43, 57
  evolving roles, 57–61, 235–237
  future possibilities, 44–61
Suspension in school, 11

Staff development experts, 142, 224
Student teaching, 129

Teacher competency
  tools to assess, 17
Team advocates, 30–31, 72, 86–90
Team agenda, 67–69
Team approaches, 65–66, 69–70, 113–114
Team building, 75–76, 154–155
Team characteristics, 74–75
Team effectiveness, 79–80
  evaluation of, 82–85
Team forming, 70–71
Team goals, 72–73
Team leadership, 76–77
Team roles, 72, 231–232
Teaming, 30, 65–90
Teamwork, 38, 67, 69–86, 108–109, 131
Technology, 29, 53–54, 57–58, 88, 89–90, 104–105, 128, 133–134, 135, 177–179, 224–227, 251
  as a powerful force, 53–54
Testing and evaluation specialist, 59–60, 207–208
Training/educating personnel, 117–148
  field/clinical experience, 124–130
  general education, 118–120
  preparation, 117–130
  professional education, 120–124
  student teaching, 129

Underachievers, 12–13
University
  providing courses, 41, 42

Vocational education, 124, 128–129

Win-win agreements, 24
Work groups, 71

Year-round education, 47–48
  affecting support services, 48–49